Traces of Paradise
The Archaeology of Bahrain
2500BC-300AD

WITHDRAWN

an Exhibition at
at The Brunei Gallery
Thornhaugh Street, London WC1

12 July - 15 September 2000

Presented by
The Ministry of Cabinet Affairs
& Information of the State of Bahrain
and
The Institute of Archaeology,
University College London

Sponsored by
INVESTCORP

With the support of
Quilter & Company Limited
The Bahrain-British Foundation
The Bahrain Society
Aluminium Bahrain (ALBA)
Visiting Arts
Batelco
Gulf Petrochemical Industries Company (BSC)
Arab Ship Building & Repair Yard (ASRY)

First published in 2000
by The Dilmun Committee, 1 Battersea Bridge Road, LONDON SW11 3BG

© 2000 The Bahrain National Museum

The right of the Bahrain National Museum as the Author of the work has been
asserted by it in accordance with the Copyright Design and Patent Act 1988

Set in Triplex, font designed for Emigre Fonts by Suzana Licko 1990
Photoenraving by Snoeck-Ducaju & Zoon, Ghent, Belgium

Printed in June 2000 by
Quadacolour Ltd, Unit 3, Kangley Bridge Road, LONDON SE26 5AR

British Library Cataloguing in Publication Data
A catalogue record for this book is available from the British Library

ISBN: 0-9538666-0-2

The Organisers of
Traces of Paradise: The Archaeology of Bahrain 2500BC-300AD
acknowledge gratefully the role of
L'INSTITUTE DU MONDE ARABE, Paris
in first bringing this collection from
THE BAHRAIN NATIONAL MUSEUM to Europe.

The cooperation of
THE FORHISTORISK MUSEUM, Moesgård, Denmark
is also much appreciated.

The principal academic sponsor of the exhibition is
THE INSTITUTE OF ARCHAEOLOGY, 31-34 Gordon Square, London WC1

Special thanks are due to
The Director of the SCHOOL OF ORIENTAL AND AFRICAN STUDIES, London University
Sir Tim Lankaster, for providing the facilities of the BRUNEI GALLERY
and to the Gallery's staff.

The exhibition is organised by
THE DILMUN COMMITTEE (Michael Rice, Chairman, Dr Harriet Crawford,
the Embassy of the State of Bahrain, London, Khaled Alsendi and Dr Nick Merriman)
1 Battersea Bridge Road, London SW11 3BG
Telephone: 020 7223 3431   Facsimile: 020 7228 4229

Traces of Paradise: The Archaeology of Bahrain 2500BC-300AD
has been designed and installed by
GRAPHIC DESIGN INTERNATIONAL LIMITED
1 Battersea Bridge Road, London SW11 3BG
Telephone: 020 7223 3431   Facsimile: 020 7228 4229

Acknowledgements

Dr Pierre LOMBARD
Principal Scientific Adviser
to the Exhibition in Paris

BAHRAIN NATIONAL MUSEUM, MANAMA
Abdulrahman MUSAMEH
Khaled ALSENDI
Mustapha IBRAHIM
Lubna AL-OMRAN
Saleh AHMAD

THE BRITISH MUSEUM, LONDON
Dr John CURTIS
Keeper, Department of Western Asiatic Antiquities

MOESGÅRD MUSEUM, DENMARK
Dr Flemming HØJLUND

Scientific committee

of the exhibition in Paris, on whose work
"Traces of Paradise" is in large part based.

Khaled ALSENDI
Superintendant, Acquisitions and Excavations,
Bahrain National Museum

Béatrice ANDRE-SALVINI
Chief Conservator and Head of the Department
of Oriental Antiquities, Louvre Museum

Serge CLEUZIOU
Director of Research, CNRS, Paris

Harriet CRAWFORD
Reader at University College London

Anja HERLING
Researcher, University of Göttingen (Germany)

Flemming HØJLUND
Researcher, Forhistorisk Museum, Moesgård
(Denmark)

Monique KERVRAN
Director of Research, CNRS, Paris

Jean-François SALLES
Director of Research, CNRS and
Director of the Maison de l'Orient
Méditerranéen, Lyon

Organising committee

THE DILMUN COMMITTEE
Michael RICE
Harriet CRAWFORD
The Embassy of the State of Bahrain
Khaled ALSENDI
Dr Nick MERRIMAN

Catalogue

The Catalogue for "Traces of Paradise" has been edited by Harriet Crawford and Michael Rice and designed by Graphic Design International Limited.

Revisions of translations from the French texts and editorial assistance by Catharine Walston.

This catalogue was produced with the generous support of Quilter & Company Limited.

Photographic Credits

Sites:
Directorate of Archaeology and Heritage, Bahrain National Museum, p. 11, 21, 36, 39-41, 137, 141, 144, 145
Danish Archaeological Expedition, Prehistoric Museum, Moesgård, p. 62, 90-92
London-Bahrain Archaeological Expedition, p. 57, 67, 94
German Archaeological Mission in Bahrain, p. 137-139
French Archaeological Mission in Bahrain, p. 109, 117-119
Pierre Lombard, p. 30, 219
Philippe Maillard, p. 13, 31

All photographs of objects are by Philippe Maillard with the following exceptions:
British Museum, Department of Western Asiatic Antiquities, p. 57 (right), 73, 75, 76, 172
Directorate of Archaeology and Heritage, Bahrain National Museum/Saleh Ahmad, p. 55 (bottom), 56 (bottom), 57 (left), 82 (right), 86, 158
Louvre Museum, Department of Western Asiatic Antiquities, p.33
Louvre Museum, Department of Western Asiatic Antiquities/M. Chuzeville, p.34, 77 (right)
Réunion des Musées Nationaux/P. Bernard, p. 16

Table of Contents

Foreword

The Institute of Archaeology is delighted to be the academic sponsor of this important exhibition. Thanks to the generosity and imagination of the Ministry of Cabinet Affairs and Information of the State of Bahrain and to the Director and staff of the Bahrain National Museum, a splendid collection of antiquities has been gathered together which bring to life the history of the Bahrain islands over a period of more than three thousand years. Bahrain has a long tradition of research into its past and Bahraini archaeologists have made distinguished contributions in this field. There has been fruitful and valuable cooperation with them in the preparation of this exhibition. It is the first time that most of the objects have left the islands and the first time that Europe has had the opportunity to learn at first hand about the civilizations of Dilmun and Tylos, the ancient names of Bahrain.

The exhibition was originally hosted by the Institut du Monde Arabe in Paris and it is a pleasure to record our debt to the Institut, to its Museum Director Monsieur Brahim Alaoui, and to the Moesgård Museum which hosted part of the same exhibition earlier this year. The work involved in mounting the exhibition in London has been undertaken by the Dilmun Committee and I would like to record my special thanks to its Chairman Mr Michael Rice, to Dr Crawford who initiated the moves to bring the exhibition to London and to the other members of the committee. We are all most grateful for the encouragement which we have received from HE Shaikh Abdul Aziz Mubarak al Khalifa, the Ambassador of the State of Bahrain in London.

The objects in the exhibition demonstrate that the tradition of the Bahrain islands as a trade centre and a cultural melting pot goes back at least four thousand years. These traditions continue today and the copper merchants of four thousand years ago would probably feel quite at home in today's vibrant market place. Bahrain has a heritage of which it is justly proud and it is a privilege to play a part in introducing this heritage to the people of London in this millennial year.

Professor Peter Ucko
Director, Institute of Archaeology

Preface

"Traces of Paradise: The Archaeology of Bahrain 2500BC-300AD" is the result of the efforts of many people and the members of the Dilmun Committee would like to express their warmest thanks to all of them. Acknowledgement must first be made to the Government of the State of Bahrain for their financial support and to HE Mr Mohammed Mutawa, the Minister of Cabinet Affairs and Information, Dr Abdullah Yateem, Bahrain Assistant Under-Secretary for Culture and Heritage, and the Institute du Monde Arabe to mount the original exhibition in Paris in 1999. The exhibition then travelled to Moesgård in Denmark and we have been able to work closely and productively with scholars in both places and are deeply grateful to them all. Without their co-operation it would have been impossible to mount this exhibition.

In Britain HE Shaikh Abdulaziz Mubarak Al-Khalifa, Ambassador of the State of Bahrain, has been unstinting in his support and in securing much of the financial sponsorship, which has made the project possible. We owe a great debt to all our sponsors and especially to Investcorp International Limited, our major supporter, and to the Institute of Archaeology, University College London, our academic sponsor. John Hollingworth and the staff at the Brunei Gallery at the School of Oriental and African Studies have facilitated our work at all times and have been a pleasure to deal with.

Our final debt of gratitude must be to the people of Bahrain through the ages who, by their skill and their imagination, by their initiative and their hard work, have made this exhibition possible. They have created a unique record of their own past and it is a privilege to be able to introduce their achievements to the people of this country at the beginning of the new millennium.

Michael Rice
Harriet Crawford

Bahrain: Two Seas, One Civilisation

Pierre Lombard, Khaled Alsendi

The thirty-three islands and islets that make up the Bahrain archipelago have recently more usually been associated, it is true, with the exploits of petroleum engineers than with those of archaeologists. It is generally forgotten that the first are almost consigned to history already, whereas the second are in the process of development... The modern State of Bahrain, which benefited in 1932 from the first flow of black gold in the Gulf - today being steadily exhausted - is already confidently established in a post-petroleum phase, true to the country's age-old tradition of adaptation and innovation.

The land of Bahrain provides a constant challenge to those who live there and have made the country prosperous since antiquity. Situated half-way between the mouths of the Tigris and the Euphrates and the Strait of Hormuz, the archipelago, which is often reduced to its two main islands - Bahrain, which gives the country its name, and Muharraq - belongs to the arid tropical zone, whose character is accentuated in this case by one of the globe's warmest seas. However, these islands have two major and complementary advantages. The first is their strategic position in the heart of the Gulf, at the crossroads of maritime routes that link the Near East to the Indian sub-continent. The second is a veritable gift of nature, due to a specific geological phenomenon. It is on Bahrain that immense freshwater reservoirs situated in the depths of the Arabian Peninsula reach the surface in the form of abundant artesian springs. This means that the two main islands have the advantage of a "second sea" of fresh water, a fact that has left its mark on the name of the country.*

Its strategic position and attractive environment enabled Bahrain, from the Bronze Age onwards, to control trade in the Gulf with ease, but above all, to impose its natural role as a trading crossroads, while at the same time serving as a useful transit point for merchandise and an agreeable one for people. These two assets, from which Bahrain still benefits today are nevertheless fragile: the vagaries of history have a habit of rendering maritime and land routes somewhat unpredictable, and geography has dictated that the "second sea", of fossil origin, will not renew itself...

Perceived by a few travellers as early as the end of the 19th century, the great archaeological interest of Bahrain was confirmed from the 1950s onwards. A Danish archaeological expedition, perhaps through loyalty to the memory of Carsten Niebuhr who, two hundred years earlier, had explored another Arabia, "inserted Bahrain into world history" by showing that the civilisation of Dilmun had really existed.

Until then, the Dilmun civilisation that was probably born in the Eastern Province of Saudi Arabia was only known through the work of philologists. It was on Bahrain that Dilmun reached its height between 2 000 and 1 800 BC.

* In Arabic, *Al-Bahrayn* means "The Two Seas"

The pioneering work of the Moesgård Museum expeditions opened the way that all archaeologists who are fascinated by Bahrain and Dilmun now follow.

Whilst our current knowledge is still too incomplete for a comprehensive inventory, the exhibition chosen here aims to evoke four important moments in the historical development of Bahrain: the culmination of the Dilmun culture (Early Bronze Age, circa 2 000 – 1 800 BC), the occupation of Dilmun by the Mesopotamian Kassites (Middle Bronze Age, circa 1 450–1 300 BC), the last centuries of Dilmun (Iron Age, from 1000 – 450 BC), and finally the era known as the Tylos period, after the Greek name for Bahrain, (Hellenistic, Parthian and Sasanian periods, from 300 BC to 600 AD). Over and above chronological or material distinctions, these diverse cultural phases are intimately linked, and constitute a continuous way of life, creating a civilisation that is unique to the archipelago as marked by its insular identity and – perhaps paradoxically – by its constant openness to neighbouring cultures and their products. The present name, Bahrain, has led us to call this the "Civilisation of Two Seas".

The most original characteristic of the Dilmun culture is the importance and the unique place attributed to its funerary customs. The main island has some of the most impressive necropoleis formed of tumuli in the world in terms of their sheer number, so widespread that at the beginning of the century it was even thought that Bahrain was an "Isle of the Dead" used by the inhabitants of the neighbouring Arabian coast. The discovery of settlement sites and several temples has today put paid to this idea, which derived in part from the reputation of Dilmun which was considered to be a pure and sacred place by the ancient Sumerians, a kind of earthly Paradise where gods and heroes enjoyed immortality. The Sumerians attributed the creation of Dilmun to one of their principal gods, Enki, lord of the "Apsû". They also believed that the sea of fresh water on which the Earth floats, according to Sumerian beliefs, surfaced at Dilmun, bestowing life and luxuriant vegetation on the land.

The coincidence of the exceptional hydrological situation of Bahrain is particularly striking, and very early on this played a role in the (partial) Identification of Dilmun with the "archipelago of the Two Seas."

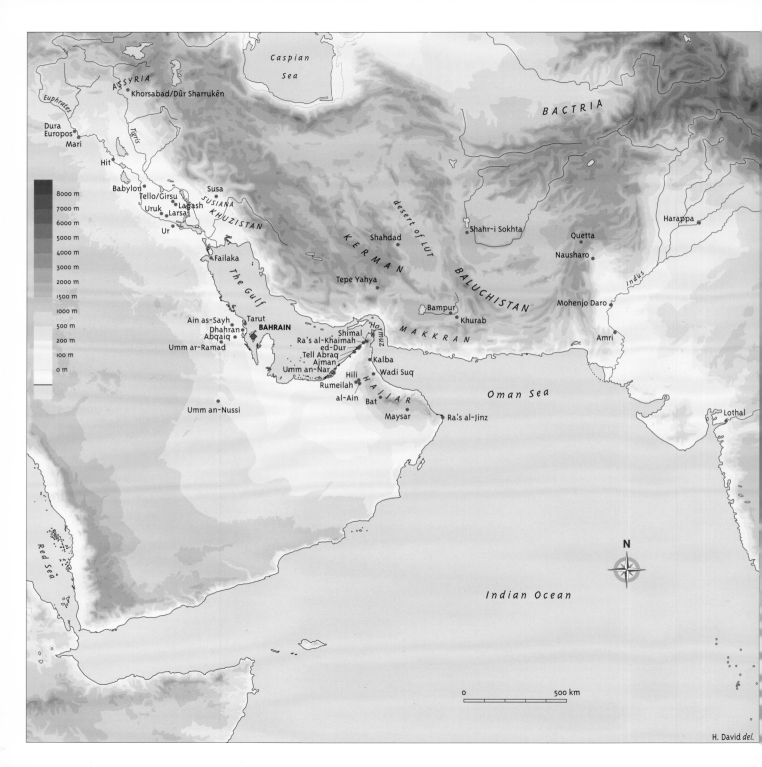

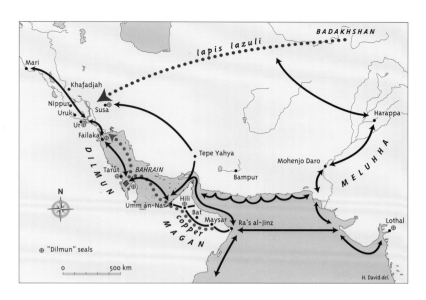

This mythical Dilmun is not, obviously, accessible to archaeologists. The Dilmun they are patiently uncovering seems both more prosaic and more real. The material found in tombs reflects the lives of men, and largely confirms the role of Bahrain as a crossroads during the Bronze Age. Pieces imported from Mesopotamia, Iran, or the Indus civilisation have been found, but also pieces made locally, of which a certain number are particularly sophisticated and original such as the "Dilmun seals". With a shape and iconography unusual in the Near East, these illustrate, more than any other category of objects, the "hidden art" of this civilisation. In parallel with the archaeologists, the philologists are compiling lists of the numerous Mesopotamian economic texts that mention the merchants and the emporium of Dilmun. The latter often appears to have been the intermediary used by its larger neighbours to access the raw materials that were essential at that time - copper and diorite from Oman; building timber, ivory, hard or semi-precious stones (diorite, carnelian, lapis lazuli) from the

Indus Valley, etc. These traded products were found side by side with local products in Dilmun - high quality dates and probably pearls, which, until 1932 remained the island's most famous product.

Towards the end of the 18th century BC, the Indus civilisation collapsed, and at the same time destroyed Dilmun's *raison d'être*. The archipelago underwent diverse trials and tribulations of which history cannot always provide us with the details. Archaeological research has, nonetheless enabled two periods to emerge. The first is from the 15th to the 14th century BC. This is the period when Bahrain was occupied by the Mesopotamian Kassites (usually known as "Middle Dilmun") and it is still relatively unknown. Recently some light has been shed upon it by the work of the French archaeological Mission at the Qal'at al-Bahrain site. Discoveries include the Kassite governor's palace, as well as a small archive of cuneiform texts, one of the southernmost examples of this writing found in the Near East.

Dilmun/Bahrain
at the crossroads
of the trading routes
of the Early Bronze Age.

Previous page.
Map of the Middle East
during the Dilmun
and Tylos Periods.

¹Votive Plaque of Ur-Nanshe, King of Lagash
Mesopotamia: Tello, ancient Girsu (Land of Sumer)
Early Dynastic III period (c. 2500 BC)
Limestone
H40 W47 TH14 cm
Paris, Louvre Museum, acc. n° AO 2344
Léon Heuzey 1893, p. 13-17; E. Sollberger 1956; E. Sollberger & J.-R. Kupper 1971, p. 44-45 (IC3c); B. André 1982 n° 167, p. 225; J. S. Cooper 1986, p. 22-23 (La.1.2)

The most ancient historical documents that mention the importance of Dilmun as a great trading centre for raw materials imported from distant lands accessible via the Gulf, belong to the first sovereign of the ancient Sumerian City-State or Principality of Lagash. Ur-Nanshe, a powerful monarch, mentioned in numerous inscriptions the relations that had developed between Dilmun and Lagash. Seven of them have been preserved. They are official inscriptions carved onto plaques with a figured relief, perforated to be hung on a wall, stone tablets, and pivot-stones destined to be placed in the foundations of temples to commemorate their construction. The most important of these monuments shows the king, in the official sheepskin robes of his religious office as a builder. As the representative of his people before the deity, he himself lays the first brick of the edifice. He carries it in the basket placed on his head, in the presence of his wife and children, shown smaller and in the presence of the holder of the cup for lustral libations, who is behind him. A second scene shows Ur-Nanshe, his family and his court, during the ritual banquet to celebrate the finishing of the building. Inscriptions carved on the skirts of the characters indicate their names, whilst those covering areas of the monument name the royal edifices evoking the power of the State. This extended its trading relations as far as Dilmun, whose inhabitants and fleet brought to Lagash the precious exotic wood used to embellish the sanctuaries for the two guardian divinities of Lagash. These were Ningirsu and Nanshe: "Ur-Nanshe, King of Lagash, son of Gunidu, son of Gursar, built the temple of Ningirsu, built the temple of Nanshe, built the Abzubanda... He had brought (to Lagash), by the boats of Dilmun, wood from distant lands".
Economic texts from the same period also mention copper imports to Lagash (Cat. 81).

The last centuries of Dilmun ("Late Dilmun") date to the Iron Age (first half of the 1st millennium BC). Apart from necropoleis which reveal contacts with the neighbouring cultures of the Oman peninsula, this phase left important architectural remains from the Achaemenian period (5th century BC) at Qal'at al-Bahrain, including an official residence and probably a temple. Diverse populations thus coexisted on the island, and new burial customs were introduced.

Finally around 325 BC one of Alexander the Great's maritime expeditions reached the main island of Bahrain, by then known as Tylos. The island then enjoyed an exceptional phase of prosperity, characterised by the development of a culture inspired by the Hellenistic and Parthian worlds. At the present time the only evidence we have of this comes to us via the necropoleis. They were noticeably better protected against pillaging than the Dilmun tumuli, and Tylos burials have been discovered intact, and in an exceptionally well preserved state.

There was generally a large amount of funeral furniture and this was often highly original, especially between the 1st century BC and the 1st century AD. Objects found include numerous glazed ceramic vases, finely worked glass vessels, alabaster vases, ivory objects, terracotta or plaster figurines, as well as jewellery and sometimes spectacular gold items.

Uncommon limestone steles represent the rare sculptures bequeathed to us by the ancient island of Bahrain. The diversity of the influences shown by this material culture demonstrates that during that period Bahrain had once more become an important crossroads in the Hellenistic and post-Hellenistic worlds.

From Dilmun to Tylos, through the phases of Kassite, Babylonian, Achaemenid and Parthian occupation, Bahrain produced a culture that is as original as it was unrecognised. For this exhibition, the National Museum of Bahrain has agreed to present more than 500 objects that represent this unique way of life, with its privileged position straddling the Two Seas. Many of them are from the most recent work undertaken by the numerous archaeological excavation expeditions in the archipelago.

We are certain that this exhibition will be a complete revelation to visitors. With their very first step, they should meditate on the French poet Paul Valéry's advice which he would have found perfectly fitting faced with the reconstructions of the enigmatic tumuli of Dilmun...

"*I will be tomb or treasure for him who passes,*
I can speak or I can keep my silence.
It is in your hands, my friend,
Enter not without desire ..."

Bahrain, a Geological Phenomenon

Rémi Dalongeville

Geography and archaeology of the Bahrain archipelago.

Close to the eastern coast of the Arabian Peninsula, Bahrain covers a little under 700 km², and groups together over thirty islands and islets spread over two groups: the Bahrain archipelago which includes the principal island, and the Hawar archipelago, further to the south. The limestone heights of Jebel Dukhan rise to 135 m (443 ft). These have served as a vital landmark for navigation in these dangerously shallow waters with a sea-bottom comprised of sand banks and coral reefs that are almost exposed at low tide.

The climate is hot and arid. The average annual rainfall does not exceed 74 mm, and the average temperature is 18.5°C in January and 39.1°C in August. But the climate is subject to random changes, and these averages hide the huge irregularities that the population has to deal with – some years are almost completely dry, with extreme temperatures (over 45°C in August and 3°C in January)…The sea, which is not very deep, does not fully play its role as a thermal regulator, even less so due to high humidity.

However it is true to say that, for a long time, this place has offered a number of specific advantages. Men from the sea or from the desert were able to exploit these to their best advantage and transform a site which, on the whole, was not particularly hospitable. Paradoxically, they made Bahrain an island whose riches have endowed it with almost mythical status as a land Of dreams - dreams of opulence and a sweet life.

This island status is both recent and uncertain. During the Quaternary Period (the last million years), and especially during the last 120 000 years, global climate fluctuations have caused this sector to be attached and then separated from the Arabian peninsula. When the earth's sea level was 120 m below the current level, 18 000 years ago, the Gulf was practically dry, and Bahrain was simply a *jebel* among many others, lost among the vast expanses of stony glacis and fields of dunes. It was only when the levels were high, on several occasions, that sandy and shelly sediments stuck to the base of the slopes and hardened. This means that Bahrain is rich in building stone which is highly sought after, being formed of calcarenite which is easy to carve and easy to transport. Coral was also used on occasions, as patch reefs abound around the island. For the last 6000 years or so, since sea levels rose to their present level, Bahrain has been surrounded by water. But the changing sand banks mean that today Bahrain is separated from Saudi Arabia by a narrow channel which, since 1987, has had a 25 km bridge across it.

The general circulation of waters in the Gulf runs in an anticlockwise direction, and the fact that the alluvial deposits carried by the Tigris and the Euphrates are thus distributed along the length of the coast, means that the coastal currents are once again threatening to join Bahrain to the continent.

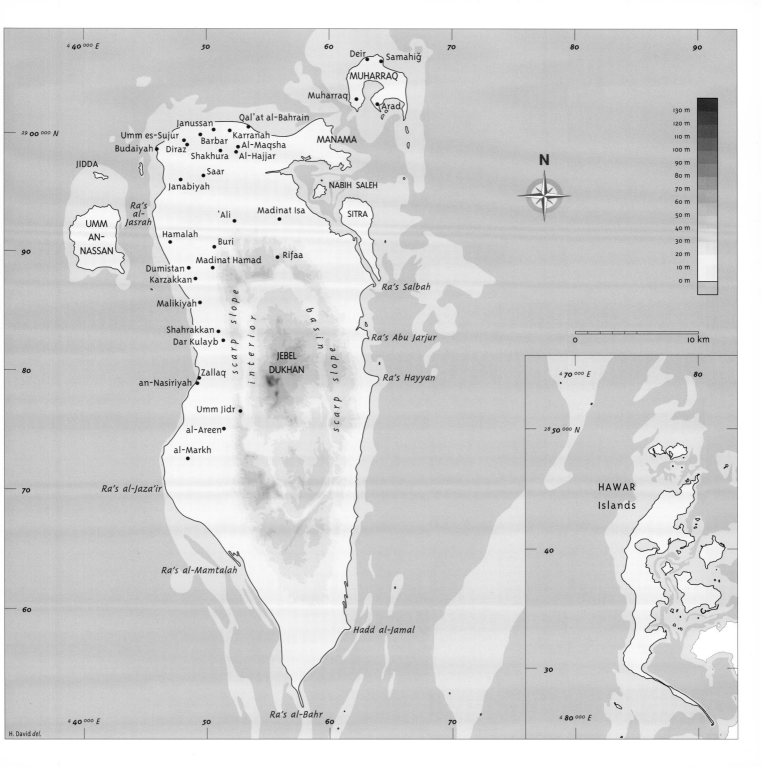

4 40 000 E   50   60   70   80   90

Deir • • Samahiğ
MUHARRAQ

29 00 000 N   Muharraq • • Arad
                Janussan •   Qal'at al-Bahrain
        Umm es-Sujur •   Karranah •   MANAMA
Budaiyah • Diraz • Barbar • Al-Maqsha •
                Shakhura • Al-Hajjar •
JIDDA   Saar •
                Janabiyah •   NABIH SALEH
            Ra's
            al-   'Ali •   Madinat Isa •   SITRA
90   UMM   Jasrah
      AN-
      NASSAN   Hamalah •
                            Buri •
                Madinat Hamad •   Rifaa •
            Dumistan •
            Karzakkan •   Ra's Salbah
            Malikiyah •
                                                        Ra's Abu Jarjur
        Shahrakkan •   scarp slope   interior   basin   scarp slope
        Dar Kulayb •   Ra's Hayyan
80   JEBEL
            Zallaq •   DUKHAN
    an-Nasiriyah •
        Umm Jidr •
        al-Areen •
70   al-Markh •

    Ra's al-Jaza'ir

60   Ra's al-Mamtalah

                        Hadd al-Jamal

                Ra's al-Bahr

N

130 m
120 m
110 m
100 m
90 m
80 m
70 m
60 m
50 m
40 m
30 m
20 m
10 m
0 m

0   10 km

4 70 000 E   80

28 50 000 N

HAWAR
Islands

40

30

4 80 000 E

H. David del.

Jebel Dukhan, the highest point on the island of Bahrain.

The northern palm grove on Bahrain island. In the foreground, the Qal'at al-Bahrain site with its Islamic-Portuguese fort.

Part of the island's geological history is due to plate tectonics. The Arabian plate, between the Red Sea, the Dead Sea trench and the Gulf, is moving northwards, where it plunges underneath the Gulf waters to pass under the Iranian plate. This explains the lack of symmetry between the northern coast of the Gulf, which is rocky and quite steep, and the southern coast which is sandy and flat. This plate dynamic, which provokes powerful earthquakes, gave birth, tens of millions of years ago, to the folded mountain chains of Iran and Afghanistan, and also to the anticline that forms the basic relief of the island of Bahrain. Here, erosion has worn away the summit, removing the softer parts, but conserving the more resistant parts. The result is an unusual relief in the centre of the island which owes its appearance to its structure – a ring-shaped depression around the foot of uplands inclined towards a central dome.

This anticlinal form, above bedrock with faults in it, is one of Bahrain's major advantages. For millions of years, the limestone layers of the centre of the Arabian peninsula have been absorbing precipitation, and have trapped, several hundred metres underground, powerful fossil aquifers that extend as far as the Gulf. Due to this anticlinal structure, the water resurfaces in Bahrain in the form of abundant artesian springs, all the more welcome as they rise up in an area with a harsh climate. Bahrain is, almost despite itself, an oasis. Thus, in the north of the island, the maximum level of freshwater in the sedimentary rock is actually 6 m *above* the highest sea level. During antiquity, there were thus veritable geysers at several points on the island (*aïn*), which ensured regular and abundant irrigation. Several springs even had their sources under the sea – until quite recently, their fresh water was periodically collected by divers equipped with leather containers.

As long as the water table has generated artesian springs, these have brought life to Bahrain, and prevented the seawater from penetrating the sediments in the lower parts of the island. However, the springs have been dwindling slowly since antiquity, and this phenomenon has rapidly accelerated since the 1920s, due to the machine drilling of deep wells. Today, the majority of these natural springs are depleted, if not dry. Man has clearly exceeded Nature's limits, and the water table is overexploited, with the level of precipitation of the present climate being insufficient to compensate. Bahrain is still an oasis, and its vast palm groves, sustained by hard work and ingenuity, are still being cultivated. But for how long? The most important of the island's riches is disappearing rapidly.

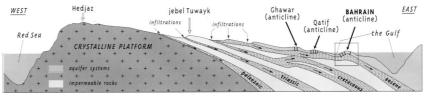
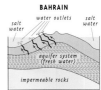

The "second sea" - diagram of the aquifer systems of the Arabian Peninsula and the Bahrain artesian springs (after P. Beaumont et al, 1988, fig.2.17, p.87)

These springs in the desert led to the establishment quite early on of the Neolithic populations of the Ubaid civilisation (around 6000 years ago), followed by those of Dilmun (around 4500 years ago). These populations left evidence of their activities - they hunted gazelle and dugong, and gathered the shellfish from the coastal mangrove forest of which just a few traces remain in Bahrain today. We know that the forest was much richer at that time, as witnessed by Alexander's admiral recorded in the narrative of his travels. The mangroves provided the local populations and those simply passing through with an abundance of varied foods, including fish, crabs, turtles, birds, and shellfish. These served as food not only for the people, but their domestic animals too. Today, the population still obtains a large part of their food from the sea.

On vast rocky flats that are uncovered at low tide, the Bahrainis have installed a special type of fixed trap, the *hadras*. These resemble long fish nets and are used by the farmers of the nearby palm groves, who come to harvest the catch using little carts pulled by mules - this is a favourite image for Bahraini postcards. Another type of harvest is made possible by the conjunction of sandy carboniferous sea floors and coral banks, remnants of a distant past. As early as the Dilmun culture, Bahrain was an important centre for pearl fishing. This industry continued over the centuries, as the ancient classical authors, and the tales of

Renaissance and modern travellers testify. However, recently (since 1930), the cultured pearl oyster industry in the Far East began to rival and threaten this local industry. Bahrain's economy bounced back almost immediately - oil was struck in the centre of the island in 1932, and supplied up to 15 million tonnes/year in 1994. Natural gas, (3.5 million m^3) also represents an important resource for the country.

Bahrain's principal source of wealth, however, is above all its people. The inhabitants who, for millennia, have succeeded one another, have known how to make the most of this small group of islands. Bahrain has always been an important centre for exchange, a place for human activity, a meeting place for land and sea-faring travellers. All these aspects combine to make Bahrain an oasis in the true sense of the word. Today, it is a country that is in tune with the times - the Bahrainis know that what made Bahrain's wealth in the past will not ensure its future, and they remain an inventive and open-hearted people.

CHAPTER TWO The Dilmun Culture
(2500–1800 BC)

Dilmun: Origins and Early Development

Serge Cleuziou

Fifteen thousand years ago the Gulf did not yet exist. A vast marshy plain, crossed by the meanderings formed by the meeting of the Tigris and the Euphrates, bordered the foothills of the mountains of Iran and separated them from the deserts of Arabia. In an environment that was as arid, if not more so than today, this plain probably drew to it the hunters of the end of the Palaeolithic period. But the rise in sea levels that, from 15 000 BC, accompanied the end of the last Ice Age, placed this entire area under water. The rise was relatively rapid, 10 m per millennium, up to the maximum, which was 2 to 3 m above the present sea level, around 6 000 BC, before oscillating from this date between 1 to 2 m above or below it. Such variations in a very flat region are not without significance. They lead to the drying out or flooding of immense areas that can, depending on the situation, be expanses of shallow water, lagoons, or desolate *sabkhas* invaded little by little by the desert sands. At around the same time, from 8000 BC, and probably more markedly between 6 000 and 4 000 BC, climatic conditions that were slightly more humid than today's allowed the development of vast areas of mangrove swamp on the borders of these coastal lagoons. The human communities of that time found extremely useful ecosystems there, enabling them to gather food all year round.

No object that can be attributed with certitude to the Palaeolithic period has been found, either in Bahrain, or the Gulf, where the most ancient known flint tools date from the 8th to 7th millennia BC. Given the environmental changes mentioned above, this is hardly surprising, as any earlier settlements, if they existed, as is probable, would be under the waters of the Gulf, a lost province of Arabian prehistory, and more or less unreachable using current archaeological techniques. These first tools, identified in Qatar in the 1950's as Group B by the Danish archaeologists, are characterised by tanged arrowheads on flint blades, and present similarities with the industries of the same era in northern Palestine and Arabia, to which they could be linked in some way. They have not yet been definitively found in Bahrain. Next, in the 5th and 4th millennia, we find tools characterised in particular by tanged arrowheads with fine pressure flaking over their entire surface, known as Group D. Several sites with this type of arrowhead are known in the western part of the island and on the west slopes of Jebel Dukhan. But this period is characterised in the numerous coastal sites of the region by the presence of sherds of painted pottery identical to that of the farming villages of the Ubaid culture of Southern Iraq. They have been found in particular in the fishing settlements of al-Markh, where excavation has revealed the marks of the posts of dwellings in light materials. Clay analyses have unequivocally shown that this pottery is of Mesopotamian origin, probably imported by boat during exchanges between the inhabitants of southern Mesopotamia and the fishermen of the Gulf banks.

At the Aïn as-Sayh site in Saudi Arabia, near Dhahran, just opposite Bahrain, fragments were recently discovered of the bitumen caulking from the reed boats that were used for these exchanges.

Some authors postulate that the presence of this pottery is an indication of cultural and social links between the inhabitants of the Gulf banks and those of Lower Mesopotamia. This hypothesis merits further study, but should be approached with caution. In any case, it is accepted that what was to become the land of Dilmun was, even as early as this period, in contact with what was to become the land of Sumer. The contacts covered the entire Arab shore of the Gulf, as pottery fragments of the Ubaid type have been found as far as the emirate of Ras al-Khaimah. Pottery, bitumen and a few fragments of obsidian came from Mesopotamia to the Gulf, but this list, the only one archaeology can at present provide, is certainly not closed. Products reaped from the sea were probably exported in return. These would have included dried fish, shellfish, shark and dugong skins, turtle shells, and perhaps pearls, which have to this day ensured the wealth and the reputation of Bahrain.

In the 4th millennium, while the state, cities and writing were developing in Mesopotamia, the Gulf was also experiencing complex and poorly understood transformations. We have no confirmed evidence for this period on the island of Bahrain, though the site at al-Markh was apparently still occupied. A certain number of sites attributed to this period exist in the Eastern Province of Saudi Arabia, opposite Bahrain. Umm an-Nussi in the Jabrin oasis and Umm ar-Ramadh in the al-Hasa oasis have shown traces of mud brick houses and, among locally produced ceramics, sherds of pottery than can be attributed to the Uruk period in Mesopotamia. Cattle, sheep and goats appeared as domestic animals, although the latter two had been present in small numbers on the coastal sites from the end of the 5th millennium. The excavators at Umm ar-Ramadh suggested that the date palm was already being cultivated there, but this has yet to be confirmed. This was a critical period in the history of Dilmun, whose name appears in Mesopotamia from the end of the 4th millennium onwards in the archaic texts of Uruk, the oldest known texts, around 3 300 BC. It is interesting to note that the name of Dilmun is often associated with copper objects, even at this early period. There were no copper mines in the Dilmun area, even in its largest possible compass, but it was, however, just at this time that the land of Magan, the Oman peninsula, began its mining activities. Thus the texts probably reflect the existence of a trade that subsequently flourished and expanded.

² Soft Stone Vessel

Saar necropolis
("Burial complex"),
Bahraini excavations 1984–85,
Grave B/EI.2
Early Dilmun, c. 2000–1800 BC
(discovery context)
Chlorite
H7.7 D MAX12.2 cm
Manama, Bahrain National
Museum, acc. n° 358-2-88
B *Bahrain National Museum* 1993,
p. 42; Crawford & Alsendi 1996

This vessel has a complex design, a mixture of geometrical patterns - chevrons, hatchings - and naturalistic elements - weaved patterns and bricks. The accepted interpretation is of a stylised building with a doorway with a curved lintel, in the style of the *mudhifs*, the reed structures that are still used in the Lower Valley of the Euphrates and the Tigris, and which are frequently found represented in Sumerian iconography in the 3rd millennium BC. These vessels with their figurative decoration were mainly produced in Iran, where the stone is available in abundance. However, several hundreds have been found on the island of Tarut, close to Bahrain, some unfinished, which suggests that Dilmun may also have been a production centre, or at least an important port of call for these vessels on their way to Mesopotamia. Their manufacture often pre-dates the building of the Bahrain tumuli by several centuries. It is likely that their exceptional character made them worth keeping from one period to the next - this is undoubtedly the case for this remarkable specimen.

The quantity of material of Mesopotamian origin found on the sites on the eastern coast of Saudi Arabia increased considerably at the beginning of the 3rd millennium, not only at Umm ar-Ramadh but also not far from there at the tombs of Abqaiq, and most of all on the off-shore island of Tarut.

These materials were mainly ceramic jars from the Jemdet Nasr and Early Dynastic periods of Mesopotamia, of which some were imported and others were local imitations. For a good part of the 3rd millennium, Tarut was undoubtedly the main site in the region. Under the fort dating from the Islamic era, there is a substantial tell, with traces of monumental architecture attributable to the 3rd millennium. Even though no major digs have been possible on the site, the island has provided a great many objects. These include a statue of a worshipper in stone of the Mesopotamian Early Dynastic period, copper and lapis lazuli, but mostly several hundreds of fragments of vases with incised decoration in greenish soft stone - steatite or chlorite. These objects were already known in Mesopotamia or at Susa, so it was first thought that they had been imported from these regions, but the presence of fragments at various stages of manufacture shows that one or more workshops must have existed on Tarut. Some patterns reproduced on these fragments recall vases made in eastern Iran, but other of the more spectacular elements were also well known in Mesopotamia - the eagle

```
0        1        2 cm
```

[3] **Tablet in Pre-Cuneiform Sumerian Script with Dilmun Ideogram**
Mesopotamia (Land of Sumer)
Uruk III Period (c. 3100-3000 BC)
Clay
H4.5 W7.2 TH1.5 cm
Paris, Louvre Museum,
acc. n° AO 29560
B R. Englund 1983, p. 35-37;
M.W. Green et H.J. Nissen 1987,
n° 77 et 729; H. J. Nissen,
P. Damerow, R. K. Englund 1990,
p. 205 n° 4.28, photograph p. 23

Accounting record concerning rations of barley allocated as payments or rations. They are represented by a stylised image of a head, representing the individual, next to a bowl similar to those, made of rough earth, found at Uruk, which had been used to hold the quantity of food allocated to a worker for one meal. This is also the symbol for bread. The reverse side of the tablet shows the total. Other administrative transactions are noted and totalled. Next to the "food ration" ideogram, the ideogram for Dilmun appears in another cell with figures. It may resemble the sign used to write the word *sikil*: "pure", the epithet associated with the land of Dilmun in the literary texts, designating the goddess of Dilmun, Ninsikila. This is attested to from the beginnings of writing in the economic texts of Uruk around 3300-3200 BC, as well as in the first contemporaneous lexical lists, which allow this identification. The most ancient economic texts allude to the trade in metals in return for grain, provided by the Sumerian authorities, and to clothes. The trading system was therefore already set up and very elaborate.

with a lion's head, the Master of the Animals, palms, etc. The question needs to be posed as to whether these objects were produced in the style of Sumer to be sold there, or whether the common themes are an indication of common cultural ground between Dilmun and Mesopotamia, hypotheses equally supported by Mesopotamian mythological texts. It would seem that lapis lazuli, a blue stone originating from the mountains in northern Afghanistan, was also worked at Tarut, which was probably the main coastal town of a Dilmun already rich from its palm groves and its role in international trade.

If there is no longer any doubt that Bahrain belonged to ancient Dilmun, it is disappointing to have found so little evidence from this period thus far on the islands. We have to content ourselves with one painted fragment of Jemdet Nasr type pottery found in backfill associated with the oldest temple at Barbar, and a white stone seal found in a much later tomb, from the Kassite era, at al-Hajjar. Towards 2 400 BC, however, the evidence of a high level of occupation grows with the settlement levels of City I at Qal'at al-Bahrain and the oldest tumuli at Buri and Madinat Hamad. This was the beginning of a particularly flourishing period, but the long prelude described here demonstrates two things about the history of Dilmun: on the one hand, this history has a continental, and not solely an insular aspect, even if the insular side began to dominate once maritime trading routes developed and Bahrain was able to combine the advantages of being an island and of having available agricultural lands as well. The other side to the history of Dilmun is that it is linked to that of southern Mesopotamia, with which Dilmun seems to have rapidly developed more than just trading relations.

"The land where the sun rises ... "
The Representation of Dilmun in Sumerian Literature

Béatrice André-Salvini

Descriptions of Dilmun appear in several Sumerian mythological compositions. A creation myth, known as "Enki and Ninhursag", or the "Myth of Dilmun", links Dilmun to the origins of the world, offering a hymn of praise to this land blessed by the Gods, graced with abundant fresh water, and renowned as an international marketplace. This land of milk and honey, whose riches were destined for Mesopotamia, was idealised as a place that was propitious for eternal life. According to the written sources available, no other foreign country seems to have aroused such intense interest from the thinkers of ancient Mesopotamia. Sumer is considered as the centre of the world, and the archetype of civilisation. Dilmun is associated with this influence, as it helped maintain it through its importance as a trading crossroads, vital to the Sumerian economy. Dilmun is mentioned in archaic official and economic texts, in relation to the importation of raw materials necessary for Sumer to achieve its greater destiny. Apart its value in matters practical, Dilmun enjoyed a unique cultural prestige. This was due to the Sumerian mind-set, which glorified the values that maintain harmony in the world, and trade formed part of these values. Other countries accessible via the "Lower Sea" – the Gulf – are evoked and praised in literary works at the same time as Dilmun. Their fabulous riches arrived regularly by boat, for over 800 years, on the quays of the capital cities of Ur-Nanshe of Lagash, Sargon of Akkad, Gudea of

Lagash, then at Ur, capital of the kings of the Ur III empire and international port of the sovereigns of the Larsa dynasty. More distant countries, such as Magan (present day Oman, and perhaps the Iranian coast of Makran) and Meluhha (the Baluchistan coast and the Indus Valley), produced the precious stones, the wood and the copper required for the construction work ordered by the sovereigns of Mesopotamia to glorify their gods and their reigns, and on which their civilisation depended. When, in the myth known as "Enki and the World Order", the Sumerian God of Wisdom decrees the destinies of Sumer and the surrounding countries, Meluhha and Dilmun receive tremendous wealth, as their prestigious role is to allow Nippur and Ur, the royal city that represents Sumer, to benefit from it: "*Let the lands of Magan and Dilmun come to me, Enki, let the anchorages be prepared to receive the boats of Dilmun; let the boats of Magan reach the horizon; let the great (cargo) boats of Meluhha transport the gold and silver of (l. 124-129)... Meluhha, oh dark land, your trees are leafy, the seats made out of them will be placed well in the palaces... your birds will all have a plumage of carnelian... your riches will be in overabundance... (Then) Enki cleaned and purified the land of Dilmun and put the goddess Ninsikilla in charge;... he gave [marshes...], so that fish could be eaten, he gave [the date palm] to its cultivated lands, so that the dates could be eaten (l.219-242)*".

There were several historical, geographical and cultural reasons to which Dilmun owed its privileged position in the eyes of the Mesopotamians. Most of the Sumerian literary texts that we have are in the form of copies written during the first centuries of the 2nd millennium, in versions that were sometimes changed or embellished. At this time, Dilmun became the only marketplace for long distance trade via the Gulf. It was a port of transit where representatives of all countries came to exchange or sell their products, controlled by the seafaring-merchants of Ur, the *alik Dilmun*. The island of Bahrain, which meant Dilmun at that time, is an ideal staging post due to its geographical position, its fresh water sources and its facilities for anchoring boats. One of the versions found of the myth "Enki and Ninhursag", from Ur, dating from year 21 of the reign of the last king of Larsa, goes into a long hymn-like digression on the prosperity of Dilmun due to its exceptional role as an import centre (UET VI/1 1 obverse II):

"*Let the land of Tukrish deliver for you the gold of Harali, the lapis lazuli...*
Let the land of Meluhha [bring for you],
on great ships, desirable and precious carnelian,
trees of Magan...
Let the land of Marhashi [bring for you] precious stones and agate (?)...
Let the land of Magan [bring for you] hard and resistant copper, diorite stones...

Let the Sealand [bring for you] ebony,
the ornament [of the throne] of royalty;
Let the Land of Tents [bring for you] wool,
and fine powder,
Let the Land of Elam transport [for you] a cargo of excellent wool,
Let the sanctuary of Ur, the seat of royalty,
the pure city,
Bring to you barley, sesame oil, precious cloths,
on great ships ...
Let the vast sea [bring you] its abundance.
In Dilmun, dwellings will be pleasant dwelling places;
Its barley will be fine barley; its dates will be large dates; its harvest will be triple...".

Dilmun was also renowned by the Sumerian poets for its rich vegetation, another source of prosperity. Royal hymns from the Empire of Ur III's lyrical works evoke Dilmun using the image of the palm tree: "*You are the beloved of the goddess Ninegal like the date palm of pure Dilmun*" is found in a hymn to king Shulgi (Hymn D). Comparing a loved one to the fruit of a tree became a literary cliché: "*my mother is a sweet Dilmun date*" wrote a poet-essayist (TCL XV pl. 81-82).

The cultural importance of Dilmun for the cultivated classes of Sumer is essentially characterised by the myth "Enki and Ninhursag". This work occupies a special place in Sumerian literature as its symbolic significance concerns a country outside Mesopotamia. It was conceived by the Eridu school of religious thought. Eridu was the southernmost city of Sumer, in the marshlands close to the mouth of the Gulf. The myth was perhaps destined to flatter the population of Dilmun, whose favourable disposition towards Sumer was important. Indeed, the myth "Enki and the World Order" shows that trading relations with the Gulf countries, for example Elam on the eastern coast, were not always easy. But this story has a deeper meaning than this. It describes Enki the divinity who protects Eridu and the freshwater ocean (Apsû), and who supports the Earth, pouring his fertilising waters onto the Earth through wells and springs. The geography of the island and the character of this god rapidly made him popular in Dilmun. Enki is associated with the goddess to whom he entrusted Dilmun – Ninsikilla, identified in this case with the Sumerian mother-goddess, Ninhursag. The text endows Dilmun's divinities with a prestigious ancestry: Ninsikilla, who was present at the beginning, even before an ordered world was born – at her request to Enki, the creator – plays the roles of wife and daughter of Enki. Inzak becomes lord of Dilmun as a reward for being one of the eight divinities brought forth by the mother-goddess Ninhursag to heal Enki, whom she had sentenced to death as a punishment for disturbing the still unstable order at the beginnings of creation. The god of Dilmun,

whose name means "the lord who does good things", or the "lord of the flank", because that was the part of Enki's body he healed, is written in Sumerian: En-sa6-ag. The choice of the sign sa6 = gishimmar "date palm", shows his power over Dilmun's favoured tree.

The myth begins with a hymn of praise to Dilmun, comparing its purity and perfection to that of Sumer (l. 1-6):
"*Blessed is the city that is bestowed upon you,*
Blessed (also) is the land of Dilmun;
Blessed is Sumer..., blessed is the land of Dilmun;
The land of Dilmun is blessed, the land of Dilmun is pure,
The land of Dilmun is luminous, the land of Dilmun is radiant.
When he settled there, the first at Dilmun,
the place where Enki settled with his wife,
this place (became) pure, this place is radiant".

This follows the Sumerian myths of creation, presenting parallels with some of the most ancient narratives that have reached us, describing the beginnings of the world, before civilisation, before Enki penetrated the world, a kind of negative image of reality. This is a land where there is not yet fresh water, without which no life can exist. It is a representation of limbo – the fringe, the potential for civilisation, and not a vision of paradise, as might be thought from an objective reading of the patterns of Sumerian

literature, guided by a search for parallels
with the Bible, might interpret it. Biblical
thought may have used it as inspiration,
but indirectly with its own interpretation.
(l. 7-30):

"At Dilmun, no crow cawed
The partridge (?) did not cackle,
The lion did not kill,
The wolf did not carry off the lamb,
The dog did not know how to herd the goats,
Nor did the wild boar know how to eat grain;
The widow spread the malt over her roof,
the birds of the sky did not come and peck at it;
The dove did not curve its neck;
No one with pain in their eyes said
"my eyes hurt",
No one with pain in their head said
"my head hurts!";
No old woman said: "I'm old!",
No old man said: "I'm old!";
Young women did not bathe, no clear water
ran through the town;
No one crossed the river shouting,
No Herald walked around his district,
No poet broke into a song of joy,
Nor sang a lamentation on the outskirts
of the town"

Even if this is not the original paradise,
a happy state at the beginnings of time
unknown to Sumerian thought, according
to which human beings were created

The gardens and palm groves
of Bahrain.

to replace the gods in performing hard
agricultural tasks, it is not the description
of total nothingness either. It is more that of life
as yet unorganised, contrary to the rules
of civilisation, a state of ignorance.
In this land without cities and without
agriculture, where the salty waters of a lagoon
stagnate, beasts and embryonic man act
in opposition to their nature. This example
is not unique. A fragment narrating
the Sumerian Flood, badly damaged,

but reconstituted using a duplicate of this passage in the Epic of "Enmerkar and the Lord of Aratta" (l.136-155), also describes the state of a country before it enjoyed the beneficial effects of civilisation:

"*…In those days, no canal [were opened]… mankind [walked about naked], in those days, there being no snakes, [being no scorpions], being no lions, being no dogs, [no wolves], mankind [had no opponent], fear [and terror did not exist]*" (Jacobsen 1981, p. 516, l.3'-5').

The style of the narrative is different, as it clearly states that wild animals did not yet exist, but its goal is the same. It aims to show a state of affairs that does not conform to the ordered laws of the universe, by establishing a catalogue, according to the Mesopotamian way of thinking, which aimed to explain things about nature by returning to the first principle that engendered the world.

Nevertheless, the notion of "paradise" can, to a certain extent, be applied to Dilmun. Dilmun is the land of eternal life, the place where the gods send the heroes they have made immortal to enjoy happy days and a peaceful eternity, in a prosperous location, towards the Orient, the place where the sun rises, where daylight is born. In the narrative of the Sumerian Flood, Ziusudra, the hero who survives the catastrophe and becomes immortal, was established by the gods in Dilmun (l.254-262):

"*Ziusudra, the king, having prostrated himself before An and Enlil… they bestowed eternal life upon him as for a god… They installed him in a country overseas: At Dilmun, where the sun rises*".

Dilmun was the trade gateway to the East, so were its heroes not chosen ones, luminous beings, radiant with saintliness, like the land of Dilmun itself? This is not the Old Testament vision of paradise (Genesis), but, paradoxically, is a vision that approaches that of the New Testament or of the Koran.

The myth then describes the birth of civilisation which explains the origin of the country's prosperity, linked to its role as an international warehouse (l. 31-64):

"*Ninsikilla spoke to her father Enki:… My city has no water in its channels [...] [Her father Enki replied to Ninsikila:] [Let the Sun make water rise up from the gates of the Earth [...] Let Dilmun have abundant water to drink! Let the saltwater wells become freshwater wells And let your city become the "house*

on the edge of the quay" (a warehouse)...
And he gave Dilmun water in abundance...
The fields and the ground produced barley...
Dilmun truly became the "house on the edge
of the quay" of the land,
And, in the sunlight of that day, it was so!".

The rest of the story probably takes place
in Enki's domain, in the marshland of Eridu,
as the composition seems to group several
narratives together, but it has a profound
resonance for Dilmun. This is how Dilmun
acquires its guardian deity, prototype
of a Sumerian sovereign, who will ensure
Dilmun's happiness and prosperity.
Dilmun becomes the perfect example
of civilisation, on an equal footing with Sumer.
Its luxurious landscape evokes a "paradisial"
place (the *paradeisos*).

Dilmun is as pure, holy and brilliant as Sumer,
and its goddess, Ninsikila,carries a name that
signifies "the Pure Lady". But the moral of the
myth is that Sumer is the source of all
civilisation, as it is the Sumerian civilised
god *par excellence*, Enki, who brings civilisation
to Dilmun. The myth thus rejoins historical fact.
After the decline of the port of Ur, and the
disappearance of the Indus civilisation,
Dilmun, whose sources of supplies were
then cut off, was no longer cited in
early Mesopotamian literature except
concerning the quality of its dates.

**4 Sumerian Creation Myth:
"Enki and Ninhursag"
or "The Myth of Dilmun"**
Southern Mesopotamia
Date of writing: end of
the 3rd millennium BC;
date of the tablet: beginning
of the 2nd millennium BC
Clay
H9.1 W7 TH2.7 cm
Paris, Louvre Museum,
acc. n° AO 6724
B S. Langdon 1915 (version
of Nippur); S.N. Kramer 1945;
C.J. Gadd & S.N. Kramer 1963,
n° 1 (version of Ur);
J.-M. Durand 1977 p. 169-171
(AO 6724: new copy
of H. de Genouillac, TCL XVI,
n° 62); A. Cavigneaux 1982,
n° 182 p. 236-237; B. Alster 1983,
p. 39-74; P. Attinger 1984,
p. 1-52; T. Jacobsen 1987,
p. 181-204; J. Bottéro
& S.N. Kramer 1989, p. 150-164

The symbolic meaning of this
myth of the origins of the world
is complex (see "The land
where the sun rises..."). It shows
that the Sumerians wished
to include Dilmun, their
privileged trading partner,
in the civilised world
gravitating around
the influence of Sumer. This is
the meaning of the introduction
to the composition, a hymn
of praise for Dilmun. The text
explains the origin of its
maritime wealth and fertile land
as the result of an act by Enki,
encouraged by the goddess
of Dilmun, Ninsikila, conflated
here with the great Sumerian
goddess, Ninhursag. The text
then recounts the divine
geneaological succession
which ends with the placing
on the throne of Dilmun the
god, Inzak (or Enzag). He is the
son of Enki, but Enki owes him
his life, since, as he was born,
like his seven brothers and
sisters from Enki's sick organ, he
delivers Enki from the curse of
death pronounced over him
by Ninhursag. The succession
of divine generations that ends
with Inzak is due to Enki lying
with three successive
generations of his own
daughters, until the mother-
goddess interrupts this process
which goes against the laws
of civilised nature. Enki's illness,
brought about by eating
poisonous plants he himself
created, shows him
the necessity of finding
harmony through the
establishment of normal sexual
relations. The lesson inflicted on
Enki is the prelude to the
establishment of order. This
myth also offers an explanation
of the beginnings of vegetation
on earth - marsh plants, edible
plants, fruits, and medicinal
plants.
Three copies of the myth
have reached us. That held
by the Louvre is partial,
and contains the tale of the
rape of his daughter Ninimma,
absent from the other versions,
and the birth of Uttu (140 ff.).

5 Sumerian Creation Myth "Enki and the World Order"

Southern Mesopotamia
Beginning of the
2nd millennium BC
Clay
H12.2 W6.4 TH3.2 cm
Paris, Louvre Museum,
acc. n° AO 6020
B C.A. Benito 1969; B. André 1982,
n° 183, p. 237-238; B. Alster
1983, p. 39-74 (bibliography);
J. Bottéro, S.N. Kramer 1989,
p. 165-188

The god of Knowledge wanted to organise things on earth to ensure abundance for the Land of Sumer whose power, held by an enlightened sovereign, would enable him to import precious materials that the kingdom was lacking. On inspecting his domain, Enki dictated to Destiny and named the wealth of the different parts of Sumer, on which he bestowed agriculture, livestock farming and a textile industry, whose fruits would be used for exchanges for imported items. To the rich foreign lands on which Sumer depended to obtain them, he bestowed raw materials: metals, wood, and precious stones. Dilmun, in the same way as Magan and Meluhha - willing, peaceful and indispensable trading partners - was endowed with a good fate (l. 238 to 241). On the contrary, the lands of Elam and Marhashi, in Iran, were obliged to contribute their wealth in the form of a tribute of war. Thus, the myth reflects the political and economic situation of the Gulf region, of which Dilmun was the crossroads. This long text, at least 464 lines long, reached us in the form of several copies from the beginning of the 2nd millennium. The version from the Louvre contains the end of the myth.

6 Bilingual Sumerian/Babylonian Vocabulary of the Date Palm and Dates

Southern Mesopotamia, Babylon
Neo-Babylonian Period,
c. 6th cent. BC
Clay
H13 L14.5 TH2.8 cm
Paris, Louvre Museum,
acc. n° AO 2131
B F. Thureau-Dangin 1904, p. 129;
B. André-Salvini 1996, p. 34-35

The fragmented text contains the canonical version of volume III of the twenty-four part series of the great Babylonian encyclopedia. It is devoted to trees, and the largest number of terms listed concerns the date palm, the only arboricultural resource of the southern part of the country, whose palms were used to make numerous everyday objects, and whose fruit was a rich food source. Two varieties of Dilmun date-palms are noted (l.284-285): "tilmun"

and "asnû". The second probably supplied sweeter and better tasting dates if we are to judge by the content of Babylonian economic texts. The "dates of Dilmun" were of great renown in Sumer, subsequently in Babylon, and this title became a sort of guarantee of vintage, in economic as well as literary texts where they are a symbol of sweetness and beauty, but also to a certain extent of social rank and civilisation. In the myth of the "Wedding of Sud", a minor goddess who became the wife of Enkil, "baskets full of Dilmun dates" (l. 120) were among the best products chosen to offer as wedding gifts by Enlil to his new wife. During his visit to the Sumer federal sanctuary at Nippur, the moon god, Nanna-Suen praised the town in the following terms: "My city where date-palms grew before Dilmun existed!" (l. 33-34).

"The World's Largest Prehistoric Cemetery..."

Jean-Yves Breuil

The "vast sea of sepulchral mounds... of some unknown race", described by J.T. Bent in 1890, is still today one of the largest burial sites of the Bronze Age. Originally estimated to number some 170,000, the tumuli have long been the essential feature of Bahrain's archaeological horizon, giving a "lunar" aspect to some landscapes. At the same time, some scholars have sought to interpret their presence as evidence that the island was a land reserved for the dead from the neighbouring civilisations of Arabia or Mesopotamia. This idea of a funerary island, which supposedly found its echo in Sumerian mythology is, however, no longer considered a possibility since several settlements have been found that were contemporary with the tombs. In parallel to this, it has been demonstrated that an island population of 10 000 people over five centuries (with a life expectancy of 40 years) would have been sufficient to occupy the tombs found.

It is sometimes difficult to date these graves due to the absence of artefacts. Overall, the construction of the tumuli covers seven centuries, between 2 400 and 1 700 BC. The tumuli are separated into ten or so "fields", which are spread over the north and the west of Bahrain in a desert-like zone bordered on one side by the central depression, and on the other by the more fertile coastal strip. These cemeteries are therefore all situated outside the cultivable areas, but probably not far from the settlements, since at least some of these were likely to have been situated where the present day villages are found. Outside these natural restrictions, the land chosen was never enclosed, and seemed to be an area large enough to allow the cemeteries to expand. The sedimentary cover is not very thick; the limestone substratum, naturally flawed and eroded, is easily accessible and provided the materials necessary for the building of the monuments.

Increased urbanisation over the last three decades has considerably reduced the number of tumuli, but at the same time, salvage digs have enabled us to understand burial practices better.

A typical tumulus has the following features: a mound of earth with limestone fragments of 1 to 4 m in height, surrounded by a circular wall on average 6 to 10 m in diameter. This wall is generally no longer visible due to the progressive subsidence of the tumulus. The top of the mound often presents a depression which is a sign of pillaging.

The tumuli all cover a central rectangular burial chamber, built with rough blocks of limestone, and covered by slabs of the same material. This chamber, usually orientated North/South, is built at ground level, or sometimes slightly dug into the substratum. Its dimensions can vary

The "vast sea of sepulchral mounds…" of the desert-like fringes of Bahrain is still impressive, despite the archipelago's increased urbanisation.

Bahrain during the Early Dilmun Period (2500-1800 BC).
Distribution of the different types of necropoleis and settlements.

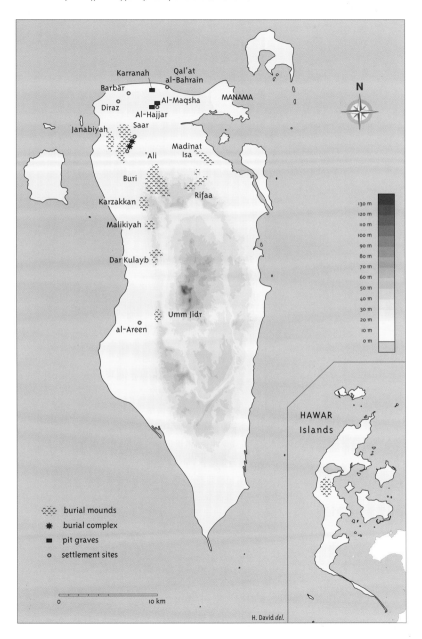

from one to several metres in length with and average width and height of approximately 1 to 1.50 m. It often has one or more lateral alcoves designed to receive the funeral furniture.

Not all of the tombs are occupied. This is basically due to the poor conditions of conservation, and any cenotaphs (monuments with no body) are purely accidental. The majority are individual tombs. The skeleton is placed on its side, with the head to the north, the legs are bent, and the hands are brought close to the face. There is no trace of any coffin-like container, and the body is not covered with earth. There does not seem to have been any discrimination: women, men, and children were all apparently entitled to the same type of tomb.

The funeral furniture is a constant element in the funeral ritual. It can consist of everyday or decorative ceramic objects, personal ornaments (jewellery sets, necklaces, seals), copper weapons and cups, stone vessels. A small amount of food in bitumen-coated baskets or ostrich egg shells may also accompany the deceased. Bones of ovi-caprids or fish (remains of the funeral meal?) are sometimes part of the offering. Systematic pillaging means that the original offering cannot always be determined, although it can be deduced that it was usually quite extensive, varying in opulence with the architectural quality of the monument itself. In any case, the deceased always received a minimum burial

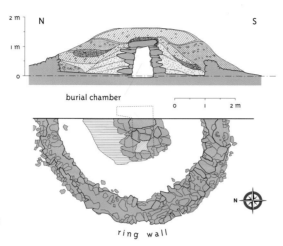

burial chamber

0   1   2 m

N

ring wall

Section and plan of a "classic" Dilmun tumulus (after Cleuziou *et al*, 1981, fig. 4, p.40).

offering. This was usually composed of local objects, although the presence of some imported objects or imitations bears witness to the contacts Dilmun had with Mesopotamia, Iran, the Oman peninsula and the Indus Valley.

The latest research has brought some new facts to light that may change the long-established and uniform image we have of tumuli, the basic, infinitely repeated pattern which indicates a deeply-anchored collective ritual... A more ancient type apparently exists, a kind of prototype for the traditional tumulus, quite low, without a surrounding wall, with an oblong corbelled chamber, generally found associated with ceramics of the "Umm-an-Nar" tradition (Oman). The first can be dated back to the start of the second half of the 3rd millennium.

The external aspect of classic tumuli has long been documented. Their present mound shape, a flared cone, is due to the collapse of the surrounding wall and its gradual disappearance with the subsidence of the monument. Originally, these monuments were of cylindrical shape with a flat or slightly domed summit, a sort of circular "tomb tower", some even with more than one level. These had a second circular wall with a smaller diameter halfway up.

The most remarkable characteristic of these tombs is that they were built in advance. We have observed that many of these monuments were built in two stages, most of the work being done in the first stage (surrounding wall, funeral chamber, inside filling), with access to the funeral chamber remaining possible (from above, or from the side, or via a shaft, occasionally a horizontal gallery). The monument was then left this way until the person died, and was only completely blocked up after the burial had taken place.

It would seem that the people of Dilmun at that time had their final resting-place built during their lifetime. There are evidently exceptions to this rule, in particular for children or adolescents, whose death is, by definition, unpredictable. This explains why we generally find them buried in adjoining tombs built according to the same model,

Top. The 'honeycomb' burial complex at Saar.

Bottom. The "royal tumuli" at 'Ali – the necropolis of the rulers of Dilmun?

each chamber surrounded by a wall
in a half-circle, a kind of semi-tumulus built
hastily and always built against a central
tumulus. In this way, several tombs can be joined
to one another starting from one original tomb.
It is probable that there was a filial or family
link between the different occupants of these
tombs, though no anthropological evidence
has yet backed up this hypothesis.
The burial monument built in advance
by its future occupant was a good indicator
of the status of the person, which takes us further
and further from the idea of a monotonous
cemetery where each tomb is a strict replica
of all the others. The cemetery at 'Ali in
particular shows great variety in the density
and nature of the monuments. It would appear
that the burial area was carefully managed,
with, in particular, in the north part of the
necropolis, twenty or so enormous monuments
well separated from one another. These
"royal tumuli" some over 20 m high with a
diameter of 25 m use the same principle of
circular construction in levels, but there is a
systematic arrangement to allow access (a shaft,
or a gallery and doors) that opens on to several,
sometimes superimposed chambers of nearly 10
m in length. These extremely well-kept,
spectacular, exclusive tombs (carefully cut
stones, plastered walls), which perhaps
betray the existence of a hierarchical system,
were the exception in that they were used
for several burials (hence the specially

Typical burial chamber
of a Dilmun tumulus
(circa 1900 BC).

constructed entrances). They number among the
rare examples of collective tombs in a single
tumulus at this phase of Early Dilmun.

The final resting places of the inhabitants
of Dilmun, some of which are almost built like
"fortresses" were all apparently pillaged
not long after the burial. The people of Dilmun
did not apparently try to fight this practice, as
though it was more important to preserve and
ensure the durability of the "building", even if it
was "unfurnished".

The digs of the last few years have shown
that during the same period, as well

as the tumuli, there were two other types
of tomb. Although these are much fewer
in number, their existence highlights
the diversity in burial practices in Bahrain.

At Saar, three burial complexes have been
uncovered near the tumuli. They are vast groups
of several hundreds of tombs that are
interconnected like a honeycomb, and can cover
areas of up to 5000 m². Each tomb surrounded by
a wall has a rectangular burial chamber,
sometimes with alcoves. The basic principle
is the same as for the tumuli, but taken
to extremes, so that no tomb can be separated
from the next. Each new tomb was added to the
existing ones, and so masked them. The group
forms a low mound. The tombs vary little,
between 1.50 m and 1.80 m in length
and around 1m high.

These burial complexes are from the same period
as the tumuli, and the burial ritual was similar.
The deceased was placed lying on their side, with
a similar funeral offering. But in other ways the
burial practice is radically different – there is no
ostentatious, individualistic attitude. Instead of
individual tumuli built in advance, each tomb
was discreetly erected almost certainly after the
person's death, and disappeared among the
others in the complex. This type of cemetery
seems to follow certain organisational principles,
since all the graves of children are grouped
together in specific areas.

The third type groups together a thousand or so rectangular graves hollowed out in the rocky substratum and covered with slabs. They have currently been found in three places situated in the heart of the northern palm groves, areas that were, until this point, not used for burial purposes, but were regularly used from then on until the Tylos era.

These cemeteries were begun in the first half of the 2nd millennium and were linked to small settlements in the immediate vicinity (al-Hajjar, for example). They seem to have developed in a concentric fashion, in circular groups. Here also, a burial offering accompanied each of the deceased, and this did not differ noticeably from that observed in the other types of necropoleis. The grave length varies from 1m to more than 4m for widths of 0.50-0.75m and depths of 0.50-1.20m.

The most recent graves seem to be the largest ones, found on the outskirts of the cemeteries, where we often find objects that originated from the neighbouring Omani "Wadi Suq" culture. These tombs were clearly destined to receive several bodies. This type of cemetery thus inaugurated and developed from around 1700-1800 BC onwards, a burial practice that was until then extremely rare - collective graves. The Kassite settlers to whom we had until now attributed the appearance of this practice actually only perpetuated an existing custom.

The Janabiyah necropolis (shown here is a collective grave with access shaft, excavated in 1998) provided the information needed to reconstruct the original appearance of the Bahrain tumuli.

It would be premature to attempt an explanation for the differences between the three types of cemeteries, which probably coexisted at some point. Do they indicate different populations? Do they simply illustrate the slow development of a multicultural society constantly enriched by new contributions?

The evidence leads us to observe that the Dilmunite attitude towards death and the dead was complex, oscillating continually between strong ritual practices and the regular assimilation of new burial practices. A century of archaeological work has enabled us only to partially understand this attitude, and the full extent of its richness is yet to be laid bare.

Early Dilmun Burial Offerings

Pierre Lombard

7, 8 Vessels in the Mesopotamian Tradition
Rifa'a necropolis,
Bahraini excavations 1996-97,
Tumulus 7
Madinat Hamad necropolis (SE),
Bahraini excavations 1984-85,
Tumulus 94
Early Dilmun, c. 2300-2000 BC
Pottery
H20.2 and 11.3
D MAX.15.3 and 8.5 cm
Manama, Bahrain National
Museum, main store,
and acc. n° 9-2-88
B *Bahrain National Museum*
1993, p. 16

This type of vessel which is found in several sizes is undoubtedly of Mesopotamian origin. They have been found in the Royal Graves of Ur in particular (Woolley 1934, pl. 253, fig. 44a; pl. 265, fig. 224) and in sites as late as the Akkad period. They are quite frequently found in burial offerings in the oldest Early Dilmun tumuli at Bahrain (Lowe 1986, fig. 6, p. 77), but also in those of the neighbouring Omani Umm-an-Nar culture (Grave N at Hili, for example), towards the end of the 3rd millennium BC (Haddu 1989, p. 64: 9), and also in the Eastern Province of Saudi Arabia (Burkholder 1984, num. 33). The form could be specific to burial use.

Contrary to what the first explorers and other more recent authors of the necropoleis at Bahrain, may have thought, nearly all of the Bronze Age tombs did contain a body, accompanied by the traditional deposit of offerings. When the culture of Dilmun disappeared there were probably various tumuli as yet unoccupied and we cannot entirely exclude the possibility that a few rare cenotaphs were erected, but we know today that pillaging - practised since antiquity, on a large scale, almost systematically - combined with natural phenomena (water seepage, fauna, flora) is responsible for the numerous empty tombs mentioned regularly in connection with archaeological digs.

When not completely pillaged, the funeral furniture was often "disturbed". This means that our information is incomplete - we know of no complete group of offerings, and archaeologists must take this into account when interpreting their discoveries.

The few complete studies of funeral furniture in early Dilmun, all of them tentative, show, nonetheless, that the offerings were generally modest, and fairly homogeneous. The most ancient tumuli often contained ceramics seemingly imported from Mesopotamia or from the Oman peninsula (Cat. 7-13, etc.). During the period that was Dilmun's apogee (approx. 2 000-1 800 BC), a specific container

(Cat. 21-25) was found in almost all tombs. This is the "cylindrical jar" or "burial jar", which is one of the most characteristic pieces of local work. We do not know whether the jar's contents were perishable, and if so what they were, or if it was empty. It is generally found associated with other storage jars (Cat. 18-20) which are found in settlements. These jars are sometimes associated with painted vessels (Cat. 26-41), of which some were perhaps specifically made for funeral purposes, and were sometimes imported from regions that traded with Dilmun. Vessels in soft stone (Cat. 42-46), also imported, must have represented a luxury item, although they were not targeted by pillagers, who obviously looked for metal objects (Cat. 47-52, 55) which were relatively rare, and jewellery (Cat. 63-64). Several deposits show that perishables were placed near the deceased - drinking receptacles (Cat. 56-57) or baskets coated with bitumen (Cat. 54). In the absence of texts from the civilisation of Dilmun, these are the only clues we have concerning a possible ritual ceremony, and a probable belief in an afterlife.

The emblematic object of local culture, the stamp-seal, is very frequently found, often in its original position, around the neck of the deceased. Found in adult graves, but also in those of children, its symbolic function probably went deeper than its simple functional and commercial role.

9, 10 Vessels in the Mesopotamian Tradition
'Ali necropolis ,
Bahraini excavations 1988-89,
Tumulus 62a and 2.2
Early Dilmun, c. 2300-2000 BC
Pottery
H18.5 D MAX15.5 cm
Manama, Bahrain National Museum, acc. n° 2454-2-90-10 and 2505-2-90-10
Unpublished

This is the second type of ceramic pot of Mesopotamian origin widely distributed in Bahrain towards the end of the 3rd millennium (Lowe 1986, p. 76 and fig. 7, p. 77). It was also found in the Royal Graves of Ur (Woolley 1934, pl. 253, fig. 40). It has been suggested that this form could have been a prototype for the traditional Early Dilmun "burial jar" or "cylindrical jar" (Cat. 21-25).

11, 12 Vessels in the Omani Tradition

Madinat Hamad necropolis,
Bahraini excavations 1982-83,
Tumulus 7.1
Saar necropolis
("Burial complex"),
Bahraini excavations 1981,
Grave B/K2.1
Early Dilmun, c. 2300-2000 BC
Pottery
^{H}15.6 and 10.5
$^{D\,MAX}$13.9 and 9.9 cm
Manama, Bahrain National
Museum, acc. n° 3-2-88
and 432-2-88
^{B} *Bahrain National Museum*
1993, p. 17, 32

Petrographic analyses carried
out on several "Umm an-Nar"
tradition vessels discovered
in Bahrain have confirmed
that their clay does correspond
to that of the Omani foothills
region. Their typology
also clearly links them to known
specimens from the Umm
an-Nar graves in this region
dating from 2300 BC
(see for example Al-Tikriti 1989,
pl. 39: d, f, g; pl. 52: a;
pl. 53: a). They were therefore
commonly exported
to the Early Dilmun sites
(Bahrain, Eastern Province
of Arabia) and probably
exchanged for the most
common type of Dilmun
"burial jar" which has been
identified on numerous
sites on the Oman Peninsula
(Cat. 21-25).

13 Ovoid Red Slip Vessel

Madinat Hamad necropolis
(BS1), Bahraini excavations 1984,
Tumulus 853
Early Dilmun, c. 2000-1800 BC
Pottery
^{H}14.8 $^{D\,MAX}$12.3 cm
Manama, Bahrain National
Museum, acc. n° 2557-2-90-2
Unpublished

This pot, especially typical of
the type of material found in
the "classic" tumuli (Ibrahim
1982, pl. 45: 4-5), is above all
characterised by its reddish
wine-coloured slip. This was
obtained from pigments from a
type of red ochre that probably
originated from the islands
or the Iranian coast
of the Hormuz Strait.
Similar slips are found
until the Kassite period
(Middle Dilmun) and are
probably of the same origin.

14, 15 Burial Jars
Saar necropolis,
Bahraini excavations 1977-78,
Tumulus 175
Madinat Hamad necropolis
(BNN), Bahraini
excavations 1984-85,
Tumulus 230.6
Early Dilmun, c. 2000-1800 BC
Pottery
H23.5 and 17.7 D MAX18 and 14 cm
Manama, Bahrain National
Museum, acc. n° 415-2-88
and 416-2-88
B Ibrahim 1982: 33; fig. 37:4;
pl. 51:3

The decoration of ridges
in relief, frequently found
on the body of globular burial
jars was often found next
to similar jars decorated to
resemble them with irregular
painted horizontal stripes.

**16, 17 Vessels with Snake
Decoration**
Madinat Hamad necropolis
(M2), Bahraini excavations 1986,
Tumulus 169.1; (BS3),
Bahraini excavations 1985-86,
Tumulus 65.7
Early Dilmun, c. 2000 BC
Pottery
H9.6 and 12.2 D MAX13.7 and 12 cm
Manama, Bahrain National
Museum, acc. n° 449-2-88
and 26-2-88
Unpublished

This type of container with its
decoration remains relatively
rare in Bahrain, where
it has been found as often
in the necropoleis as
in the layers of City IIb
of the Qal'at al-Bahrain
settlement site. The snake,
however, is a recurrent theme
in the iconography
of the cultures of the Arabian
Peninsula and the Arabian Gulf,
in the Bronze Age and in later
periods.

18, 19 Jars with Filter
Saar necropolis,
Bahraini excavations 1984-85,
Tumulus 243.11
and tumulus unspecified
Early Dilmun, c. 2000-1800 BC
Pottery
H28.4 and 36.5
D MAX26.2 and 25.7cm
Manama, Bahrain National
Museum, acc. n° 1154-2-88
and main store
Unpublished

It is still not clear how the globular jar with a permanent filter inside the neck (length and narrowness varies in the examples so far discovered) worked, and what exactly it was used for. Either the jar was completely immersed in a tank or basin containing the liquid to be separated from its suspended particles (barley wine or beer?), or the liquid was carefully introduced into the filter, which is effectively placed in a hollow. Once clear, the liquid could then be poured or drunk using a straw passed through the filter (cf. the traditional representations of "beer drinkers" on the Dilmun stamp-seals). This type of vase seems however to be found more frequently in burial contexts than associated with domestic equipment.

20 Jar with Ridged Body
Madinat Hamad necropolis
(BS2),
Bahraini excavations 1984-85,
Tumulus 149.37
Early Dilmun, c. 2000 BC
Pottery
H39 D MAX22.5 cm
Manama, Bahrain National
Museum, acc. n° 25-2-90-10
Unpublished

21-25 "Burial Jars"
'Ali necropolis,
Bahraini excavations 1989-90,
Tumulus 65.2A
Madinat Hamad necropolis,
Bahraini excavations,
seasons and graves unspecified;
1986-87, Tumulus 1; 1984-85,
Tumulus 92
Early Dilmun, c. 2000-1800 BC

Pottery
H21, 17.6, 14.6 and 10 D MAX.12,
13.7, 10 and 8.5 cm
Manama, Bahrain National
Museum, acc.n° 2231-2-90-10,
3-12-2-90, 555-2-88, 2699-2-
90, 2693-2-90
Unpublished

Sometimes also called
"cylindrical jar", this type
of receptacle was especially
frequent in graves, but was also
occasionally found
in settlements. It represents
the most common type of burial
offering and it can be
considered, in the same way as
the famous circular stamp-seals

(see below), as a "type fossil"
for the Early Dilmun culture,
with a slight change
in the shape of the receptacles
between 2000 and 1800 BC
(cf Velde 1998, p. 248,
fig. 2: 1-4; p. 252, fig. 3: 1-7).
These Dilmun "burial jars"
were exported as far as Larsa
in Iraq, but especially

to the south of the Gulf,
on the Oman Peninsula
(Shimal, Kalba, Tell Abraq;
Méry et al. 1998, p. 178).
It is quite possible
that these vessels contained
a special liquid reserved
for burial rites.

26-28 Burial Vessels
Madinat Hamad necropolis (BS2),
Bahraini excavations 1984–85, Tumulus 157.8
Saar. Bahraini excavations 1988–89, Tumulus 238.A4
Dar Kulayb necropolis, Bahraini excavations 1994–95, Tumulus 89.17
Early Dilmun, c. 1900–1800 BC
Pottery
H 19.2, 17 and 24.7
D MAX. 15, 12.7 and 16.3 cm
Manama, Bahrain National Museum, acc. n° 90-2-88, 1841-2-89 and main store
Unpublished. Comp.: Velde 1998, p. 252, fig. 3: 9-10

29-33 Miniature Burial Vessels
Madinat Hamad necropolis (BS2),
Bahraini excavations 1984–85, Tumulus 2.80, Tumulus 107.20; season and grave unspecified; (NBH4), 1989, Tumulus 10.30
Early Dilmun, c. 1900–1800 BC
Pottery
H 5.7, 6.3, 10.5, 8.7 and 10.6
D MAX. 5.7, 6.3, 12. 8,8 and 10.4 cm
Manama, Bahrain National Museum, acc. n° 3937-2-91, 19-2-88, 90-7-1, 1990-2-89, 5308-2-91
Unpublished

35-36 Burial Goblets
Saar necropolis, excavations
1977-78, Tumulus 100 and 54
Early Dilmun, c. 2000-1800 BC
Pottery
H13.2 and 10.2
D MAX.12.8 and 9 cm
Manama, Bahrain National
Museum, acc. n° 410-2-88
and 411-2-88
B Ibrahim 1982: 71; fig. 38:2
and 38:1; pl. 49.1 49:2

34 Suspension Vessel
Madinat Hamad necropolis
(BSW1),
Bahraini excavations 1986-87,
Tumulus 4
Early Dilmun, c. 1900-1800 BC
Pottery
H14.3 D MAX.10 cm
Manama. Bahrain National
Museum. acc. n° 433-2-88
Unpublished. Comp.:
Bahrain National Museum 1989.
n° 33; Velde 1998. p. 254.
fig. 4:18.

This strangely shaped vase
with four lateral pierced lugs
was probably designed
to be suspended. It belongs
to a type that was widespread
during the Isin-Larsa period
(beginning of the
2nd millennium BC) in Southern
Mesopotamia (Larsa. Ur),
in Iran (Susa), and has even
been found in a context
from the same period in Oman.
We can consider it to be
an excellent chronological
indicator.

37-39 Burial Vases
Madinat Hamad necropolis
(BS2),
Bahraini excavations 1984-85,
Tumulus 153.3; (BSW) 1985-86,
Unspecified tumulus ;
(BH/65-60), 1982-83,
Unspecified tumulus
Early Dilmun, c. 2000-1800 BC
Pottery
H26.5, 13 and 18.3
D MAX.22.2, 12.5 and 16.8 cm
Manama, Bahrain National
Museum, acc. n° 86-2-88,
561-2-88 and 84-2-88
Unpublished. Comp.:
Bahrain National Museum 1993,
p. 40; Velde 1998, p. 254,
fig. 4: 20

**40 Ring-Base
Suspension Vessel**
'Ali necropolis,
Bahraini excavations 1994,
Tumulus 7B
Early Dilmun, c. 2000-1800 BC
Pottery
H19.2 D MAX.14.5 cm
Manama, Bahrain National
Museum, acc. n° 94-1-1
Unpublished

This piece is so far the only
one of its kind found
in Early Dilmun burial offerings
at Bahrain. It could be
a late Harappan import.

41 Suspension Vessel Decorated with Figures

Saar necropolis,
season and grave unspecified
Early Dilmun, c. 1900-1800 BC
Pottery
H23.3 D MAX.13.5 cm
Manama, Bahrain National
Museum, acc. n° 97-2-52
B *Bahrain National Museum*
1993, p. 32

This remarkable piece
has a particularly
heterogeneous style:
The shape is more or less
inspired by the Mesopotamian
suspended vessels from
the Isin-Larsa period (Cat. 34).
The thickened shoulder
of the vessel, is rather unusual,
as is the long vertical neck
which evokes the neck of the
traditional Dilmun "burial jar"
The decoration is geometrical
and also shows animals
(caprids, cattle). It is organised
in panels and on several
registers. This is reminiscent
of the iconography of
Indo-Iranian regions at the
beginning of the
2nd millennium BC. If it were
not for the quality of the clay,
which is clearly superior to that
of Dilmunite productions, we
would be tempted to look on it
as a local design, a synthesis
of the diverse technical
and artistic influences to
which the Island of Bahrain
was subject at that time.
This type of suspended vessel
which also, paradoxically, has
an integrated annular support,
is rather intriguing. We can also
see two or more perforations
in the middle of the body
of these two vases, which means
they could not be used to
transport any liquids. These
holes could have been used as
air vents for a kind
of suspended incense burner
used in the same way as modern
religious censers.

42 Soft Stone Vessel with Compartments and Incised Decoration
Saar necropolis
("Burial complex"),
Bahraini excavations 1984-85,
Grave B/E3.1
Early Dilmun, c. 2000-1800 BC
(discovery context)
Chlorite
H6.2 L9.7 W4.3 cm
Manama, Bahrain National
Museum, acc. n° 306-2-88
Unpublished

This is another shape almost
exclusively associated
with "Umm-an-Nar"
manufacture. This rectangular
box with a slightly
wedge-shaped profile is
divided into two compartments
by an internal partition.
It also has the characteristic
decoration of this production
(cf for example Vogt 1985,
pl. 27: 16; Al-Tikriti 1989,
pl. 55: b). Boxes of this type,
whose exact use and contents

are not known, were often
associated with a flat lid
with a central lug which
is missing here.

**⁴⁶ Soft Stone Vessel
with Incised Decoration**
Saar Necropolis
("Burial complex"),
Bahraini excavations 1984-85,
grave B/Fɪ.2
Early Dilmun, c.2100-1900 BC
(discovery context)
Chlorite
ᴴ12.8 ᴰ ᴹᴬˣ·10.4 cm
Manama, Bahrain National
Museum, acc. n° 359-2-88
Unpublished

This cylindrical goblet
with a very slightly flared base
is typical of the chlorite vessels
made in the Oman Peninsula in
the "Umm-an-Nar" period, in
the second half of the 3rd
millennium BC (cf for example
Vogt 1985, pl. 27: 19). The Hajjar
mountain chain contains a
large number of soft stone
(chlorite, steatite) deposits
which were the preferred
materials for the production of
these vessels. The dotted double
circle pattern traced with a
compass, spaced out in rows is
also characteristic. Stone vases
were a common offering in
graves in the Gulf region,
but, curiously, only appeared
sporadically in the Bahrain
tumuli.

**⁴³ Soft Stone Spouted
Vessel with Incised
Decoration**
'Ali necropolis,
Bahraini excavations 1989-90,
Tumulus 65.2
Early Dilmun, c. 1900-1800 BC
Chlorite
ᴴ5.8 ᴰ ᴹᴬˣ·16.5 cm
Manama, Bahrain National
Museum, acc. n° 1987-2-90
Unpublished

This flat-bottomed bowl
with a pouring spout is another
typical shape from
the "Wadi Suq" period.
Its decoration combines
horizontal lines, small dotted
circles and chevrons,
supplemented this time
with a fish bone pattern
which is a little rarer.
It is carved out of a fine grained
chlorite which is matt
and of a brown colour,
demonstrating the variety
of sources of raw materials
that were used in the Oman
Peninsula.

**⁴⁴, ⁴⁵ Suspended Soft
Stone Vessel with Incised
Decoration**
Al-Maqsha necropolis,
Bahraini excavations 1992-93,
Grave ɪ
Madinat Hamad necropolis (BS2),
Bahraini excavations 1984-85,
Tumulus 149.45
Early Dilmun, c. 1900-1800 BC
Chlorite
ᴴ6.5 and 14.8 ᴰ ᴹᴬˣ·9.8 and 15 cm
(vase); 6 x 10 cm (lid)
Manama, Bahrain National
Museum, main store
and acc. n° 145-2-88
Unpublished

Equipped with four vertically
pierced lugs which were used

to hold strings to suspend
them with, these vessels are
particularly typical
of the "Wadi Suq" chlorite vases
from the Oman Peninsula,
appreciably later than those of
Umm-an-Nar. Large numbers of
specimens have indeed been
found in graves from the end
of the Early Dilmun period
in Bahrain. The decoration
is classically organised around
groups of horizontal lines
separating rows of dotted
circles under the lip from series
of chevrons between the lugs.
This typical pattern is also
engraved on the lids of
the vases.

47-49 Metal Vessels
'Ali necropolis ,
Bahraini excavations 1988-89,
Tumulus 101.5 and 103.11
Madinat Hamad necropolis
(BS1), Bahraini excavations
1986-87, Tumulus 1
Early Dilmun, c. 2000-1800 BC
Copper or copper alloy
H8.5, 9.5 and 5
D MAX.10.8, 13.2 and 8.4 cm
Manama, Bahrain National
Museum, acc. n° 2888-15-90,
2884-15-90, 2882-2-90
Unpublished

Either due to grave robbery or
corrosion, metal objects
have been found in smaller
quantities in the Early Dilmun
necropoleis than ceramics
or soft stone vessels.
These three bowls are
exceptionally well preserved,
but are however rather
insignificant chronologically
speaking. Similar specimens
have been found
in Mesopotamia, at Susa,
in the Indus region
and in Bactria (cf Tallon 1987,
p. 209-210).

53 Incense Burner
'Ali necropolis,
Bahraini excavations 1988-89,
Tumulus 101.16
Early Dilmun, c. 2000-1800 BC
Pottery
H19.8 D MAX.10.9 cm
Manama, Bahrain National
Museum, acc. n° 1831-2-89
Unpublished

Examples of this type of object
(which does not seem to have
been produced locally)
are very rare amongst the burial
offerings found in the Early
Dilmun tumuli. It was perhaps
associated with a ritual that
took place at the time of burial.

50-52 Spearheads
Saar necropolis
("Burial complex"),
Bahraini excavations 1984-85,
Grave A/13.3;
Season and grave unspecified
Early Dilmun, c. 2000-1800 BC
Copper or copper alloy
L11, 19.7 and 17.2;
W MAX. 2.6, 2.7 and 2.5 cm
Manama, Bahrain National
Museum, acc. n° 2923-3-90,
main store and 2924-2-90
Unpublished

Bronze Age weapons have also
only been found sporadically in
Bahrain. This type of spearhead
with a socket was a type that
was widespread in the Gulf
and also in Mesopotamia,
at the beginning
of the 2nd millennium BC.
They have been found
in graves and in settlements.

54 Bitumen-coated Basket
Saar necropolis,
season and grave unspecified
Early Dilmun, c. 2000-1800 BC
Bitumen
H12.9 D MAX.13.5 cm
Manama, Bahrain National
Museum, acc. n° 292-2-88
Unpublished

Small "baskets" or receptacles woven in palm leaves which were then coated inside and out with a layer of bitumen to make them waterproof were commonly placed in the Bahrain tumuli. There are basically two models of basketry in this category: this type of container with two lugs for suspension, and smaller goblets, which were perhaps provided for the deceased to be able to drink (Højlund 1995). Bitumen itself was commonly used in the ancient Near East as an adhesive or for waterproofing. In the desert zone to the south of the *Jebel Dukhan*, the island of Bahrain possesses a limited source of natural bitumen, but, curiously, this does not seem to have been exploited during antiquity. Archaeometric studies have shown that the bitumen used in Bahrain came either from Mesopotamia (Hit, especially), or from Iran (Connan *et al.* 1998).

55 Dagger with Crescent-shaped Pommel
Madinat Hamad necropolis,
Bahraini excavations 1998-99,
Tumulus 422
Early Dilmun, c. 2200-2000 BC
Copper or copper alloy
L47 Lhandle 11; Wpommel 13;
Wblade 3.6 cm
Manama, Bahrain National
Museum, main store
Unpublished

Two examples have so far been found in Bahrain of this type of long dagger characterised by its marked central rib, its thin hilt and the well developed flat crescent-shaped pommel. They were found in two tumuli in the section of the Madinat Hammad necropolis which, like other cemeteries on the island, contained very few weapons.

The rest of the burial offerings found with these burials were unexceptional. This elegantly shaped specimen seems to be relatively rare within the weapon typology of the Bronze Age in the Near East.

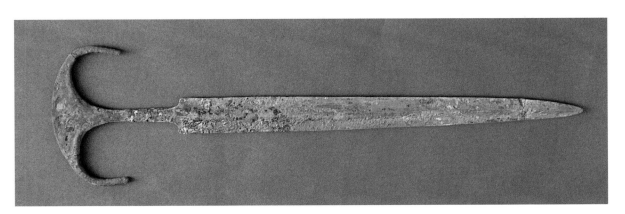

56, 57 Ostrich Eggs

Saar necropolis,
Bahraini excavations 1989-90,
Tumulus 107
Madinat Hamad necropolis (BS1),
Bahraini excavations 1994-95,
Tumulus 8.22
Early Dilmun, c. 2000-1800 BC
Shell
^{H}13.5 and 15 $^{D\,MAX}$12 and 12 cm
Manama. Bahrain National
Museum. acc. n° 2084-2-90
and main store
Unpublished

Ostrich egg shells were
frequently part of burial
offerings. They are all open
at the top and were often
painted in a faded red to light
brown colour on the body.
They were probably used
to drink out of, although
they may have contained
some sort of a liquid for the use
of the deceased, or perhaps
performed a function during
the burial ritual (funeral meal).
Their decoration. which evokes
the architectural motifs
of certain soft stone vessels
(Cat. 2) indicates that they
perhaps belonged to an ancient
regional tradition. The ostrich.
which was common on
the Arabian Peninsula during
antiquity. was still hunted
locally until the 19th century.
Today it has disappeared
from the region.

58-62 Various Stamp-seals

'Ali necropolis,
Bahraini excavations 1988,
Tumulus 24.1
Madinat Isa necropolis,
Bahraini excavations 1981,
Tumulus 18
Al-Hajjar necropolis,
Bahraini excavations 1993,
Mond 3, Grave 1
Shell
^{H}1.6 and 1.4 ^{D}3.2 and 2.7 cm
Manama, Bahrain National
Museum, acc. n° 3171-10-90
and 3179-10-90
^{B} Al-Khalifa 1986: fig. 81,
and unpublished

Stamp-seals, rather than
the Syro-Mesopotamian
cylindrical seals, were used
throughout the Early Dilmun
culture, and remain the most
original material representation
of this culture. Dilmunites
were often buried with
their personal stamp-seal,
whose carved side always
showed a unique iconography,
probably defined by the owner
when the stamp-seal was made.
From the simple stamp-seals
carved from the apex
of a shell (of type *Conus*)
to the characteristic specimens
in soft stone (chlorite
or steatite), several traditions
of stamp-seals seem to have
co-existed in Bahrain,
and they are not always easy
to distinguish chronologically
(cf below "The Hidden Art
of Dilmun...")

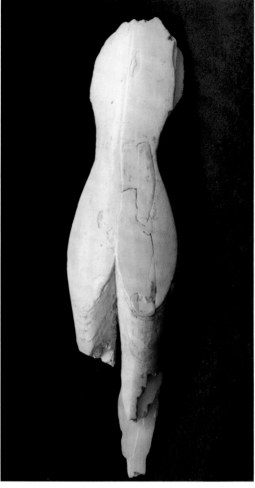

63-64 Necklaces
Madinat Hamad necropolis,
season and grave unspecified
'Ali necropolis.
Bahraini excavations 1994.
Tumulus 92
Saar necropolis.
Bahraini excavations 1988-89.
Tumulus 326.21
Varied shells (*Dentalium.*
Engina mendiceria); fine stones
(carnelian, agate), copper
Early Dilmun, c. 2000-1800 BC
L38 and 94 cm
Manama, Bahrain National
Museum, main store
Unpublished

Many of the elements used
to make the Early Dilmun
adornments were not available
in Bahrain. It is thought,
however, that these necklaces
were produced locally,
where craftsmen put together
shells from the Gulf
or the Indian Ocean with
other elements obtained
through transit trade
(carnelian and agate beads
from the Indus region
– probably imported
unworked – copper from Oman,
etc.). The discoloration of the
agate and carnelian beads is
more likely to be due to natural
alterations resulting from
the environment in which
they were preserved
than from any specific
treatments (heating, for
example).

**65 Ivory Figurine of Nude
Female**
Found at A'ali, Bahrain from
upper chamber of tomb 12.
H21 W5 T3.5cm
British Museum. BM no. 130595.
Reg. no. 1926-10-8,11.
Courtesy of the Trustees of the
British Museum.
B Mackay, Petrie and Harding –
Bahrain and Hemmamieh p. 22,
pl 1.1; Bossert – Assyrien,
fig.1283; Barnett – Catalogue of
Nimrud Ivories U.15, p.227,
fig.90; ECL During-Caspers,
1989, – 'Mackay's Ivory Figurine
from Tumulus 12 at 'Ali Bahrain'
Iranica Antiqua 24, 159-74; JE
Reade and R Burleigh, 1978 –
'The Ali Cemetery: Old
Excavations, Ivory, and
Radiocarbon Dating' Journal of
Oman Studies 4, 75-83, pl.31-34.

Back only, lacking head and
feet and part of buttocks.

"At Dilmun, the dwellings will be pleasant dwelling places..."

Pierre Lombard

The discovery in the 1950s of settlement sites in Bahrain satisfied a number of archaeologists who were sceptical about the theory of the "necropolis island" advanced by the first explorers. Nevertheless, 40 years later, funerary archaeology remains the principal focus of salvage work by the Bahrain Directorate of Archaeology. Only two settlement sites, Qal'at al-Bahrain and Saar, are currently being excavated, under the aegis of foreign missions. This low number may seem surprising, although in the past there have been others: the site at Barbar and its temple (excavated between 1954 and 1961), that of Diraz, which, unfortunately, was destroyed a few years ago, as well as the small settlement at al-Hajjar, discovered by chance in 1993 underneath a Hellenistic cemetery. Two other sites have also been located by surface survey, the first close to Saar and the second not far from Jebel Dukhan, at al-Areen.

It is certain, however, as several demographic studies have shown, that the people living in these few sites could not have produced all of the tumuli so far discovered. We must therefore suppose that the settlement pattern of the island has only changed slightly since the early Dilmun period, and the numerous present-day villages in the palm grove areas actually cover more ancient settlements. The distribution of the tumuli themselves, in several distinct areas, as well as the probable situation of these settlements close to springs and cultivated areas, reinforces this hypothesis.

The two sites currently being excavated appear to be quite different, but, as such, usefully complement one another.
The interest of Qal'at al-Bahrain, sometimes identified as being the capital of the land of Dilmun, lies in particular in the thickness of its archaeological layers (almost 8 m), which illustrate a sometimes discontinuous occupation between 2 200 BC and the 16th century AD. Paradoxically, this precious stratigraphy, the veritable "memory" of the island, limits our access to the Bronze Age levels. Buried at the base of the tell, we have, until now, only been able to access limited sectors, but these have revealed very elaborate defensive and public architecture, certainly inspired by a state-based organisation.

The Saar settlement, smaller in area, and probably less important in its function, is, however, easily accessible to archaeologists. This small town, whose apogee was apparently around 1 900 BC, was abandoned some 200 years later, and never rebuilt. Its ruins, covered by a sandy layer no more than 1.50 metres thick, have been the object of extensive excavation by the London-Bahrain Expedition.
These excavations have provided us with a unique image of a highly organised early Dilmun settlement.

Qal'at al-Bahrain in the Bronze Age

Flemming Højlund

The largest archaeological site in Bahrain is the tell of Qal'at al-Bahrain, on the north coast of the main island. The tell measures 700 m by 400 m and rises to a height of *c.* 8 m. It is crowned by a fort from the 16th century AD, Qal'at al-Bahrain, which has given its name to the tell.

The tell of Qal'at al-Bahrain was identified as the probable site of the ancient capital of Dilmun in 1954, and from then until 1978 excavations were carried out here by P.V. Glob and Geoffrey Bibby of the Danish archaeological mission, which have been continued since 1977 by Monique Kervran and Pierre Lombard of the French archaeological mission. The tell comprises the remains of a considerable city occupied at many periods over the past four to five thousand years. The study of these remains has formed the basis of the chronology of Bahrain and has, indeed, played a prominent role in the archaeology of the Arabian Gulf. It is worth noting, however, that though excavations have taken place here for almost 50 years, no more than a fraction of the surface of the tell has been uncovered. Qal'at al-Bahrain is, thus, still hiding most of its secrets below its barren surface.

The Earliest Occupation

The earliest remains of human occupation found at Qal'at al-Bahrain date back to c. 2 200 BC and were located by the northern side of the tell facing the sea. This small settlement is the only one from this period in Bahrain and, indeed, in all of eastern Arabia.

The finds show subsistence at that time already relied on a fully developed oasis agriculture with palm trees and cereal cultivation in the nearby fields, supplemented by herding of cattle, sheep and goats and by fishing.

People lived in small houses with several rooms with plastered floors. The walls were built of rough stone set in clay or mortar.

There are indications that complexes of houses were separated by streets.

Only a few pieces of chipped flint were found during the excavation, so stone was hardly of much, if any, importance as a raw material for artefacts. Conversely, a socketed spearhead, a fish hook and numerous small fragments of copper, bear witness to an abundance of metal.

Indeed, a large workshop where copper casting took place, covering an area of at least 15 x 35 m, was uncovered. Many open moulds intended for casting simple plates of copper coupled with the lack of two-piece-moulds and lost-wax moulds, seem to indicate that copper artefacts were primarily shaped by hammering and annealing and not cast.

Most crucibles are rather small, with an estimated volume of 300–800 cm^3, but a few large crucibles with a volume of around 4 000 cm^3 suggests large-scale production, indicating that the presence of full-time specialists.

Top. Bird's eye view
of Qal'at al-Bahrain tell.

Bottom. Plan of Qal'at al-Bahrain.
City wall and central warehouses
of the Bronze Age (after Højlund
and Andersen 1997, fig.4, p.11).

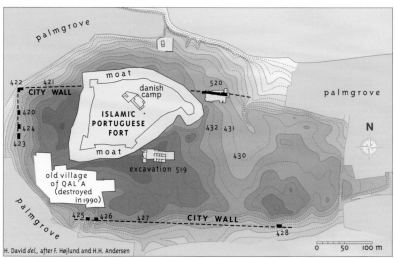

Copper from one of the crucibles has been analysed and shown to be compatible with copper from the Oman peninsula.

There can be no doubt that the occupants of Qal'at al-Bahrain were engaged in large-scale transportation of copper from Oman to Mesopotamia and apparently also in processing the metal.

The pottery consisted mostly of local, hand-made cooking pots, supplemented by storage vessels and pots for eating and drinking, imported from Mesopotamia and Oman. A number of other objects suggest connections with Mesopotamia, (a cuneiform inscription and a haematite weight) and with Oman (steatite bowls). Relations with the Indus civilisation are indicated by carnelian beads, a stone weight and a few potsherds.

The Walled City

An important event in the history of Qal'at al-Bahrain took place by the end of the 3rd millennium BC. A fortification wall was built around the settlement. The wall has been located on the northern, western and southern slopes of the tell, but on the eastern slope no excavation has till now been carried out. The walls follow the cardinal directions and are at right angles to each other; they enclose an area of about 15 hectares, but all of this area does not seem to have been built up. The wall has been closely investigated on the northern side. It was constructed of rough stones laid in clay and mortar. The front was built of larger blocks than the rear. Originally, it had a thickness of 2.30 m, but it has been subsequently reinforced everywhere. There was a 1.25 m wide gate through the wall, enough to allow a loaded donkey or even a camel, but not a vehicle to pass through. Owing to the build-up of the ground level inside the wall, the wall was rebuilt several times, so that four different successive gates can be distinguished. In the latest gate, two pivot-stones were found, of a black, fine-grained material that must have been imported. Both had shallow sockets in the top to hold a double-leafed gate, with a width of 2.30 m at this period. On the western side the outer face of the wall was intact and visible along a length of thirty feet. It was built of regular and well-laid large squared stones. The procurement of the stone material for such a monument and the construction of the wall entailed a very substantial input of labour that is likely to have been mobilised by some form of public organisation.

The same organisation may have been responsible for a complex of monumental buildings that were erected at the centre of the city. On both sides of a 12 m wide, north-south oriented street, several buildings of apparently identical ground plan and construction were erected. The ground plan of one building has been established in its entirety: its entrance faced the street, and it had eight rooms arranged on both sides of a central hall, which served rather like a central passage. The walls were huge, at least 4.5 m high and 1.1 m thick, built of limestone ashlars. The buildings lay parallel along two axes, so they must have been laid out according to an overall plan and have constituted a single entity. The style of construction is magnificent, of a magnitude and lavishness not to be surpassed in Bahrain or anywhere else in the Gulf till the Islamic period.

This well-planned complex of warehouses situated on a commanding location in the centre of the tell may be interpreted as part of a palace. This, then, was probably the centre of economic organisation of the kingdom of Dilmun. Here goods were stored before they were distributed locally or traded internationally. Towards the north, the street led to a huge gate, that may have opened into other parts of the palace.

Within the northern city wall and in the area of the gate, a cluster of modest houses equipped with wells has been excavated. Several streets divided the houses, one leading to the gate. These houses are of much the same size and building technique as those of the preceding period and must have been inhabited by the ordinary population.

The pottery gives a strong impression of continuity. The local tradition became even more dominant as the import of pottery from Mesopotamia and Oman – mainly forms suitable for storage and for eating

Qal'at al-Bahrain. Western city-wall.

Qal'at al-Bahrain.
Northern city-wall with gate.

and drinking – was reduced. This was matched
by a development of similar functional types
in local pottery.
Among the interesting finds from this period,
the stamp seals of the Dilmun type must
be mentioned, as well as the cuboid
and spherical shaped Indus weights
and a cuneiform tablet of Mesopotamian type.
The walled city at Qal'at al-Bahrain flourished
for several hundred years, but sometime
after 1 800 BC problems arose and habitation
came to an end. The buildings were abandoned
and slowly filled with drift sand.

The Dilmunite Settlement at Saar

Jane Moon

Location and Main Characteristics

The Early Dilmun settlement of Saar is strung
out along the eastern slope of a low ridge
running parallel to the west coast of Bahrain.
In the flat, intensely hot and humid landscape
this slight elevation (c. 13 m) catches
any available breeze. Just to the east there
is fresh water and cultivable land,
while on the west the barren sand-covered
limestone, then covered with thousands
of grave mounds, stretches towards the sea,
3.7 km distant. Archaeobotanical
and faunal remains from the settlement show
that the economy of the town was heavily
biased towards the exploitation
of marine resources, and it is possible
that the eastern seaboard, now 7 km distant,
may have been nearer. Even recent maps
show an inlet coming to within 3.6 km of Saar.
The settlement runs for about 250 m
along the ridge, ending abruptly some 30 m
north of the temple. The maximum width
is about 100 m, mostly less, and the whole
occupies about 2.5 ha.
Communications with neighbouring settlements
would not have been difficult, even on foot: just
250 m to the south-west is a settlement of around
40 000 m², at least partly contemporaneous.
Diraz and Umm es-Sujjur lie 3–4 km
to the north-west, Barbar just 2 km further,
and Qal'at al-Bahrain itself only 6 km distant.
The artefacts, and particularly the pottery
from the main excavated settlement,
are essentially comparable with material
from Qal'at al-Bahrain City IIB, and a few items
with City IIC. Small soundings into deeper
levels have produced pottery of City I date.
The origins of the settlement can therefore
be placed around 2 300 BC, the main phase
beginning around 1 900 BC, and perhaps
enduring for around 200 years.
The characteristics of the town are: a wide main
street with subsidiary pathways running off
approximately at right angles; a temple
on the highest point; houses built in blocks,
sometimes arranged around an open square;
and a pattern of domestic architecture
which repeats a basic two-to-three roomed
plan, although with many variations.
There is a well on the eastern flank.
The only building with a clearly defined
special function is the temple.

The Buildings

Houses were built of roughly hewn local
limestone, roofed with wooden poles and date
leaves or date-leaf mats. The latter can be seen
as impressions in the covering gypsum plaster,
and the poles can be presumed to be also
of palm. There are no indications of stairways,
and the amount of collapsed stone encountered
in excavation suggests single storey dwellings.
The buildings were grouped into blocks,
consisting of three or more separate dwellings
in a line. In some cases, rows were arranged
around a common open area. This arrangement

makes environmental sense, as it would minimise the exposure to the weather for each dwelling. What social significance the groups had we can only conjecture: nothing in the material found suggests grouping according to profession. Parallels with modern Near Eastern villages point to the likelihood of near neighbours being near relatives.

Among the house plans is a repeated basic pattern of a rectangular unit divided into an L-shaped area and a single inner room. The latter was definitely roofed, while the L-shaped area had a dirty, uneven surface which suggests it was open, or perhaps partly shaded. The pattern is seen most clearly in Block G, Houses 100-110. Most of these have an entrance at the rear as well as from the street, and the door to the inner room is placed to allow maximum privacy. Some houses have only a single entrance, such as House 57, while others have a second courtyard at the back, such as Houses 3 and 205, and others share one, as with House 4, 5 and 8, and Houses 202-204. There are innumerable slight variations to the basic plan, such as the double inner rooms of Houses 60-61, and one or two buildings which are quite anomalous, such as the much larger House 53, and the more complex Houses 301 and 56.

Many of the domestic features show a regularity of construction and position too.

Typically, there is a basin just inside the door, with a jar-stand next to it. The inner rooms are general clean and empty, and must have been sleeping or sitting areas, or for storage of bedding or similar. They rarely show signs of activity. Cooking was nearly always done in the L-shaped courtyard. There are some simple hearths, but many houses have a sophisticated 'kitchen range' built against a wall: a semicircular hearth at ground level, with a set of tripod legs next to it. A bread-oven may be adjacent or separate. Other kitchen equipment often found in a house includes a large quern, and usually several grindstones and pounders. As with the ground plans, the placement of installations has a certain regularity, but also some dramatic variations. In Houses 4 and 7, for instance, it was in fact the inner room which contained the cooking equipment, and in House 222 the inner room contained many vessels, lids, and stone tools.

Artefacts

The numerous small variations in ground plan are not, on present evidence, reflected in the general distribution of artefacts, which is very uniform. The exception to this is the occurrence of clay sealings, which only occur in a few houses. On the other hand, most houses have produced at least one stamp seal.

Apart from potsherds, the largest artefact class is stone tools, accounting for 20-25 % of registered objects. These are pounders

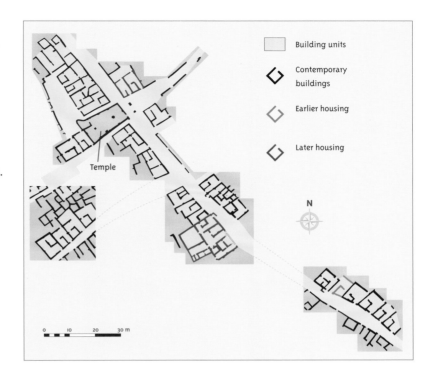

Saar. Overall plan
of the excavations (as of 1994).

Building units

Contemporary
buildings

Earlier housing

Later housing

Temple

N

0   10   20   30 m

and rubbers, many of local limestone,
but about a third of imported black igneous rock.
Every building had several of these.
Flint tools were less common, and included
flakes as well as crushing tools.
Casting slag from copper was common,
and a small number of ingots have been
discovered. There is no evidence for smelting,
and no moulds have been found, suggesting
that manufacture was confined to small items
such as pins and fish-hooks, fragments
of which are fairly frequent. There are a small
number of larger copper implements, including
a hoe, 3 spearheads, chisels, tweezers
and augurs. Copper jewellery is limited
to a few rings and pins, and indeed jewellery
generally is sparsely represented in
the settlement, by a small number of beads
and some small pearls.
Bitumen fragments are also common, testifying
to the importance of what must have been
the only reliable waterproofing substance.
Most pieces are the remains of bitumen-coated
palm-leaf baskets, but there are also
large 'beads', perhaps floats for fishing nets.
Pottery is almost all hand-made, and assumed
to be locally produced, although it has
not proved possible to find matching modern
clay sources. The commonest shape is
the globular cooking pot, blackened fragments
of which are found in just about every
context. Jars with shallow ribs on the body,
and sometimes an integral sieve, large ribbed

storage vats, and shallow open dishes are
the other main constituents of an essentially
plain, domestic repertoire. Painted fragments
only occur occasionally, and some
of the characteristic decorated pottery types
familiar from the tombs, such as red fine-ware
flasks and painted chalices, are virtually absent,
showing an interesting dichotomy between
the funerary assemblage and that used at home.
Whereas Mesopotamian pottery types still
occur at Qal'at al-Bahrain at this period,
albeit in reduced quantities, none have been
recognised at Saar. Only a minute number
of possible Wadi Suq sherds have been found,
emphasizing the essentially local nature
of the ceramics. There are a few Indus-related

fragments, and one instance of a large storage jar decorated with polychrome Indus motifs. A single square Indus weight further testifies to an Indus connection, and the one cylinder seal discovered shows a Mesopotamian or Syrian inspiration in form, though not in decoration, which is entirely in the local style. The material, too, is steatite, of the same type used to make the stamp seals, which, apart from two mutilated animal figurines, constitute the Saar people's only surviving art form.

Over 80 stamp seals have been found at Saar. Detailed study is in progress, but it can be said that they bear the motifs and scenes familiar from seals found at Failaka, and elsewhere on Bahrain, including contemporary tombs: repeated favourites are horned animals, hunting scenes, palm trees and crescent moons. Only a small minority of the seals are of the more simple 'Arabian Gulf style'. Sealings, which concentrate in Houses 201, 207, 211, 220 and 224 are stamped with very similar seals.

Society and Subsistence at Saar

It will be evident that most of the population lived in the same sorts of houses, used the same kinds of domestic equipment, and used it in much the same way, surely indicating a society devoid of elaborate stratification. While the population cannot be estimated with any accuracy, a settlement of over 70 dwellings would have needed some form of leadership, and the temple must have required someone to perform religious duties. We can presume a village chief, or one or more 'bigmen', and we can say that neither their wealth nor their prestige merited a dwelling much different from their neighbours'.

Over 90% by weight of bone recovered from Saar is of marine fish, the rest being mainly sheep/goat, with a little cattle and gazelle. Sea shells are common, but not over-abundant. Plant remains have been difficult to recover, but show overwhelming evidence for date-palm cultivation. The diversity of this plant for use as food, for building and craft material is well documented from contemporaneous examples, and there is little doubt the Saar people used it widely. Hunting was not important economically, though it may have been an important social activity. As to non-subsistence activities, there is no evidence that the people made anything they did not need for themselves.

That some trade and exchange was involved in their lives is shown by the presence of imported items such as copper from Oman, bitumen from Iran, carnelian from India, and by the seals.

No defensive arrangements can be detected from the excavations: there is no outer wall, and there are few weapons. When Saar was finally abandoned, for whatever reason, it was evidently a peaceful and a gradual operation.

Typical Saar dwelling,
with covered room and a courtyard.

Domestic activity area.

Saar is at present unique, in that no comparable
settlement has been extensively excavated.
That means that many questions remain
to be explored. How, for instance, did the village
fit into Dilmun society as a whole, and what
was its relationship with the capital?
It is to be hoped that ongoing study
of Qal'at al-Bahrain will elucidate these as well
as other aspects of society in the Ancient Gulf.

66, 67 Storage or Transportation Jars

Madinat Hamad necropolis (BS2), Bahraini excavations 1984-85, Tumulus 149.34; (BSWL/5), 1995-96, Tumulus 22
Early Dilmun, c. 2000-1800 BC
Pottery
H36 and 34 D MAX 29 and 28.5 cm
Manama, Bahrain National Museum, acc. n° 8673-2-91 and 5593-2-91
Unpublished. Ibrahim 1982, p. 145, fig 36; p. 212, pl. 50

These jars with finely ridged bodies, made locally out of a good quality yellow clay are also found in the settlement. One has clearly been repaired with bitumen, which would seem to indicate that these jars were not without a certain value in the eyes of those who used them.

68 Mortar and Grinder

Saar settlement, Jordanian excavations 1984-85, House unspecified
Early Dilmun, c. 2000-1800 BC
Limestone
H18 D MAX 25.5 cm
Manama, Bahrain National Museum, acc. n° 685-2-88
Unpublished

The fine-grained material, the elaborate shape and the careful finishing of this piece suggest that it was being re-used, and that its initial function was different. It was found in a house, together with other grinders.

69 Mortar and Grinder

Saar settlement, Jordanian excavations 1984-85, House unspecified
Early Dilmun, c. 2000-1800 BC
Limestone
H9.5 D MAX 31.5 cm (mortar);
H6 D MAX 7 cm (grinder)
Manama, Bahrain National Museum, main store
Unpublished

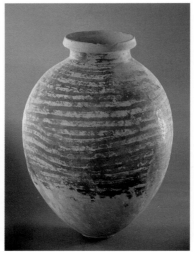

⁷⁰ Storage Jar
Umm es-Sujjur spring,
Japanese excavations 1995-96
Early Dilmun, c. 2000-1800 BC
Pottery
^{H}48 $^{D MAX}$55.5 cm
Manama, Bahrain National
Museum, acc. nº 93-3-1
Unpublished.
Comp.: *Bahrain National
Museum* 1989, nº 11;
Højlund & Andersen 1994, p. 89,
fig. 174

This type of container with thick
ridged sides and a rounded
bottom may have been partially
buried in the floor or courtyard
of Early Dilmun houses; it may
have been used to store water or
grain.

**⁷¹ Storage
or Transportation Jar**
'Ali necropolis, Bahraini
excavations 1989-90,
Tumulus 65.1
Early Dilmun, c. 1900-1800 BC
Pottery
^{H} 38.4 $^{D MAX.}$ 26.2 cm
Manama, Bahrain National
Museum, acc. nº 2036-2-90
Unpublished. Comp.: Højlund &
Andersen 1994, p. 166, fig. 697

This jar, found in a burial
context, is nevertheless exactly
like those found in most of the
settlement sites currently
known on Bahrain. It is egg-
shaped, has a short neck with a
triangular section and its body
is covered with horizontal
painted bands, to give a ridged
effect, making it one of the
most common forms of
domestic pottery found at the
end of the Early Dilmun period.
It was certainly made locally.

⁷², ⁷³ Cooking Pots
Saar settlement, British
excavations 1991 (16:22:31),
House 203;
Jordanian excavations 1985
(IIIK28)
Early Dilmun, c. 2000-1800 BC
Pottery
^{H}25 and 12.3 $^{D MAX}$17.3 and 25 cm
Manama, Bahrain National
Museum, main store
and acc. nº 70-2-88
Unpublished

74, 75 Cooking Pots
'Ali necropolis,
Bahraini excavations 1989-90,
Tumulus 65.1
Madinat Hamad necropolis
(BS2), Bahraini excavations
1984-85, Tumulus 205.13
Early Dilmun, c. 2000-1800 BC
Pottery
^{H}8 and 6.5 $^{D\,MAX}$18.8 and 19.5 cm
Manama, Bahrain National
Museum, acc. n° 2617-2-90
and 39-2-88
Unpublished;
comp.: *Bahrain National
Museum* 1993, p. 40; Velde 1998,
p. 248, fig. 2:5.6

These flat-bottomed pots are
a lot rarer than the previous
type (Cat. 72, 73), but have
been found at Saar and at
Qal'at al-Bahrain. On one
of them, we can see
an ingenious system with
a removeable handle
(here reconstituted in wood)
that can be fitted to a lateral
notched tenon, a curious
prototype of a
similar device well-known
to today's cooks!

76 Boat Anchor
Qal'at al-Bahrain,
Danish excavations 1970,
Northern City-wall
Early Dilmun, c. 2000-1800 BC
Limestone
^{L}52 $^{IW\,MAX}$37 cm ^{WE}28.8 kg
Manama, Bahrain National
Museum, main store
Unpublished

Stone anchors, along with
a few stylised representations
of boats on the soft stone seals
and rare fragments of bitumen
caulking are the sole evidence
that remains of the famous
boats of Dilmun mentioned
frequently in the Mesopotamian
economic texts. This anchor
was found not far from the gate
of the Northern city-wall
of Qal'at al-Bahrain, which
opened directly onto the beach
and the mooring area where
the numerous boats waiting
to be loaded or unloaded
were anchored.

Bahrain: Warehouse of the Gulf

Harriet Crawford

The Bahrain islands are not rich in raw materials, but they are ideally placed to acquire the goods they lack as they lie about half way down the upper Gulf off the eastern coast of Arabia. The islands have plentiful supplies of fresh water and sheltered harbours to offer to sailors and traders from better endowed regions. These attributes allowed Dilmun to acquire the goods it needed for its own consumption, and also to gain considerable wealth by acting as a vital warehouse on the sea route which linked Mesopotamia with countries as far away as the Indus valley.

Dilmun's own priority was raw materials, such as good quality stone and metal. The locally grown date palm provided an inferior quality wood, and the stands of mangrove apparently present on the island in the past provided some wood of a higher quality, but more seems to have been needed, perhaps to build the boats used for trade. Local flint was used for tools, while local limestone was widely available as a building material, but for finer work stone had to be brought in. Hard stone was imported to face monumental buildings and to make many of the pounding and grinding stones found on sites of this period. More decorative stones like carnelian and lapis lazuli, and the softstone used for the stamp seals manufactured at sites like Qal'at al-Bahrain and Failaka island, all had to be imported, as did the copper

which was processed locally in relatively small amounts to produce simple tools and ornaments. The evidence for this can be seen in the droplets of copper found widely on sites of this period, the remains of copper melting and casting.

A few manufactured goods were also imported of which the softstone vases are perhaps the commonest. These range from a few examples in the figurative Intercultural style which becomes rare by the end of the 3rd millennium, to the many simple pots, bowls and lids decorated with a dot and circle motif which originated in the Oman peninsula. A few distinctive pottery vessels with non-local origins are also found. Local potters were skilled enough to copy such decorative vessels themselves so the identification of genuine imports is not always easy. Exotic objects like the famous bull's head from the Barbar temple may also have been imported, together with other copper artefacts and alabaster vessels from the same site.

The sources of these imports were many and varied. The copper and the softstone, as we have seen above, appear to have come from Oman, ancient Magan. Painted pottery came from eastern Arabia and Iran, pottery and carnelian from the Indus valley, while lapis originates in Badakshan, part of modern Afghanistan. The contacts with the Indus appear to have been especially significant as some of the earliest seals found in the islands, the so-called Arabian Gulf seals, show clear signs of influence from the Harappan civilisation. The seals are decorated with motifs such as the humped bull, which are native to the Indus valley. Some even bear short inscriptions in the Indus valley script although epigraphists suggest that the inscriptions are in the local language rather than that of the Indus. There are even hints of contacts further afield with Central Asia which may have been the origin of the bull's head and the other objects from the Barbar temple mentioned above.

Dilmun's developing role as a warehouse at the end of the 3rd millennium BC was apparently the trigger for its rapid development in the early second millennium, but the only aspect of this trade for which there is extensive written documentation is that with ancient Mesopotamia and from the cuneiform tablets we learn that the pattern of trade shifted frequently in the period from about 3 200-2 000 BC.

The first written references to Dilmun in the Mesopotamian tablets refer to copper artefacts and long predate the first towns and cities on the Bahrain islands.
The name Dilmun at this early date around 3 200 BC seems to refer to the copper producing areas of Oman. References continue infrequently throughout the third millennium to copper

An extensive correspondence, addressed to Ea-Nasir an Urite merchant trading with Dilmun and possibly resident there, survives in the form of clay tablets excavated from the remains of his house in Ur. The correspondence is often acrimonious with Ea-Nasir's partners and "financiers" in Ur, often expressing alarm at the way in which he conducts his business. This tablet from Nanni, complains that the wrong grade of copper has been delivered after a shipment from Dilmun and further complains about the mis-direction and delay in another delivery.

and fine wood arriving from Dilmun, often for the building of temples by rulers like Ur-Nanshe of Lagash, but by about 2 400 BC the name seems to refer to the Eastern Province of Arabia rather than to Oman, while the mining region in Oman is now referred to as Magan. By the end of the 3rd millennium during the hundred years or so in which the Ur III kings were in power in Mesopotamia, Dilmun is barely mentioned and contact is entirely between merchants in the capital of Ur and copper producing Magan (Oman).

By 2 000 BC we see another change and the tablets talk only of Dilmun, a name which is certainly now given to the Bahrain islands. A little later it also includes Failaka and the Eastern Province of Arabia. We do not know why this change took place or how the Mesopotamian boats were diverted from Magan to Dilmun, though it was obviously easier and cheaper for them to end their journeys on Bahrain and to acquire supplies there than to go all the way to Magan. Perhaps the merchants of Dilmun were able to undercut their competitors in Magan (it seems unlikely that force was used by the people of Dilmun to capture this lucrative market as there is little evidence of weapons from the islands.). Perhaps some improvement in the size of the Dilmun boats or in their speed may have enabled Bahrain to steal a march on its competitors and cut prices. On the other hand, there is some evidence for major disruption in Magan itself as a result of which it may have lost overall control of the trade, although copper continued to be mined.

Happily we know rather more about the workings of the trade between Ur and Dilmun because excavations at Ur uncovered the records of a man

called Ea-Nasir who lived at the very beginning of the 2nd millennium and was a merchant who specialised in trading with Dilmun. Such merchants were known as the alik Dilmun or "those who go to Dilmun". These men seemed to have worked for the temple at Ur which provided the capital for their expeditions to Dilmun so that they could acquire copper, by then an essential commodity rather than a luxury, and various other goods, which probably included tin, wood, semi-precious stones, ivory, and exotic animals. The importance of copper to the Mesopotamian economy is demonstrated by the very large quantities mentioned in some of the texts. One consignment weighed 18.33 tons. Other commodities were less significant in terms of quantity.

In addition to the merchants travelling from Ur it also seems likely that some Dilmunite merchants travelled north and lived at Ur as a number of the typical Dilmun seals have been found there. They seem to have ventured even further afield as there are references to people from Dilmun in the famous Mari letters found in Syria on the middle Euphrates. These Dilmunites are referred to as messengers and in one text there is mention of a lugal or king of Dilmun to whom a present of oil is sent. From other scraps of information such as the Dilmun seal impression on a tablet from Susa, and a few tablets, we know that Iran

78 Neo-Sumerian Receipt for Garments
Mesopotamia: Ur III period, reign of Ibbi-Sin.
Clay
H4.3 W3.9 TH1.7 cm
British Museum. BM 130462.
PRN: WCT395.
Reg no. 1948,0423.362.
B UET III 1507.
Courtesy of the Trustees of the British Museum.

A receipt for garments sent by boat to Dilmun.

was also involved in this complex network of trading relationships and the presence of a temple dedicated to the Dilmunite god Inzak in Susa may suggest that merchants from Bahrain were resident here too.

It is strange that, while the texts tell us a great deal about the goods coming into south Mesopotamia, we know little about the goods being sent to Dilmun in return. It used to be thought that grain formed a significant proportion of these exports, but recently doubt has been cast on this because grain is difficult to transport in bulk and of relatively low value. It now seems more likely that higher value, lighter goods like textiles and oils, also mentioned in the texts, played the major role and that other perishable goods, including some cereals, were involved as secondary items. There are also references in the cuneiform texts to bags and other objects made of leather. None of these perishables would leave much evidence in archaeological records. One more durable commodity was, however, involved – bitumen from Hit on the Euphrates has recently been identified at Qal'at al-Bahrain. There are few manufactured objects from early Dilmun which can be shown to be of Mesopotamian origin, but the seals show some motifs of Mesopotamian origin such as a god wearing the typical horned helmet of the Mesopotamian pantheon. Other motifs seem to be Syrian in origin.

A trading network of the volume and complexity of that between Mesopotamia and Dilmun requires relatively complex administrative techniques for weighing, pricing and recording the transactions. While we have cuneiform texts from Mesopotamia, as we have seen, there are no comparable documents from Dilmun. If a local writing system existed, it would seem that it used perishable materials like ink and skins which have not survived. However, we do have evidence for two systems of weights and measures in use on the islands, one deriving from Mesopotamia, loosely based on the sexagesimal system, and the other a binary system from the Indus valley. Weights on the former system are bullet shaped and often made of haematite while those on the latter are cubes of fine veined stone, both apparently used with a pan balance of a type used in the Gulf in living memory by the pearl merchants. Arguably the most important administrative device of all was the stamp seal decorated in the distinctive early Dilmun style. These seals served to identify the parties involved in a transaction and were also used as devices with which goods could be secured.

The best evidence for the way these seals were used comes from the impressions that were made by them. A study of the marks on the backs of the pieces of clay on which seal impressions were made suggests that most of them were used

to seal packets tied with string, the necks of jars, boxes, and even possibly doors. A large number of these sealings were found at the site of Saar and all bear impressions in the Dilmun style. This strongly suggests that the goods from which they came were originally packed up within Dilmun itself. There is no textual evidence at all for this type of local exchange and as many of the goods appear to have been consumables there is no archaeological evidence either, so we have here from the evidence of the glyptic a whole unrecorded aspect of economic life.

In addition to the seal impressions discussed above, there are a small number of so-called 'tokens' from Bahrain whose purpose is unknown, but which seem to have been another administrative device as they may have been used as authorisations or receipts. They are button or disk-shaped pieces of clay, carefully made, sometimes pierced for suspension and stamped with seal impressions on one or two sides. It is interesting that in at least one case the design, of looped concentric circles, is the same on examples from at least three sites on Bahrain, Qal'at, the Barbar temple and Saar.

The first three hundred years of the 2nd millennium marked the height of Dilmun's prosperity and its greatest geographical expansion. The island of Failaka at the mouth of Kuwait bay, was settled soon after 2 000BC

presumably to make the transfer of goods to the cities of south Mesopotamia easier and quicker. Copper remained the staple commodity traded northwards until the network largely ceased to function around 1 700 BC. Three main factors seem to have brought about the decline of Dilmun; Ur, the main port of entry for Dilmun copper in south Mesopotamia was destroyed in the course of local revolts against the central government under Hammurabi of Babylon's son; the potential market for copper in south Mesopotamia dried up, due to depopulation of the area in the wake of this unrest and the increasingly easy availability of alternative sources of cheaper copper from Anatolia and Cyprus undercut the Gulf suppliers.
The classic response to this sort of economic situation would have been for Dilmun to look for new markets, but sadly, the contraction in the economy of the Indus valley limited the possibilities for diversification.
Of all the surrounding regions, only Susa remained sufficiently prosperous to be able to maintain the traditional links for a limited period of time. After this Dilmun sank into historical limbo for two or three hundred years until it emerged into written history again as a Kassite province.

80 Cylindrical Seal with Inscription and Showing a Scene of Presentation to a Deity

Al-Maqsha necropolis, Bahraini excavations 1991-92, Grave 27/a
Ur III period
(end of 3rd millennium BC)
Haematite
H 0.5 D 2.6 cm
Manama, Bahrain National Museum, Main Store
Unpublished. For comparison, see for example M.V. Nikolskij, 1908

The scene must have shown a kneeling figure being "presented" by a guardian goddess to a bearded god sitting on his throne, behind which an eagle with its wings spread hovers over two intertwined standing lions. The beast facing to the left is holding a staff. This iconography is characteristic of the Ur III Period.
The object was re-carved shortly after its manufacture to allow a stone cutter to add a three-line inscription in a frame, thus eliminating the worshipper figure. The right arm of the goddess, bent back to take the character by the hand is cut off by the frame

of the inscription, as are the feet of the standing lion facing to the right and the staff that it must have held to make the scene symmetrical.
The harmony of the scene is thus destroyed.
The inscription, written in Sumerian, gives two proper names and one title: "Kaga, 'the man of the great boats', son of Abbagula". The title mentioned (*lú má gal-gal*), is uncommon, but it, and the type of boat with which it is associated (*má gal-gal*), appears several times in administrative texts of the Early Dynastic III Period (c. 2400 BC). These are lists of boats, sailors, and boatman, and it is placed first (e.g. Nikolskij, 1908 n° 12.1 and 306.1), which underlines its importance. It could be translated as "master mariner" and must have commanded a high status amoung the seafaring merchants of Dilmun.

81 Sumerian Administrative Document referring to the Arrival of Copper from Dilmun in Lagash

Mesopotamia: Tello, Ancient Girsu (Land of Sumer)
Early Dynastic III period: year 1 of the reign of Enentarzid (c. 2365 BC)
Clay
H 6 W 6 TH 2.5 cm
Paris, Louvre Museum, acc. n° AO 3999
B F. Thureau-Dangin 1903, n° 26; M. Lambert, 1953, p. 60-61

Economic texts from Lagash show that the merchant Ur-Enki played an important role in the maritime trade between Lagash and Dilmun. This receipt shows that he brought 214 minas of copper, 85 kg, to Dimtu, the wife of Enentarzid.
Grain and wheat were the merchandise for which it was traded.

82 Purchase Note for two Royal Officials Returning from Dilmun

Mesopotamia: Tello, Ancient Girsu (Land of Sumer)
IIIrd Dynasty of Ur, reign of Shulgi (c. 2080 BC)
Clay
H 2.5 W 2.5 TH 1.4 cm
Paris, Louvre Museum, acc. n° AO 3474
B F. Thureau-Dangin 1902, p. 75 and 93; F. Thureau-Dangin 1903, n° 337; T. Fish 1954, p. 84

Even if the sovereigns of the Ur Empire obtained their copper directly from Magan, beyond Dilmun, they nonetheless continued their relations with Dilmun. This note grants 2 litres (2 *sila*) of flour to Ur-Dumuzi, the messenger, who is returning to Lagash with two subordinates who are sick. Agaushlugal is granted a half-*sila* of flour only.

83 Sumerian Administrative Document that Mentions Products from Dilmun

Mesopotamia: Tello, Ancient Girsu (Land of Sumer)
Early Dynastic III period
(c. 2380-2350 BC)
Clay
H 5.2 W 5.2 TH 2.5 cm
Paris, Louvre Museum,
acc. n° AO 13611
B F. Allotte de la Fuye 1913:
DP 405

Account of edible plants from the gardens of Girsu, among which we find "Dilmun garlic". Along with dates, also mentioned in texts from the archives of Lagash, these bulbs were cultivated at Dilmun, then exported, and the Sumerians considered them to be choice produce.

84-86 Copper Ingots

An-Nasiriyah, chance discovery
Early Dilmun, c. 2000-1800 BC
Copper
L 16.5, 13.5 and 10.5
MAX W 4.8, 6.5 and 3.4 cm
Manama, Bahrain National Museum, main store
Unpublished

These ingots, which occur in several shapes ranging from the nearly spherical cap to the truncated cone, are of the plano-convex type, extremely common in the ancient Near East. Their shape is the result of a production process that seems to have consisted of the following: at the site of the mining operation, the metal was extracted in a crude oven dug in the earth; once the fusion temperature was reached (approx. 1083°C), the copper, freed of its gangue of ore and separated from its slag, flowed towards the bottom of the oven, and accumulated at the bottom of the depression, which gave the bars their irregular shape. It was probably in this form that copper was exported from the mining areas of Oman. It may have been refined by successive recastings in crucibles before being sold - it is not impossible that this could have taken place in Bahrain itself. The famous "Vase à la Cachette" of Susa, c. 2450 BC, provided similar ingots, and these had already been subject to a significant degree of refining (Tallon 1987, p. 195-196).

88 Soft Stone Vessel
Al-Hajjar necropolis,
Bahraini excavations 1979,
Grave 2
Early Dilmun, c. 2000-1800 BC
(discovery context)
Chlorite
H 5 MAX D. 8.8 cm
Manama, Bahrain National
Museum, acc. n° 3183-4-98
Unpublished

This small cylindrical recepticle
is one of the rare examples
from Bahrain of vessels in stone
probably of Iranian origin.
The decoration that covers
the entire surface and is deeply
incised, is a naturalistic
representation of a woven
pattern, and can be associated
with textile production that
developed during the second
third of the 3rd millennium BC.
It was largely exported from
the mountains in the centre
of Iran to Mesopotamian sites,
and to a lesser degree to the
Gulf where examples are often
found in much later contexts.

87 Painted Jar
Madinat Hamad necropolis,
season and grave unspecified
Early Dilmun, c. 2000-1800 BC
Pottery
H 20.5 D MAX. 23.2 cm
Manama, Bahrain National
Museum, acc. n° 302-2-88
Unpublished

The potters of Dilmun were
experts in copying certain types
of ceramics which reached
the island of Bahrain as part
of the transit trade, and it is
often difficult to tell the original
productions from their local
imitations. This type of globular
vessel reproduces a style
of decoration that was common
to eastern Iran and even
the Indus region, but it may
also have been produced
locally.

89 Painted Vessel
Saar necropolis, Bahraini
excavations 1989, Tumulus 178
Early Dilmun, c. 2000-1800 BC
Pottery
H 16.3 D MAX 16 cm
Manama, Bahrain National
Museum, acc. n° 2066-2-90
Unpublished

The painted decoration
of this small globular jar, made
out of high quality clay,
recalls the decoration found
on items from the rich ceramic
production from Shahdad
cemetery, in Kerman in Iran
(cf Hakemi 1997, p. 584-604).

**90 Truncated Cone-
Shaped Soft Stone Vessel**
Al-Hajjar necropolis,
season and grave unspecified
Early Dilmun, c. 1800 BC
Chlorite
H 9 D MAX. 9.5 cm (vase);
H 6 D MAX. 4.5 cm (lid)
Manama, Bahrain National
Museum, acc. n° 195-2-88
Unpublished

The highly accentuated
truncated cone shape of this
elegant chlorite vessel imported
from the Oman Peninsula,
and that of its curved lid,
together with its decoration
(simple circles with dots
together with its series
of straight lines) are also
representative of the period
known as "Wadi Suq". The lack
of a handle on the body
would place this vessel in a late
period of the culture.

**91 Spouted Vessel
in the Omani Tradition**
'Ali necropolis, Bahraini
excavations 1988-89,
Tumulus 101.16
Early Dilmun, c. 1900-1800 BC
Pottery
H 17 D MAX. 18.5 cm
Manama, Bahrain National
Museum, acc. n° 2017-2-90
Unpublished. Comp.: *Bahrain
National Museum* 1993, p. 33

The Omani culture known
as "Wadi Suq" (after the valley
where it was first discovered)
which followed that of Umm-
an-Nar in the 2nd millennium
BC, produced abundant
quantities of this type of
globular jar with no neck and a
pouring spout (Donaldson 1984:
fig. 8-9, p. 288-289). We know
from archaeometric analysis,
that these were also copied by
Early Dilmun potters, in
Bahrain's local clay, as is the
case for the vase presented
here.

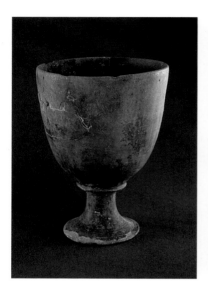

92 Chalice on Pedestal
Saar necropolis, Bahraini
excavations 1977-78, Tumulus
100
Early Dilmun, c. 2000-1800 BC
Pottery
^{H}13.2 $^{D\,MAX.}$9.2 cm
Manama, Bahrain National
Museum, acc. n° 413-2-88
^{B} Ibrahim 1982: 32; fig. 38: 3;
pl. 49: 3

This type of chalice in fine grey
clay, with its characteristic
cordon underlining the link
between the foot and the body
was probably imported from
the Indus region. We know
of examples with a very similar
shape, made out of a light
brown clay, associated
with levels of Mehrgarh Period
VIII in Pakistan around 1900 BC.
(Jarrige *et al.* 1995, p. 356,
fig. 7.27: c; Catalogue *Les Cités
oubliées de l'Indus*, n° 131).

**93 Painted Vessel
in Indus Style**
Dar Kulayb necropolis,
Bahraini excavations 1994-95,
Tumulus 12.
Early Dilmun, c. 2000-1800 BC
Pottery
^{H} 11.9 $^{D\,MAX.}$ 9 cm
Manama, Bahrain National
Museum, acc. n° 94-6-1
Unpublished

This small vase was certainly
produced in the Indus Valley,
perhaps in the Amri region, as is
indicated by its characteristic
peepul tree leaf decoration,
traditional in Harrappan
iconography, but also by its
shape. An identical piece
was discovered in the Eastern
Province of Saudi Arabia
(Bukholder 1984, n° 30).

**94 Set of Beads
from the Indus Region**
Madinat Hamad necropolis,
Bahraini excavations 1998-99,
Tumulus 420
Early Dilmun, c. 2200-2000 BC
Carnelian
^{L} from 0.55 to 3
^{W} or ^{D} from 0.5 to 1.7 cm
Manama, Bahrain National
Museum, main store
Unpublished

This set includes "etched beads"
with a geometrical design
obtained by "engraving"
or by partial discoloration
using an alkaline paste.
This type of production is
characteristic of the Indus
civilisation which exported
them to Mesopotamia, to Susa
and to the Gulf (Reade 1979).
The design most commonly
found in Bahrain (a pair of
juxtaposed concentric circles)
generally dates from between
2300 and 2150 BC according
to Reade.

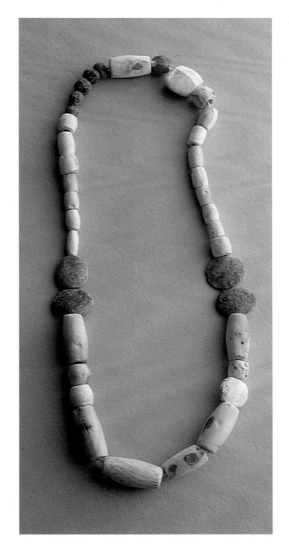

95, 96 Miniature Soft Stone Vessels
Al-Maqsha necropolis,
Bahraini excavations 1992-93,
Grave 4
Early Dilmun, c. 2000-1800 BC
Chlorite
^{H}4.6 and 5.5 $^{D\,MAX.}$2.7 and 5.5 cm
Manama, Bahrain National
Museum, acc. nº 93-1-2
and main store
Unpublished

These two miniature vessels are
typical examples of imports
that originated from Iran.
The first, in the shape
of a miniature bottle with
a square body and round neck,
the sides decorated with circles
with dots belongs to a type
discovered in the north of
Bactria south of Kerman, as well
as at Susa (South-West Iran). Its
presence in Bahrain as well as
on the Oman Peninsula (Grave
A, Hili North) shows the scope
of the inter-regional exchanges
during the Bronze Age.
The shape of the second,
with the body covered
with a fishscale pattern
characteristic of this type from
the 3rd millennium BC,
has exact equivalents among
the large sized vessels
unearthed in Iran, Mesopotamia
and on the island of Tarut.

97 Necklace
Saar necropolis, Bahraini
excavations 1978-79, Tumulus
267.5
Early Dilmun, c. 2000-1800 BC
Carnelian, lapis-lazuli, copper
^{L} 29.5 cm
Manama, Bahrain National
Museum, acc. nº 1809-2-8
Unpublished

This jewellery distinguishes
itself by the presence of four
discoidal lapis lazuli stones,
which originate from
Badakhshan (Afghanistan). It
could, however, have been
assembled in Bahrain, by local
craftsmen.

⁹⁸ Chalice with Concave Sides on Pedestal
Saar necropolis, Bahraini excavations 1988, Tumulus 140
Early Dilmun, c. 2000-1800 BC
Pottery
ᴴ 20 ᴰ ᴹᴬˣ· 12 cm
Manama, Bahrain National Museum, acc. n° 1843-2-89
ᴮ *Bahrain National Museum* 1993, p. 22

This elegant chalice, made out of extremely fine clay and with a carefully painted geometrical decoration, has been linked with the Harrappan tradition of footed chalices of Mehrgarh Period VII, although these are heavier, and older. (Cf for example Jarrige *et al.* 1995, p. 171:c) They have similarities to later examples in alabaster, in the Quetta region. It would be just as appropriate to look for the origin of this type in Western Bactria, where chalices that resemble it more closely, although not decorated, have been found in the graves of Dashly Tepe 3, for example, dating from the very beginning of the 2nd millennium BC (Francfort 1989, p. 355, fig. 37: type III, 1). A similar specimen in copper, from the same period, was also discovered in a tumulus in Bahrain (Crawford 1998, fig. 5.4, p. 85).

⁹⁹ Bowl
'Ali necropolis, Bahraini excavations 1988-89, Tumulus 2
Early Dilmun, c. 2000-1800 BC
Banded calcite ("alabaster")
ᴴ 5 ᴰ ᴹᴬˣ· 9.8 cm
Manama, Bahrain National Museum, acc. n° 1835-2-89
Unpublished

This shape of very thin calcite bowl is found in Mesopotamia as well as in Iran, the region from which it most likely comes.

¹⁰⁰⁻¹⁰³ Spindle-shaped Weights
Saar necropolis, Bahraini excavations 1991, Tumulus 4
Early Dilmun, c. 2000-1800 BC
Haematite
ᴸ2, 4.1, 4.1 and 8,3
ᴰ ᴹᴬˣ 0.8, 1.2, 0.85 and 1.8 cm
ᵂᵉ3.02, 16.40, 8.08 and 81,87 gr
Manama, Bahrain National Museum, main store
Unpublished

¹⁰⁴, ¹⁰⁵ Two Duck-Shaped Weights
Saar necropolis, Bahraini excavations 1991, Tumulus 4
Early Dilmun, c. 2000-1800 BC
Haematite and veined limestone
ᴸ3 and 2.3 ᴰ ᴹᴬˣ1.9 and 1.3 cm
ᵂᵉ24.50 and 5.12 gr
Manama, Bahrain National Museum, main store
Unpublished

¹⁰⁷⁻¹¹¹ Commercial Sealings
Saar settlement,
British excavations
1992 (1045:01), 1991 (H13:12:1),
1992 (1042:19), 1991 (F17:75:1),
1992 (1596:01), House 211
and Temple
Early Dilmun, c. 2000-1800 BC
Clay
ᴰ ᴹᴬˣ2.5 to 3.2 ᵀᴴ 0.8 to 1.2 cm
Manama, Bahrain National
Museum, main store
ᴮ Crawford & Matthews 1997,
p. 58: 28; p. 56: 13

¹⁰⁶ Weight
from the Indus Region
Saar settlement,
British excavations 1992-93
(I12:5019:01), House 223
Early Dilmun, c. 2000-1800 BC
Flint stone
ᴴ 1.5 ᴸ 1.2 ᵂ 1.2 cm ᵂᵉ 6.8 gr
Manama, Bahrain National
Museum, main store
ᴮ Crawford et al. 1997, fig. 91.
Comp.: Højlund & Andersen
1994, fig. 1985, p. 395

In the Indus system, this type
of cubic weight was often
found with other spherical
weights, examples of which
have also been found at
Qal'at al-Bahrain or al-Hajjar.
This example from Saar
corresponds to exactly half
the value of the base unit
of the Indus weight system
(13.625 gr).

¹¹²⁻¹¹⁴ Stamped Tokens
Saar settlement,
British excavations
1995 (6539:01), 1994 (2665:06),
1992 (2126:01), Houses 60, 53, 57
Early Dilmun, c. 2000-1800 BC
Clay
ᴰ ᴹᴬˣ2.1, 2.05 and 1.5
ᵀᴴ0.9, 0.84 and 0.8 cm
Manama, Bahrain National
Museum, main store
ᴮ Crawford 1998, p. 52, pl. 2;
p. 54, fig. 1-2; p. 57-58

"The Land of Dilmun is Holy…"

Pierre Lombard

Ancient religious life in Bahrain is a subject which both attracts and frustrates historians and archaeologists.

Most specialists agree that the Mesopotamian myths that describe the land of Dilmun as "pure" and "luminous" confirm the immense and age-old prestige that Dilmun had in the eyes of the Sumerians. For Sumer, Dilmun was an indispensable partner, all the more impressive for to its specific hydrological and environmental situation: the rare place where the Apsû of fresh water mixed with the salt waters of the Gulf, where two seas meet…Due to this powerful image, the perfect illustration of Sumerian cosmogony, probably related by generations of sailors and merchants, it is hardly surprising that the land of Dilmun was progressively idealised as a place conducive to eternal life. It was where the gods of Sumer placed the survivor of the Flood, Ziusudra as his place of residence, the only human being worthy of this exceptional gesture.

The numerous religious buildings discovered in Bahrain have also led us to believe that the sacred character of Dilmun was paramount. Even the attitude of the Dilmunites towards death, full of respect and the impetus behind the collective energy which fuelled the construction of tens of thousands of tumuli can be considered as the expression of a profound religious feeling. However, the scarcity of texts or inscriptions discovered in Dilmun immediately limits the interpretation of archaeological finds, and we have to admit that our knowledge of the local religion is very limited.

Buildings

One is struck by the number of "temples" that have so far been discovered, and this in a limited area of the north of the main island of Bahrain. The best known building is naturally the Barbar temples complex (see below), one of the first discoveries by the Danish expedition to Bahrain in 1954. Its function seems unquestionable. The same is true for the remarkable edifice with colonnades unearthed at Diraz in 1973 by a British team, whose findings are as yet unpublished. In the same way as the latter, the temple discovered at Saar (see below) is totally integrated in the settlement, of which it is in some ways the keystone. Alleys and streets apparently all converge on the temple. It is also thought that the two wells at Umm es-Sujjur may have been sacred, suggested by the hundred or so blocks of carved stone that are scattered in the immediate vicinity. It is highly probable that they constitute the remains of an impressive building that was destroyed in the 7th century AD on the orders of the Ummayad Caliph Abdul al-Malik bin Marwan. This building would have been the place of worship for a pagan cult whose origins were perhaps in Early Dilmun - several discoveries by the Japanese mission that studied the site in 1993-1994 date from this period, including a remarkable limestone altar (Cat. 118).

A Religion Connected with Fresh Water?

The sacred wells at Umm es-Sujour, connected to one of the most important artesian wells in Bahrain reinforce the tempting idea, which we will look at later, of a close association between the Barbar Temple II and its wellspring, assuming the existence of a Dilmunite religion that was directly related to the Apsû of Sumerian religious texts. We are perhaps running before we can walk here, in the sense that we do not know which divinity(ies) were worshipped at Barbar or Umm es-Sujjur. The connection between Enki, God of Deep Sweet Waters and Dilmun is well-known; (see above), it is Enki who brings life to Dilmun by authorising Utu to supply the country with fresh water, and choosing to save Ziusudra from the Flood and install him in the Paradise of Dilmun. However, nothing indicates that Enki was venerated in Bahrain, where the temples identified are perhaps more likely to have been dedicated to the son of Enki, Inzak, traditionally presented as the protector (nabû) of Dilmun, and to his wife Meskilak. Members of the Dilmunite diaspora had even dedicated a temple to Inzak as far away as Susa (Iran). We can also observe that neither the temple at Diraz, nor that at Saar have revealed wells or other installations connected with water.

Iconography of Seals

We will see later on how the iconography of the seals of Dilmun appears to be highly symbolic. It includes numerous elements related to the beliefs and religious activities of the Dilmunites. People are regularly portrayed consorting with figures wearing the traditional horned head-dress of the Mesopotamian gods (Cat. 125), whereas others seem visibly engaged in religious scenes before altars or tables of offerings (Cat. 127). Other scenes, which we do not yet understand, probably illustrate, in the same way a scene of piety, familiar episodes in local religion; recurring erotic scenes (Cat. 123), which often use characters placed on podiums or altars, could, rather than being simple profane representations, belong to the same category.

The Barbar Temples

H. Hellmuth Andersen, Flemming Højlund

When P.V. Glob was carrying out his first archaeological survey of Bahrain in 1954, he came across a low tell just south of the little village of Barbar, a few hundred metres from the coast. A large squared stone block protruding from the tell caught Glob's attention, and in order to gain an impression of the mound's construction a trench was driven through the centre from north to south. Within a few days it was clear that the tell at Barbar contained the remains of very important temples, and every year up to 1961 large-scale excavation took place here, directed primarily by Hellmuth Andersen and Peder Mortensen.

Three successive temples were built here, Temple I-III, with five building stages (Ia-b, IIa-b and III). The first temple was placed on a low mound sloping down towards a depression in the southwest where a freshwater spring gushed. A little towards the northeast a further temple was found.
The general structure of Temple I and II is that of a 'high temple' with a double stepped platform, an upper trapezoidal one and a lower oval one, and two wing-structures, a well chamber to the west and an enclosure to the east.

Temple II was the best preserved, constructed of finely worked limestone, perhaps quarried on Jiddah island. From the surrounding ground level a stairway led to the lower platform.

The upper platform, of trapezoidal shape, was enclosed by a 2 m high retaining wall. The floor was covered by slabs and in the centre of the sanctuary proper was a double circular altar. A number of altar stones with holes were found standing on the floor. They may have been used when tethering animals for sacrifice.

Buried in a pit below the floor a number of spectacular objects were found: cylindrical alabaster jars, a copper mirror-handle shaped as a human figure, a small copper bird and the most famous object from the Barbar temple, a bull's head of copper. This head may originally have fitted onto the sounding box of a lyre, as is known from the Royal graves at Ur, and seen on a Dilmun stamp seal. Sheets of copper were commonly found which were originally fastened with nails to wooden structures.
The well chamber appeared at the foot of the oval platform to the west as a chamber sunk below ground level, enclosing a freshwater spring. It measured 4 x 2 m and was encased in high ashlar walls. Upon excavation the water stood 1 m high. Three large subterranean channels lead the water out into the surrounding gardens. A staircase, 15 m long and almost 2 m wide, with about 30 steps, led from the basin to the upper platform, an ascent of 7 m. At the foot of the retaining wall of the upper platform the stair was flanked by a double line of eight great socket stones, each stone pierced

Bird's eye view of the Barbar
complex, after re-excavation
in 1983.

with two holes. In the holes were traces of wood faced with copper sheets, probably remains from cult statues, perhaps in the shape of four-legged animals or standards with cult symbols. Within the enclosure to the east, large-scale sacrifices took place, attested by massive deposits of dark, grey ashes containing burnt bones of animals. A ramp connected the enclosure to the upper platform.

Temple III was originally much larger than the preceding two temples, but it was very damaged and plundered of stone material. Elevated on the covered remains of Temple II, it featured a right-angled square platform, with a height of at least 4 m. Temple III presents a remarkable break with tradition, inasmuch as there is no evidence of the previous wing structures, i.e. the well chamber and the sacrificial enclosure. It is interesting to note, however, that the temple well at the south-west corner, a little east of the well chamber, goes through five distinct building stages following the five stages of the temple. Contemporary with Temple III we have, 15 m to the northeast of the main tell, a smaller tell with the remains of another temple, the Northeast temple, but in a heavily plundered state. Here, also there was evidence of two platforms, of which at least the upper one was a perfect square and a large robber-hole in the centre indicated a deep-lying structure, probably a well chamber, presumably the

main sanctuary of this temple.
We have thus through the addition
of the Northeast temple the conception
of a double-temple, and perhaps
a separation of cults that earlier were integrated
within the same temple. The ruined state
of the temples is due to demolition in connection
with the re-building of the successive phases,
but also to plundering of later times.

The temples can be dated to the centuries
around 2 000 BC and are contemporary
with the appearance of the stamp seals,
the "royal mounds" and the earliest walled city
at Qal'at al-Bahrain. The oval shape
of Temple I and II may reveal old traditions
going back to Sumerian temples like the temple
of Al-Ubaid in southern Mesopotamia.
A special type of conical beaker found
in large numbers in the foundation of Temple I
– apparently remains from a libation ceremony -
may also indicate a Mesopotamian connection.
Which deity was worshipped at the Barbar
temple? The question cannot be answered easily,
as no inscriptions or identifiable statues were
found during the excavations. But there are some
striking features of the Barbar temple, which
must be stressed. The temple was situated at a
freshwater spring, indicating the numinous
power which gave the impulse for the cult at
Barbar. Over this spring a chamber was built, and
we know that a water cult took place here. This
puts one in mind of the Mesopotamian god, Enki.

Barbar. Monumental
well of Temple II.

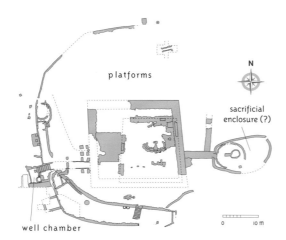

platforms

N

sacrificial
enclosure (?)

well chamber

0   10 m

Barbar. Plan of Temple II.

Enki was the god of the subterranean
freshwater ocean, called apsû. The temple-apsû
is well known from the written sources, but it has
been extremely difficult to identify in
excavations. From cuneiform inscriptions found
in Failaka and Bahrain and from written sources
in Mesopotamia there is however no evidence
that Enki was worshipped in Dilmun,
whereas it is clear that the main deity of Dilmun
was Inzak, whom the Mesopotamians introduced
into their own pantheon as the son of Enki.
Maybe these two gods were related, because
Inzak in Dilmun was also the god of fresh water?

We cannot know whether the Barbar temple,
the greatest temple ever excavated in Dilmun,
was a temple for the tutelary deity of Dilmun,
Inzak. Other gods may have been served there,
as well, for instance Inzak's spouse Meskilak.
After excavation the Barbar temple was covered
with sand in order to protect the site.
On the occasion of the *Bahrain through the Ages*
Conference in 1983 it was uncovered once again
and made accessible to the public.

The Dilmun Temple at Saar

Robert Killick

The Dilmun Temple at Saar stood in an elevated position in the middle of the Bronze Age settlement at the junction of the two main streets. It was built around 1900 BC, when the settlement was extensively remodelled during the City IIb period, and remained in use for 150-200 years, by which time many of the adjacent houses had already fallen into disrepair.

The temple was built of rough limestone, quarried locally, in contrast to the well-cut masonry of the Barbar Temple. The irregular shape of the building has no known parallels but may be partly explained by the need to fit between existing buildings. However, we are at a loss to explain the curious loop of wall in the west corner. Immediately in front of the temple were some circular stands or offering tables which can be paralleled at the nearby, contemporaneous temple at Diraz. The temple has a single entrance leading into the main chamber, with a subsidiary room in the west corner. Three buttresses in the long walls and one each in the centre of the short wall indicate where the main roof beams were placed. These were also supported by three central columns. No roofing material was recovered from the temple, but it was probably made of layers of palm frond laid over beams and poles, and sealed with a mud plaster. The temple underwent a series of modifications during its lifetime, some major and some minor. However, for most of its life, it had only

Saar. The temple and the adjacent residential quarter.

the main chamber and subsidiary storeroom. All the activities connected with the worship of the gods of the settlement must have been conducted in this central room. In the absence of texts we are left only to speculate on what these might have been, though some have preserved traces in the archaeological record.

The principal focus of ceremony within the temple was a group of benches in the north corner that were approached by two small steps. This area received preferential treatment: the floor was kept very clean; some surfaces

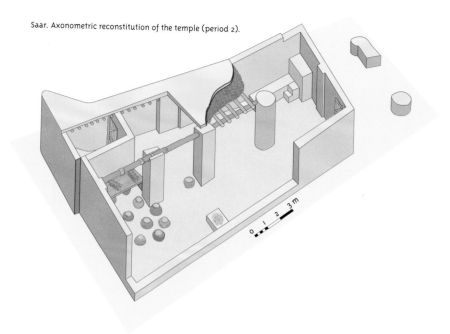

Saar. Axonometric reconstitution of the temple (period 2).

Saar. West part of the temple.

were covered with matting; and the walls coated in crimson plaster. The main bench in this group was an immutable part of the temple furnishings, surviving intact throughout the lifetime of the building. It was important not in itself but because of whatever sat on top, perhaps the statues or cultic symbols of the deities worshipped at Saar.

A second focus of cultic activity was the two temple altars, one against the central column and one on the southern wall. Both altars were of similar construction with stone built bases and curved backs. The curved motif may represent a stylised crescent moon or perhaps bull's horns. Both altars served a similar function and were used to burn food offerings, and perhaps incense, in honour of the gods.

Why two altars were required is not known, but there are many possible explanations: perhaps the level of offerings and rituals was such that one altar alone was not sufficient; or perhaps two separate deities were worshipped, and each allocated their own altar.

In contrast, the rear of the temple, furthest away from the entrance, was used for storage. It was here that jars and boxes containing food and other substances required for the temple rituals were kept. Many broken sealings were found here, discarded when the containers were broached. The small room in the west corner provided additional storage space, perhaps for the more valuable temple paraphernalia.

Externally, the stands or offering tables in the public street must have had some religious function. These were set in the loose sand, without any associated burnt debris or signs of scorching, suggesting that they did not fulfil the same function as the internal altars. If they were offering tables, then they may have been where individuals placed their private donations and offerings to the temple. An alternative interpretation is that they were pedestals for the public display of the statues or symbols of the gods, either permanently or, more likely, on special occasions.

The role of the temple in the religious life of the settlement is unequivocal. Its elevated position and the special architectural treatment it received alone suggest that it was central to the religious beliefs of the inhabitants. What that belief system entailed is difficult to ascertain but we can say that it shared some characteristics with neighbouring countries: worship required a particular building (there are no household shrines at Saar) and acts of devotion which included propitiation through offerings of food and drink. Religious symbolism, as seen on the seals, borrows heavily from Greater Mesopotamia, though the underlying meanings may of course have metamorphosed in transition. It is thus dangerous to make too close an association with particular deities, and, in any case, we would hazard a guess that given the rustic nature of the temple it may not have been a particularly important member of the Dilmun pantheon that was worshipped at Saar.

Did the temple also play a part in the economic and political life of the community? All that can be said is that there is no evidence that the temple stored and redistributed goods to the community or that the temple officials also functioned as an administrative elite, but whether this is also a reflection of the broader picture of Dilmun society is debatable.

¹¹⁵, ¹¹⁶ Ritual or Foundation Vessels

Barbar, Danish excavations, 1954 (517.BX, 517.YL), Temple IIa, central platform
Early Dilmun, c. 2000-1800 BC
Banded calcite ("alabaster")
^{H}12.5 and 17.5
$^{D\ MAX}$12.2 and 13.2 cm
Manama, Bahrain National Museum, acc. n° 604-2-88 and 606-2-88
^{B} Glob 1959, p. 140, fig. 31, and p. 139, fig. 2;
Bahrain National Museum;1989, n° 36a, b

These two vessels were part of a group of objects ritually placed in the foundation deposit of Temple II. The specimen with concave vertical sides comes from a well-known tradition in Eastern Iran (at Shahdad, in Seistan and at Khurab, cf Casanova 1991, type IVc, p. 34 and pl. IV, n° 48), the region from which both very probably originated. This type of alabaster vessel, that was widespread in the Near and Middle East in the 3rd and 2nd millennia, and is generally considered a luxury product which was part of a system of exchange that was both economic, political and symbolic.

¹¹⁷ Cylinder-Seal Representing a Cult Scene?

Madinat Hamad necropolis (BS3/D), Bahraini excavations 1991-92, Tumulus 20
Early Dilmun, c. 2000-1800 BC
Soft stone (steatite?)
^{L}3 $^{D\ MAX}$1.3 cm
Manama, Bahrain National Museum, main store
^{B} Denton & Alsendi 1996, fig. 1-2

Deeply engraved on one of the rare cylindrical seals found in the Early Dilmun levels at Bahrain, this scene associates a principal female figure, apparently bare-chested with delineated breasts, perhaps a goddess, before whom a figure of indeterminate sex is prostrated. The goddess (?) is apparently holding out a goblet to a male figure who is reaching out to take it. The composition of the scene does not enable us to say whether this last figure is placed in the background or whether he is standing on the back of the kneeling figure, which, if the latter is the case, would indicate an inferior or vanquished position. This cylinder clearly illustrates two iconographical traditions, that of the Southern Gulf (sheep or goats with long necks, plus the decoration of circles with dots on the two parts of the cylinder, which recalls the style of the reverse of the Dilmun stamp-seals), and that of Iran (Dasht i-Lut region, cf Amiet 1986, fig. 132: 6-10, 12). It has been suggested that this piece could have been made in Bahrain, either by an Iranian craftsman passing through, or by a Dilmunite craftsman, on request from a merchant originating from central Iran, who would have specified the iconography.

¹¹⁸ Altar (?)

Umm es-Sujjur, Japanese excavations 1994, Well II
Early Dilmun, c. 2000-1800 BC
Calcaire
^{H}43 ^{L}60 ^{W}33 cm
Manama, Bahrain National Museum, main store
^{B} Konishi 1996, fig. 6:7

This enigmatic block of sculpted limestone, with a fairly elaborate shape, was interpreted by its excavators as an altar associated with the access stairway to the second well at Umm es-Sujjur. The curved shape of its upper part does indeed resemble the coated stone altars from the temple at Saar. If this identification is confirmed, the two wells at the site must have had the same sacred significance as those used at Barbar, and we cannot exclude the possibility that religious activities may have taken place there. The presence in previous times of a large building, as well as the desire to destroy all traces of pagan cults at the beginnings of Islam would also make this plausible.

119-122 Conical Footed Goblets
Barbar, Danish excavations 1955
(517.DE, .CS2, .DG, .CS1),
Temple Ia, central platform
Early Dilmun, c. 2000-1800 BC
Pottery
H12, 13, 11.2 and 8.8 D MAX8.5, 7.5,
8.8 and 8 cm
Manama, Bahrain National
Museum, acc. n° 593-2-88,
592-2-88, 594-2-88
and 591-2-88
B Glob 1955, p 182: fig. 5;
Bahrain-National Museum 1989,
p. 14

125 Bull's Head
Barbar, Danish excavations
(517.FJ), Temple IIa,
central platform
Early Dilmun, c. 2000-1800 BC
Copper
H18 D MAX15 cm (horns)
Manama, Bahrain National
Museum
B Glob, P.V. 1955b, p. 191;
Bibby 1969, pl. V;
E.C.L. During-Caspers 1971;
Bahrain National Museum 1989,
n° 44

This "star" piece of the Dilmun culture (today frequently reproduced on the State of Bahrain's banknotes and stamps...) is generally considered an element of decoration for the body of a lyre or small harp, similar to those on instruments from the Royal Graves at Ur (Woolley 1934). It comes, in fact, from a long tradition of objects that have been found from Mesopotamia to Southern Turkmenistan (Masson 1976, p. 16-17 and pl. I), including Eastern Arabia and the Gulf. It is difficult to determine whether the example from Barbar is the work of a local metal smith or whether it is one of the objects acquired through the trade networks in which Bahrain participated.

123 Stamp-seal Representing an Erotic Scene

Qal'at al-Bahrain, Danish
excavations 1957 (520.LA),
Northern city-wall
Early Dilmun, c. 2000-1800 BC
Soft stone (chlorite/steatite)
H1.1 D2.7 cm
Manama, Bahrain National
Museum, acc. n° 2825-2-90
B Glob 1958: 143, fig. 13a;
Bahrain National Museum 1989,
n° 267; Alsendi 1994, n° 221;
Kjaerum 1994: 331-332, fig. 1743

Stamp-seals representing erotic scenes are not rare in Early Dilmun, and have been discovered both in settlements and graves. This one shows a naked man on a podium/altar, his genitals clumsily carved at knee height (!), and placed opposite a partner with legs wide apart and arms outstretched. Behind the man there is an antelope upside down, and behind the woman a scorpion, and opposite her face an indeterminate object, probably a vase. In equivalent scenes on numerous other Dilmun seals, the woman is often drinking from a jar using a straw, and is often associated, as in this case, with a scorpion. The podium represented on this stamp-seal, as well as other specific symbols commonly found on erotic scenes, suggest that the scene takes place in a temple. We can therefore very probably conclude that it is evoking a ritual or sacred scene.

124 Stamp-seal with Representation of Enki?

Barbar, Danish excavations,
Temple IIb, Well chamber
Early Dilmun, c. 2000-1800 BC
Chlorite or steatite
H0.9 D2.2 cm
Manama, Bahrain National
Museum, acc. n° 4097
B Andersen 1986, fig. 43a;
Alsendi 1994, n° 203

The naked man shown here in a sort of sanctuary is carrying two jars of water that actually form part of the sanctuary walls. He is probably identifiable as Enki, the god reigning over the *apsû*, the underground freshwater sea, and who allowed the land of Dilmun to enjoy its benefits. In Mesopotamia, the "walls" of his sanctuary or chapel are often represented in the form of a flow of life-giving water linking the two jars.

¹²⁶ Stamp-seal Representing a Mythological Scene
Saar settlement,
British excavations 1994
(5168:01), House 220
Early Dilmun, c. 2000-1800 BC
Chlorite or steatite
ᴴ1.1ᴰ2.54 cm
Manama, Bahrain National Museum, main store
ᴮ *Ancient Saar*: 34; Crawford, Killick & Moon 1997: fig. 32

This stamp-seal very probably evokes a mythological scene, probably familiar to the seal's owner, but which remains enigmatic for us in the absence of any textual reference. We see a god sitting on a throne with a back, the right hand raised facing a man placed before him. The man is apparently touching the god's chest with his left hand (possibly armed with a stick or a sword). Behind the deity a subordinate is raising his right hand. The foreground consists of the figure of a bull.

¹²⁷ Stamp-seal Representing a Cult Scene
Saar necropolis,
Bahrain excavations 1991-92,
Tumulus 99
Early Dilmun, c. 2000-1800 BC
Chlorite or steatite
ᴴ1.2 ᴰ2.7 cm
Manama, Bahrain National Museum, acc. n° 2889-2-91-3
Unpublished

This stamp-seal, *a priori*, is apparently separated into two "registers". The upper register features two podia or altars, placed on a line that represents the ground, and flanked by two antelope protomes. In the centre, a naked man grasps the horns of both animals and there is a jar beside his head. In the lower register, there is a fully-dressed man lying down, holding an architectural symbol (?) in his left hand behind his back, his right hand touching the line of the ground of the upper register. The interpretation of this scene, probably religious, is rendered difficult by its iconographical mode of composition. If we decipher the system of representation conventionally adopted by the Dilmunite craftsmen for complex scenes, the two "registers" should in fact be placed vertically to make the scene coherent – this places the man lying down opposite the naked man, possibly a priest officiating between two altars and their symbolic protomes.

The Hidden Art of Dilmun: the Stamp-seals

Poul Kjærum

The earliest local seals in Bahrain were manufactured in about 2 050 BC and are one of many indications of a structural change in the Dilmun society. It was at this time that Dilmun's ancient capital, the city at Qal'at al-Bahrain, was fortified with heavy stone walls, the temples at Barbar, Saar, and Diraz were founded and the Royal Tombs at 'Ali were constructed. The seals themselves were a means of organising trade and the administration of the society, used by private individuals as well as officials. Stamped on documents of all kinds, on contracts, on tags and sealings attached to goods, they certified authenticity or ownership.

More than 400 stamp-seals from the Dilmun period are at present known from Bahrain, where they are found in temples, houses and graves. With a few exceptions they are monofacial stamp-seals of the same basic form with a flat circular obverse disc and a domed reverse boss. At the foot of the boss there is a V-perforation intended for a string or a copper ring for suspension of the seal on a pin or a necklace and used when impressing the seal. The preferred material for the seals is steatite, a soft, homogenous stone which is easy to carve, but hardens when heated, so, when finished, the seals were baked and glazed. This process not only ensured that nothing could be altered

or added to the motif, which of course was important, but the glossy surface also made the appearance of the seal more attractive and easier to print in wet clay. While the shape of the seals in principle is the same throughout the four hundred years or so when the stamp-seals were produced in Dilmun, the ornaments on the reverse and the style and motifs on the obverse did change.

The earliest seals from Bahrain, from the time just after the fortification of the Qal'at-al Bahrain city, are called *Arabian Gulf seals*. Typical for these is a reverse ornament consisting of 1 to 3 grooves across the reverse, perpendicular to the perforation. The motifs on the obverse consist of different animals; bulls, antelopes, goats and lions, while human figures are rare. There is usually no evident connection between the single animal figures, placed either perpendicular to each other or oriented to the periphery as if it was the baseline (Cat. 128-131). Besides the large animals, birds of different kinds and scorpions

Stamp-seal
in the "Arabian Gulf style".

128 Stamp-seal
Saar necropolis,
Bahraini excavations 1988,
Tumulus 122
Early Dilmun, c. 2000 BC
Chlorite or steatite
H1.2 D2.6 cm
Manama, Bahrain National
Museum, acc. n° 2626-2-90
B Alsendi 1994, n° 134

129 Stamp-seal
Madinat Hamad necropolis,
Bahraini excavations 1987-88,
Tumulus 3
Early Dilmun, c. 2000 BC
Chlorite or steatite
H0.8 D2.1 cm
Manama, Bahrain National
Museum, acc. n° 2720-2-90
Unpublished

130 Stamp-seal
Dar Kulayb necropolis,
Bahraini excavations,
season and grave unspecified
Early Dilmun, c. 2000 BC
Chlorite or steatite
H1.3 D2.2 cm
Manama, Bahrain National
Museum, main store
Unpublished

131 Stamp-seal
Qal'at al-Bahrain,
Danish excavations 1965
(520.ALX), Northern City-wall
Early Dilmun, c. 2000 BC
Chlorite or steatite
H1.3 D2.1cm
Manama, Bahrain National
Museum, acc. n° 52-2-90
B Bibby 1967, fig. 4d;
Bahrain National Museum 1989,
n° 251; Alsendi 1994, n° 177;
Kjaerum 1994, p. 325, fig. 1732;
Barbar 1983, p. 38 (attributed
wrongly to the Barbar Temple)

132 Stamp-seal
Qal'at al-Bahrain,
Danish excavations 1970
(520.AZS), Northern City-wall
Early Dilmun, c. 2000 BC
Chlorite or steatite
H1.45 D2.85 cm
Manama, Bahrain National
Museum, acc. n° 3011-11-90
B Alsendi 1994, n° 279;
Kjaerum 1994, p. 322, fig. 1725;
Parpola 1994: p. 307, n° 5

are present, often depicted in the same size
as the ruminants, and in between are symbols
in the shape of a foot (Cat. 129) or more
often astral signs like stars and the crescent
moon. The elements in the designs seem
unrelated as remarked by Edith Porada
(1971 p. 335) on the meaning of the designs:
"Each one may have had a separate propitious
significance from which the seal owner believed
that he could profit". A few seals of this group
are exceptional in having inscriptions
in the still undeciphered Indus script depicted
above a ruminant, closely connected
to the Indus style (Cat. 132). This style was
adapted and used alongside the native
repertoire. Seal carving was at that time still
a new art in Bahrain and reflected foreign
influence as well as the carvers' individual
sense of art. The style varied from simple,
but firm linear carvings, to boldly modelled
reliefs of an almost naturalistic character.
There are few motifs with human beings.
They occur as protectors of the flocks,
in contest with lions or more peacefully,
seated drinking beer from a tube (Cat. 133, 134)
or as fishermen in a boat. These motifs
are known from the Mesopotamian cultural
sphere, but in Dilmun are executed in a rather
crude, local style.

During the first century of the 2nd millennium BC
the style of the motifs and decoration
of the reverse was gradually changed

133 Stamp-seal
Madinat Hamad necropolis
(BS2), Indian excavations
1984-85, Tumulus 1812
Early Dilmun, c. 2000 BC
Chlorite or steatite
H1.3 D2.75 cm
Manama, Bahrain National
Museum, acc. n° 2842-2-90
B Srivastava 1991, p. 27; fig. 55a:
2; pl. XXXIX: b; Alsendi 1994,
n° 10

134 Stamp-seal
'Ali necropolis,
Bahraini excavations 1981-82,
Tumulus 48
Early Dilmun, c. 2000 BC
Chlorite or steatite
H1.4 D2.4 cm
Manama, Bahrain National
Museum, acc. n° 3892-2-91-10
Unpublished

and standardised. The principal shape
of the seal was retained, but the reverse
decoration was standardised to four drilled
circles, two on either side of three diagonal
lines, and as a stylistic fingerprint,
the heads of the animals were drilled circles
to which snout, horns and ears were added,
and the centre point constitutes the eye.
The motifs are minutely carved reversed,
in intaglio, so when stamped they render the true
motif in relief. Parallel to this alteration,
the Indus features disappear, and the motifs
become consistent, characterised by a marked
interaction between all the single main figures,
whether animals or men. Seals of this type,
called *Dilmun seals*, are found in great numbers,
a total of around 800, from all over the Dilmun

¹³⁵ Stamp-seal
Abu Saybi necropolis (?),
season and grave unspecified
Early Dilmun, c. 2000-1800 BC
Chlorite or steatite
ᴴ0.55 ᴰ2.55 cm
Manama, Bahrain National
Museum, acc. n° 2808-2-90
ᴮ Alsendi 1994, n° 68

Stamp-seal
in the "Dilmun style".

¹³⁶ Stamp-seal
Al-Hajjar necropolis,
Bahraini excavations 1974 (?),
Grave 28/29
Early Dilmun, c. 2000-1800 BC
Chlorite or steatite
ᴴ1.3 ᴰ2.5 cm
Manama, Bahrain National
Museum, acc. n° 2832-2-90
ᴮ Alsendi 1994, n° 69

¹³⁷ Stamp-seal
'Ali necropolis,
Bahraini excavations 1988,
Tumulus 24.3
Early Dilmun, c. 2000-1800 BC
Chlorite or steatite
ᴴ1.2 ᴰ2.8 cm
Manama, Bahrain National
Museum, acc. n° 2839-2-90
ᴮ Alsendi 1994, n° 63

territory which by about 2 000 BC had expanded
towards the north with the foundation
of a trading station on Failaka island in Kuwait.
Dilmun's far-reaching commercial relations
are further illustrated by single seals found
as far south-east as the Indus port of Lothal,
and to the north as far as the Diyala river in
Mesopotamia. In the cities Ur and Susa
– commercial centres of Mesopotamia and Elam –
several of these seals have been found,
besides trade agreements certified with stamps
of Dilmun seals.

The figure repertoire on the Dilmun seals
is to a great extent eclectic, adopted
from the surrounding civilisations
in Mesopotamia, Iran and Syria and adapted
in Dilmun, modified stylistically as well
as in the interrelation between the figures,
to accommodate them to local practice.
It has to be assumed that the motifs
were understood by the Dilmunites,
so these miniature reliefs on the seals must
illustrate aspects of beliefs, rituals,

¹³⁸ Stamp-seal
Saar necropolis,
Bahraini excavations 1989-90,
Tumulus 26
Early Dilmun, c. 2000-1800 BC
Chlorite or steatite
ᴴ1 ᴰ2.9 cm
Manama, Bahrain National
Museum, acc. n° 2146-2-90
ᴮ Alsendi 1994, n° 60

¹³⁹ Stamp-seal
'Ali necropolis,
Bahraini excavations 1987-88,
Tumulus 4
Early Dilmun, c. 2000-1800 BC
Chlorite or steatite
ᴴ1.3 ᴰ2.6 cm
Manama, Bahrain National
Museum, acc. n° 2747-2-90
Unpublished

¹⁴¹ Stamp-seal
Al-Maqsha necropolis,
Bahraini excavations 1992-93,
unspecified grave
Early Dilmun, c. 2000-1800 BC
Chlorite or steatite
ᴴ1.2 ᴰ2.7 cm
Manama, Bahrain National
Museum, main store
Unpublished

¹⁴⁰ Susian Administrative Tablet with Gulf-style seal impression

Susa
Beginning of
the 2ⁿᵈ millennium BC
Clay
ᴴ6.3 ᵂ4.7 cm
Paris, Louvre Museum,
acc. n° Sb 11221 + Sb 12404
ᴮ V. Scheil 1939, n° 436;
P. Amiet 1970, p.109;
M. Lambert 1976, p.71-72

At the time when the seafaring merchants of Ur navigated to the emporium of Dilmun, Iran on the eastern side of the Gulf coast participated in the international trade. The people of Dilmun may have had an installation at Susa or in the back country of Elam. This text found at Susa is a contract mentioning the receipt of 10 minas (5 kg) of copper, which was exchanged for one ox and 10 [? text unreadable]. A certain Tem-Enzag, is mentioned. His name is composed with that of the god of Dilmun - Enzag (or Inzak). The Gulf stamp imprinted belongs to the ancient series. It represents animals with their legs folded under them.

ritual furniture and daily life in Dilmun. Except for a few sculptures in bronze and steatite this is the only surviving figural art. Thanks to this, we get an impression of the world as imagined and observed by the Dilmunites. Animals were still popular, such as the large ruminants, domesticated bulls and goats, together with gazelles, antelopes and even lions as well as birds of different kinds. These animals are conspicuous figures in the motifs, related to cult objects on a par with men and demons, being cult objects themselves - presented as idols on podia - or interacting with gods and men. In addition, dissociated foreparts or heads and necks are attached to altars as *pars pro toto* symbols of holy animals (Cat. 145), or composed in peculiar patterns of dissociated heads and necks joined in the centre of the seal, like spokes in a wheel (Cat. 144). Parts of different kinds of animals could also be joined in a monster shape. A serpent monster with snake body - though often with legs - horned head and jaws with teeth like a lion is amply represented, central in the motif like a standard or related to a god.

¹⁴² Stamp-seal

Buri necropolis,
Bahraini excavations 1987-88,
Tumulus 19.5
Early Dilmun, c. 2000-1800 BC
Chlorite or steatite
ᴴ1.2 ᴰ2.3 cm
Manama, Bahrain National
Museum, acc. n° 2819-2-90
ᴮ Alsendi 1994, n° 189

¹⁴³ Stamp-seal

Saar necropolis,
Bahraini excavations 1993,
Tumulus 14
Early Dilmun, c. 2000-1800 BC
Chlorite or steatite
ᴴ0.8 ᴰ2.4 cm
Manama, Bahrain National
Museum, main store
Unpublished

¹⁴⁴ Stamp-seal

Barbar, Western platform
of Temple II,
Danish excavations (517.ALE)
Early Dilmun, c. 2000-1800 BC
Chlorite or steatite
ᴴ0.85 ᴰ2.1 cm
Manama, Bahrain National
Museum, acc. n° 4098-18-90
ᴮ *Barbar* 1983, p. 38; Al-Khalifa
1986: fig. 82. Alsendi 1994,
n° 186

¹⁴⁵ Stamp-seal

Madinat Hamad necropolis
(MR), Bahraini excavations
1985-86, Tumulus 94
Early Dilmun, c. 2000-1800 BC
Chlorite or steatite
ᴴ1 ᴰ2.2 cm
Manama, Bahrain National
Museum, acc. n° 3023-2-90
ᴮ Alsendi 1994, n° 232

¹⁴⁶ Stamp-seal
Saar settlement, British
excavations 1990 (P19:1:10).
House 100, area 101
Early Dilmun, c. 2000–1800 BC
Chlorite or steatite
ᴴ1.32 ᴰ2.6 cm
Manama, Bahrain National
Museum, acc. n° 2989-3-90
Crawford 1991: 261 (c);
Alsendi 1994, n° 19;
Ancient Saar, p. 35;
ᴮ Crawford, Killick & Moon 1997,
p. 90, fig. 88

The ritual and mythological scenes are usually reproduced in a kind of tableau, centred around cult objects or rendered as an interaction between gods or between gods and men. These tableaux must have given the initiated spectator a hint of the spiritual meaning of the depiction. The gods wear a horned cap, like their Mesopotamian counterparts, though here simpler, just consisting of a single pair of bull's horns, and most of them with a coiffure shown as a double neckcurl. They are garbed in a dress, usually just a skirt, looking like an imitation of a flounced robe (Cat. 141). The most impressive depiction shows a god seated on his throne, probably a statue or an idol in a temple (Cat. 146). He is drinking – probably beer – through a tube, attended by a nude acolyte and facing an antelope. In other motifs the god is drinking with a companion, or depicted as the master or protector of animals, probably symbolising the people. The crowned gods are few, while the next step in the hierarchy – men dressed in the same flounced dress – are multiple. They are often depicted in scenes similar to those mentioned for the crowned gods,

and they are even faced by worshippers. More often, however, they are associated with various ritual performances by cult objects such as standards topped with various astral symbols – the crescent moon, sun and stars – and by altars. The altars are often adorned with protomes of ruminants as *pars pro toto* representations of holy animals, and on the altars are symbols, such as standards, palm fronds or an animal. The latter may be either a cult statue or a sacrificial animal. Nude men are the most numerous and are seen in various functions. They serve as attendants to gods and garbed men or are depicted as worshippers in front of them, often with a palm frond in their raised hands or grasping a standard. They are also depicted as heroes, fighting with lions, as masters of animals, as priests attending gods or performing rituals of different kinds and apparently as common people in everyday occupations (Cat. 149). As such they act as water carriers with a yoke, as donkey riders and in erotic scenes (Cat. 123). These functions, however, are also defined as either mythical or ritual by the symbols attached to them. The water carrier may

**¹⁴⁷ Quadrangular
Stamp-seal**
Saar necropolis
("Burial complex"),
Bahraini excavations 1984–85,
Grave A/E8.4
Early Dilmun, c. 2000–1800 BC
Chlorite or steatite
ᴴ1.3 ᴸ2.9 ᵂ2.1 cm
Manama, Bahrain National
Museum, acc. n° 2735-2-90
ᴮ Alsendi 1994, n° 50

¹⁴⁸ Stamp-seal
Al-Hajjar necropolis,
Bahraini excavations,
season and grave unspecified
Early Dilmun, c. 2000-1800 BC
Chlorite or steatite
ᴴ1.4 ᴰ2.8 cm
Manama, Bahrain National
Museum, acc. nᵒ 4060-4-90
ᴮ Alsendi 1994, nᵒ 47

¹⁴⁹ Stamp-seal
Al-Maqsha necropolis,
Bahraini excavations 1992-93,
Grave 1
Early Dilmun, c. 2000-1800 BC
Chlorite or steatite
ᴴ1.2 ᴰ2.6 cm
Manama, Bahrain National
Museum, main store
Unpublished

¹⁵⁰ Stamp-seal
Al-Maqsha necropolis,
Bahraini excavations 1991-92,
Grave 25
Early Dilmun, c. 2000-1800 BC
Chlorite or steatite
ᴴ0.9 ᴰ2.5 cm
Manama, Bahrain National
Museum, acc. nᵒ 4219-2-91-7
ᴮ Alsendi 1994, nᵒ 81

¹⁵¹ Stamp-seal
ˈAli necropolis,
Bahraini excavations,
season and tumulus unspecified
Early Dilmun, c. 2000-1800 BC
Chlorite or steatite
ᴴ1.2 ᴰ2.8 cm
Manama, Bahrain National
Museum, main store
Unpublished

be either the watergod himself or his acolyte and the erotic scene a fertility rite – the sacred marriage between fertility gods. A demon, in the shape of a bull with human head and torso but taurine lower part and legs, wears the same headdress as the gods. His Mesopotamian counterpart is the attendant of the sun god. In Dilmun he usually grasps a standard, only occasionally topped with a sun disc, usually with a crescent standard (Cat. 151). As local written sources are almost unknown, interpretations of the spiritual contents of the seal images are hampered. We only know the name of a single divine couple – Inzak, the tutelary god of Dilmun and his spouse Meskilak – but not even their attributes. Through the many images of ritual or cultic character we catch, however, a glimpse of formal religious practice – like a traveller who attends a religious ceremony in a foreign culture.

The Occupation of Dilmun by the Kassites of Mesopotamia

Pierre Lombard

152-159 Group of Kassite Style Vessels
Al-Maqsha necropolis,
Bahraini excavations 1988,
Grave 10
Madinat Hamad necropolis
(BSW1), Bahraini excavations
1986-87, Tumulus 2; (DS3),
1984-85, Tumulus 3.1; (BS2),
1984-85, Tumuli 47.D, 153.24
and 153.27
Middle Dilmun, c. 1350-1300 BC
Pottery
L from 6.5 to 25 cm
D MAX. from 6 to 15 cm
Manama, Bahrain National
Museum, acc n° 2395-2-90-7,
5388-2-91, 2621-2-90,
10101-2-88, 7095-2-91,
9518-2-91, 9515-2-91
and main store
Unpublished

These diverse specimens,
representative
of "caramel ware", which was
identified for the first time
at Qal'at al-Bahrain ("City III")
by the Danish mission, were
found in various necropoleis
of the Middle Dilmun period.
Many types are commonly
found in burial contexts,
but rarely in the settlement
levels, which makes them
difficult to date (Denton, 1994).
The abundance of this type
of pottery on Bahrain,
and also the fact that sandy
temper was used in their
manufacture suggests they were
produced locally, directly
inspired by Mesopotamian
models.

The economic and strategic decline of Bahrain
from 1800 BC was the result of a series
of events. These included the disappearance
of the Indus civilisation, but the major economic
retreat of Southern Mesopotamia
and the emergence of new trading centres,
competing with Dilmun, also played
an important role. Historians and archaeologists
can easily measure this decline, since the name
of Dilmun disappears for about two centuries
from Mesopotamian historical and economic
texts, and we also see the progressive
abandoning of a number of sites that were
representative of the apogee of the culture
of Dilmun. These include the temple
at Barbar and the settlements at Diraz and Saar.
The archaeological layers at Qal'at al-Bahrain
bear witness to a hiatus in the occupation
of this "type site".

When the island of Bahrain reappeared
on the Near East scene towards the middle
of the 2nd millennium BC, Qal'at al-Bahrain,
and probably the whole land of Dilmun,
was occupied by a population that originated
from Mesopotamia, the Kassites.
The Kassite dynasty, took advantage
of the instability at the beginning
of the 16th century BC to take the throne. This
followed the capture of the capital, Babylon
by the Hittites. The Kassites remain one of the
least known dynasties in Mesopotamian history,
despite retaining power for nearly 450 years. We
do know however, that successive sovereigns
consolidated their power in Babylonia
by securing the northern frontier separating
them from Assyria, and also by unifying
Southern Mesopotamia under their authority.
It was precisely this final conquest
of "the Sealand", the swampy region around
the mouths of the Euphrates by Kastiliashu III
in around 1490 BC that led the Kassite powers
to take an interest in Dilmun and its islands,
Bahrain and Failaka. We suppose that
from 1600 BC, "the Sealand" had subjugated
Dilmun, thus facilitating the task of the future
Kassite invaders.

In incorporating Dilmun into their kingdom,
the Kassite kings were motivated firstly by
economic issues – the rich environment
and strategic position of Bahrain (even if there
was competition and it had become a little

marginalised) had not escaped them.
The new network of trading routes that was
slowly establishing itself in the second half
of the 2nd millennium could be controlled
from the island of Bahrain. During this period,
a major part of the lapis lazuli from Badakhshan
and maybe Pakistan, the highly sought-after
precious stone that Kassite Babylonia supplied
to the Hittites and the Egyptian Pharaohs
of the New Kingdom had to transit via Bahrain.
The Kassites thus transformed Bahrain
into a Babylonian colony, installing a ruling
administration under the authority
of a "governor" (shakkanaku). Through
tablets of his official correspondence
found in Nippur, in Iraq, we even know
the name of one of them, Ili-Ippashra,
and the difficulties he encountered in
Dilmun in the 14th century BC.

By 1956, the Danish archaeologists had
identified a level at Qal'at al-Bahrain ("City III")
characterised by a specific type of pottery,
of a light brown colour with a sandy temper,
known as "caramel ware". Today,
this remains the best indicator of the Kassite
phase of Bahrain's history, Middle Dilmun.

The Kassite Palace
at Qal'at al-Bahrain

Today it seems clear that the Kassite
colonisers chose the city of Qal'at al-Bahrain
to establish their administration
and, undoubtedly, their governor's residence.
A major building programme began,
which consisted of the restoration, of
the centre of the site, and of the monumental
buildings of Early Dilmun. In this period they
had probably housed the seat of power and,
very probably, a place of worship,
which was also renovated. Following on
from the Danish mission's excavations,
the French archaeological mission's work
confirmed that this architectural complex
had been re-used and extended. They
also completed a part of the plan of the
complex – an access way revealed the threshold
stone of a monument made from conchiferous
limestone (approx. 3.60 m x 1.30 m); one of the
largest ancient monolithic stone slabs on the
island. A large part of the building remains
buried to the east, whereas the north and west
parts disappeared when the foundation trenches
of the neighbouring Islamo-Portuguese fortress
were dug in the 15th and 16th centuries AD.

In 1995, the discovery of a large number of cuneiform tablets confirmed that this new 'palace' was used for administrative purposes. The economic role of the complex is also evident. It housed, in particular, a series of *madbasa*, a sort of date press designed to accelerate the maturation of the fruit and recover its juice. So this typical local equipment, hardly found on the island before this, made its earliest appearance in the Kassite palace at Qal'at al-Bahrain. Several of the cuneiform tablets found at the site also seem to hint that there was a temple in the immediate vicinity. Evidence has been found in this monumental palace of a violent fire that destroyed the building, probably around the beginning of the 14th century BC. Largely in ruins, it was probably re-occupied by 'squatters', but was never rebuilt. It is quite possible that, from this time, the seat of the Kassite administration at Dilmun was transferred to the island of Failaka (Kuwait).

The "Kassite" Tombs on the Island

Several necropoleis in Bahrain have revealed tombs that date from the same period as the Middle Dilmun layers of occupation of Qal'at al-Bahrain ("City III" in the Danish chronology). It also seems that tumuli from Early Dilmun at Saar, or 'Ali, for example, were also re-used sporadically during this period.

Collective burial seems to have been the common practice for these tombs. Until recently, we believed that this practice, in theory a complete departure from the tradition of individual burials characteristic of the tumuli of the previous phase, had been introduced by the Kassites. Today, we know that, from the end of the Early Dilmun period, this rite was already established in some places, always associated with large rectangular graves, dug into the bedrock and covered by rough slabs. This is exactly the type of tomb that was wide-spread during the Kassite period, during which more complex forms developed. These collective tombs found at al-Hajjar, al-Maqsha or Madinat Hamad usually contained several dozen burials; the remains of as many as 36 individuals were counted in a tomb at Madinat Hamad. The funeral furniture apparently always consisted of numerous vases, the production of which was particularly influenced by Mesopotamian styles, mostly made in the "caramel ware" typical of the period. Cylinder seals and an occasional personal object are also present, but metal objects did not usually survive the frequent pillaging of these tombs.

160-161 Cylinder-seals
Al-Hajjar, Bahraini excavations
1992-93, Mound 7, Grave 8
(intrusive in the Early Dilmun
Settlement)
Middle Dilmun,
mid-second millennium BC
"Frit"
H 2.7 and 2.2 D 1.1 and 1 cm
Manama, Bahrain National
Museum, main store
B B. Denton 1999, fig. 26 and 25

These two seals, which appear
to have been made locally,
were inspired
by the Syro-Mesopotamian
Mitannian examples
of the Middle Bronze Age.
The iconography of the first
is well-known in the "Common
Mitannian Style" (Collon 1986,
num. 31, 36-45, for example):
two rows of men wearing
loin cloths and helmets
marching in a military style
past a standing person, evoking
a ritual dance or military
parade. The four line
inscription, clumsily written,
is a prayer to Marduk:

"May he be blessed,
he gives life,
Marduk the merciful."
Most of the inscriptions
on cylinder-seals
from the Kassite period
bear a similar invocation.
Although there is no inscription,
the second seal belongs
to the same group as the first,
usually associated
with the oldest Kassite ceramics
found on the island.
Two female figures, with both
hands raised are placed
on either side of a symbolic tree
with a circle over it.
Behind them there are
five standing gazelles
or antelopes, and a ornamental
pattern runs along the upper
edge of the seal. This type
of seal, influenced
by the Mitannian tradition,
is well represented
on Bahrain and Failaka,
and dates generally
from between 1450 and 1350 BC.

**162 Tall Kassite Style
Goblet**
Al-Hajjar necropolis,
Bahraini excavations 1974,
Site 1, Grave 25
Middle Dilmun, c. 1300 BC
Pottery
H 30.6 D MAX.8.5 cm
Manama, Bahrain National
Museum, acc. n° 2196-2-90
B Bahrain National Museum
1993, p. 34

This type of goblet, found both
in graves and settlements,
is of a shape that is particularly
typical of late Kassite
pottery, in Lower
Mesopotamia, but also
on Failaka (Kuwait) and Bahrain,
where it is found mostly at
Qal'at al-Bahrain and al-Hajjar
(cf Denton 1994, p. 126,
Type IA).

The Cuneiform Tablets of Qal'at al-Bahrain

Béatrice André-Salvini

The fifty or so tablets and fragments with inscriptions discovered in 1995 and 1996 by the French archaeological mission in the great Kassite building at Qal'at al-Bahrain, constitute part of one or possibly two local archives, which fall into distinct groups. These texts are a considerable addition to the meagre corpus that was already known. This consists of nine complete tablets and fragments, and a tag (unpublished) that came from the Danish mission's archaeological digs. These digs took place at the beginning of the 1960s, in another part of the complex, and the findings were recently published (Eidem, 1997). These documents have only been partially studied, but it would appear useful to give a presentation of them here, even if much remains unstudied, as this is indeed a significant find.

163 Bilingual Sumerian/Akkadian (Babylonian) Vocabulary
Qal'at al-Bahrain,
"Palace of Uperi" area,
French excavations 1995
(QA94.390)
Middle Dilmun, c. 1450 BC
Clay
^{H}5.75 ^{L}5 TH4.3cm
Manama, Bahrain National
Museum, main store
Unpublished

This fragment of a large tablet
with several columns
contains extracts from various
Babylonian lexical lists which
made up the classic works used
to teach scribes. For each term
in Sumerian, a language
that was dead but still known
to scholars when this copy
was written, there is a
corresponding term
in Akkadian, spoken
in Mesopotamia and written
in Dilmun, at least in court

circles, where missionaries
and officials from Babylonia
must have been quite
numerous. There are selected
pieces from the two major
encyclopaedic series here:
- the fourth tablet of the large
series in twenty-four volumes,
listing data on nature
and civilisation, called
HAR.RA=*hubullu*. The terms
here mainly deal with luxury
clothing
- the list dedicated to people
and their titles and professions.
The terms enumerate official
functions (prince,
administrator, etc.).
The reverse has been destroyed.

164 Letter
Qal'at al-Bahrain,
"Palace of Uperi" area,
French excavations 1995
(QA94.57)
Middle Dilmun, c. 1450 BC
Clay
^{H}4.2 ^{L}4.1 TH1.7 cm (original
dimensions: c. 12 x 8 cm)
Manama, Bahrain National
Museum, main store
Unpublished

The tablet is highly
fragmentary, and all that
remains is the beginning
of a few lines. We can however
recognise that this was a letter
addressed to an important
person, a king or governor.
A town, and a confiscation,
perhaps linked to some fields,
are mentioned:
"*[…] in the town of Ar[…],
until the field… [that] my lord
t[ook]… [they] confiscated…
my, [I have] 100 [?..], my lord
[…]*"

165 Administrative Document
Qal'at al-Bahrain,
"Palace of Uperi" area,
French excavations 1995
(QA94.421)
Middle Dilmun, c. 1450 BC
Clay
^{H}3.5 ^{L}5 TH2.1 cm
Manama, Bahrain National
Museum, main store
Unpublished

This document, found under the
pivot-stone of the threshold to
the great door was uncovered
on the site in 1993 and could
have been placed there
accidentally or for symbolic
reasons. It is a record of
workers, 40 labourers
and 36 servants [?].

166 Ovoid-Shaped Tag
Qal'at al-Bahrain,
"Palace of Uperi" area,
French excavations 1996
(QA96.98)
Middle Dilmun, c. 1450 BC
Clay
^{H}2.4 ^{L}5 TH2.4 cm
Manama, Bahrain National
Museum, main store
Unpublished

This object, pierced so that
a link could be passed through
it, was destined to be attached
to a basket containing flock.
The record was made on the
twelfth day of the twelfth and
last month (February-March) of
a year that was marked by
the particular sweetness
of its honey!

167 Administrative Document
Qal'at al-Bahrain,
"Palace of Uperi" area,
French excavations 1994
(QA94.56)
Middle Dilmun, c. 1450 BC
Clay
^{H}2.4 ^{L}3.3 TH1.6 cm
Manama, Bahrain National
Museum, main store
Unpublished

Message from the Palace
mentioning a delivery,
during the eighth month
of the year (the beginning
of November). The tablet
is burnt.

168 Administrative Receipt
Qal'at al-Bahrain,
"Palace of Uperi" area,
French excavations 1995
(QA94.49)
Middle Dilmun, c. 1450 BC
Clay
^{H}2.5 ^{L}4.3 TH1.5 cm
Manama, Bahrain National
Museum, main store
André-Salvini and Lombard,
1997, p. 167

Record of a delivery of
condiments, sesame and black
cumin (*nigella sativa*),
during the second month
of the year (beginning of May)
in Year 4 of the King of Babylon,
Agum (III?). Date:
"*month of aiaru, 19th day,
year 4 of Agum*".

169 Delivery Note
Qal'at al-Bahrain,
"Palace of Uperi" area,
French excavations 1996
(QA96.155)
Middle Dilmun, c. 1450 BC
Clay
^{H}2.2 ^{L}3.35 TH1.35 cm
Manama, Bahrain National
Museum, main store
Unpublished

Part of a harvest delivered.

These small, irregular-shaped tablets are written in a Medio-Babylonian cuneiform script which is very cursive and badly formed. Very few complete documents remain, but the state of the numerous fragments has enabled us to confirm that the economic documents, which make up the vast majority of the find, were dated in a traditional way according to the Babylonian calendar. The day, the month, and the year of the sovereign's reign are noted with accuracy. These elements lead us to believe that these tablets are invoices and accounts from an administrative office of the "palace", which is mentioned several times, and which was probably the seat of the governor of the province. Simple administrative operations consisting of "provisions" (Cat. 169) and "receipts" (Cat. 168) of merchandise were recorded on a daily basis.

One lot of texts mentions the name of the king under whose reign these transactions took place. The very small number of full date formulae has enabled us to narrow down the possible lifespan of this archive to a period of two years, i.e. the third and fourth years of the reign of this sovereign, which we can in all probability identify as the Kassite king Agum III (Cat. 168). These tablets also confirm that Dilmun was at that time a vassal of the kings of the dynasty that ruled over Southern Mesopotamia. The few proper names that are mentioned are mostly Babylonian. Historically, Agum III is only known via a Babylonian source long after his reign, which relates a military expedition he led against "the Sealand", in around 1465. Some documents may have a different dating formula, but they belong to a similar period. The tablets from the Danish digs, although un-dated, can be attributed to the same cultural phase.

The elements found from archives certainly do not constitute the entire collection of documents hidden in the great Kassite building at Qal'at al-Bahrain. We have observed several different styles of writing on the tablets that have been found, which would lead us to believe that there was a veritable scribal workshop and a local school there.

The Danish expedition discovered one, perhaps two school exercises. This supposition is reinforced further by the presence, among the texts discovered in 1995, of a bilingual Sumero-Akkadian vocabulary. This included a choice of extracts copied by a Dilmun scribe or apprentice scribe, who was careful to assemble the terms useful for his profession and the specific types of texts he had to write (Cat. 163).

One tablet, made of finer clay and with neater writing than the others could be a letter from outside, as far as we can tell from its fragmented state (Cat. 164).

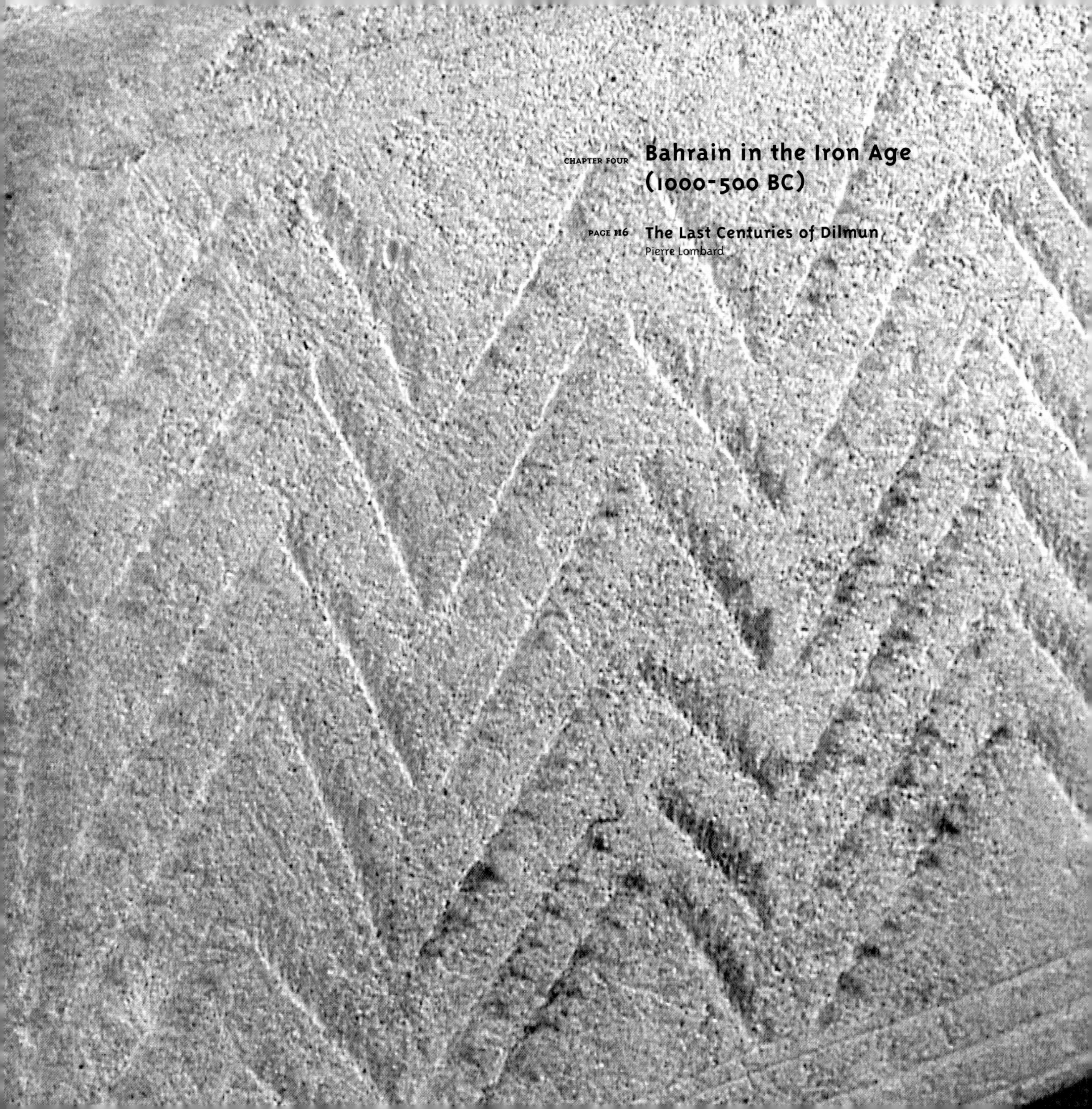

CHAPTER FOUR

Bahrain in the Iron Age (1000-500 BC)

The Last Centuries of Dilmun

Pierre Lombard

Even before the end of the Kassite dynasty, in the middle of the 12th century BC, Dilmun once again lost its historic importance. As early as 1225, the Assyrian king Tukulti-Ninurta I marched on Babylon, capturing the Kassite king Kashtiliash IV, whom he brought to Assur, with, in an act of supreme sacrilege, the statue of Marduk, which he had removed from the city's major temple, the prestigious E-sa-Gila. He added "King of Dilmun and Meluhha" to his titles to symbolise the significance of his military and political booty. But Dilmun was far from Assyria, and Bahrain was no longer of any real economic importance in his eyes… We can therefore only hypothesise about the fate of the island at that time. Assyrian political control was probably just a matter of form, and we can suppose that the country slowly rebuilt its own political and economic base, but history and archaeology provide no evidence from this period.

The Reappearance of Dilmun

500 years later, the name of Dilmun reappeared in a spectacular manner. In Khorsabad, in the heart of Assyria, the great Sargon II finished the construction of a monumental palace guarded by the famous winged bulls now exiled in the Louvre and in Chicago. Around 709 BC, in the great Neo-Assyrian tradition, the sovereign had the bas-reliefs of the walls, the paved parts and the thresholds inscribed with the annals of his reign, i.e. the, somewhat subjective, narrative of his battles and his great achievements. Here we find, no less than seven times, the episode of the "subjugation" of Uperi, "King of Dilmun, whose abode is situated like a fish, thirty double-hours away, in the midst of the sea where the sun rises", and who, in awe of the all-powerful might of Sargon II, apparently sent him gifts.
This series of references to Dilmun, whose language coupled with the vivid geographical indications found in Neo-Assyrian annals, enable us to associate them perfectly with Bahrain, are of great significance. Rather than an act of submission, Uperi's gesture should doubtless be interpreted as a skilled and prudent act of diplomacy, which fits well with the image of Dilmun as a small, prosperous

170 Compartmented Soft Stone Vessel
Al-Hajjar necropolis, Bahraini excavations 1970, Site 1, Grave 3
Late Dilmun, 10th /7th cent. BC
Steatite
H14 L9.6 W6.5 cm
Manama, Bahrain National Museum, acc. n° 188-2-88
B *Bahrain National Museum* 1989, n° 123

The compartmented Iron Age vessels are the direct descendants of specimens already imported from the region of Oman at the end of the 3rd millennium BC (cf Cat. 42). An example that is surprisingly similar to this one was found in a contemporaneous level at the Tell Abraq site in the United Arab Emirates (Potts 1990, p. 117-118: fig. 143, 144).

Qal'at al-Bahrain,
"Palace of Uperi" area.
Street and monumental gate.

Qal'at al-Bahrain,
"Palace of Uperi" area.
Room with pillars
uncovered in 1992-93.

autonomous kingdom which did not hesitate to approach, even seduce, the new Mesopotamian ruler in order to ensure its economic future.

But Bahrain was no longer the great international crossroads that it had been during the Bronze Age, and its position, faced with its dominating and imperialist neighbour, remained fragile during the 8th century BC. Esarhaddon, during his reign (681-668 BC) "ordered" from Qanaia, one of Uperi's successors "*the tribute that he owed as (his) subject*". A few years later, at around the middle of the 7th century BC, Assurbanipal had Bahrain listed officially as an Assyrian province, thus definitively sealing Bahrain's fate. In case any doubt remained, a text by the last Neo-Babylonian king, Nabonidus, confirms that in 544 BC, the country was under the authority of a *bêl pihati*, i.e. a resident administrator.

We imagine that the Achaemenids from Persian inherited Dilmun when they conquered Babylonia, but historical sources give no direct indication of this. However, as we will see later on, the Qal'at al-Bahrain archaeological digs have provided a large amount of information which documents this period, during which the archipelago was particularly prosperous.

The Search for Uperi

The episode of Uperi's unrewarded gesture has always been present in the minds of the archaeologists (first the Danish, then the French) working at Qal'at al-Bahrain. This brief repetitive text is, because of the date of its discovery, the first that brought up the name of Dilmun, forgotten for 2 400 years, in the last century. But they rapidly associated it with the new monumental complex built on the ruins of the Kassite palace, in the city centre, which was strategically situated between the Middle Dilmun levels from the mid-2nd millennium and those from the Hellenistic period. This new building ("City IV" in the Danish chronology) could have been contemporary with this historic event, and was perhaps even Uperi's residence at the end of the 7th century BC. Unfortunately, the long years of archaeological investigations have failed to provide a clear confirmation of this hypothesis.

Qal'at al-Bahrain,
"Palace of Uperi" area
(State at the end of 1996).

The levels of "City IV" illustrate several stages of occupation that cannot always be dated with accuracy. The oldest, which could indeed correspond to Uperi's era, shows impressive monumental architecture, both in terms of the quality of the building work, and its conservation, but it has provided hardly any archaeological material that can be accurately dated. A set of objects contained in a more recent layer of backfill could however come from this first period, and be associated with the place of worship that the French team place to the west of the edifice. It consists of a large number of ceramics, but mostly of curious fragmented male figurines, including some horsemen. Their unexpected number (almost a hundred) would lead us to think they are ex-votos. The presence, next to these, of a cylindrical fenestrated ceramic stand identical to a type of traditional Iron Age religious object from Palestine or the Levant, reinforces the hypothesis that there was a temple in the immediate vicinity.

Several tombs discovered at al-Hajjar and Madinat Isa date, however, from the first half of the 1st millennium BC. They often re-used more ancient tombs, and have proved particularly rich in material (painted ceramics, soft stone vases, bronze weapons, seals, etc.) These offerings bear witness to the close links with the Iron Age cultures of the neighbouring Oman peninsula. Certain pieces, practically identical to those found in settlements and tombs in the Oman region, indicate that perhaps a community of traders from Oman lived in Bahrain at that time.

The Achaemenid Phase

Under the later influence of the Achaemenid from Persia, the country probably lost its political independence, but remained economically prosperous. The archaeological levels from this period show evidence of this. The impressive residence of City IV at Qal'at al-Bahrain was again restored and extended, but we don't really know if it was still being used as a palace. Its ground plan is, however, characteristic of the luxurious residences found in numerous regions of the ancient Near East. In the same way as examples from Ur or Babylon, it is divided into public and private areas. It has a central courtyard, and a very elaborate sanitation system. The possible religious function of the west wing of the complex, also restored, is confirmed during this period. In several different places, fifty or so bowls were discovered hidden in the floors. Each of these bowls contained the skeleton of a sacrificed snake, placed there according to a ritual found nowhere else in the Near East. The public use of this area is

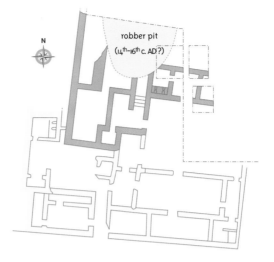

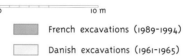

Qal'at al-Bahrain.
Plan of the Achaemenid
period residence (state in 1994).

■ French excavations (1989-1994)

□ Danish excavations (1961-1965)

also shown by the fact that eight latrines (which could also have been ablution areas) were installed there.

At the end of this Late Dilmun period, we can observe that, at Qal'at al-Bahrain, the dead and the living were neighbours. Children buried in earthenware jars, as well as many adults buried in pit-graves or in earthenware "bathtub-sarcophagi" have been discovered under the floors of dwellings. This practice is totally alien to Bahraini burial traditions, where, since the Bronze Age, cemeteries had been placed away from towns and villages. This was, however, common practice in Mesopotamia around the middle of the 1st millennium. This gives, therefore, another indication that there was probably a Babylonian colony living in Bahrain.

The end of the Dilmun civilisation saw the coexistence of diverse populations from neighbouring regions. These populations were apparently assimilated with no particular problems, and Bahrain rediscovered some of the cultural plurality that it enjoyed during its apogee in the Bronze Age. Brought under the yoke of the successive great Empires that surrounded Bahrain, the archipelago remained an exceptional meeting place for men, and for merchandise. This is what impressed Alexander the Great's admirals when they discovered Bahrain a century later.

Votive deposit
of "snake bowls".
Qal'at al-Bahrain, 1993.

171-173 Spouted Vessels
Al-Maqsha necropolis,
Bahraini excavations 1978,
Grave 4
Madinat Isa necropolis,
Bahraini excavations 1968 (?),
Grave unspecified
Late Dilmun, 10th /7th cent. BC
Pottery
H9. 8.5 and 6.4 D MAX11.8. 11.4
and 15 cm
Manama, Bahrain National
Museum, acc. n° 3769-2-91-7,

168-2-88 and 169-2-88
B *Bahrain National Museum*
1989, n° 93, and unpublished

These elegant vessels with long
gutter-spouts, made
of high quality clay with
a carefully polished surface
are reminiscent of the Iranian
Iron Age ceramic traditions.
However, in contrast with
the previous exhibit, these
do not seem to have originated

from the Oman Peninsula
where this shape is unknown.
This type does not appear
in the Late Dilmun settlement
levels at Qal'at al-Bahrain
either, even though these
are rich in different types
of ceramics. These could have
been made on the Iranian
plateau, perhaps specifically
for burial use.

120

¹⁷⁴ Spouted Vessel
Al-Hajjar necropolis,
Bahraini excavations 1971,
Site I, Grave 21/22
Late Dilmun, 10ᵗʰ /7ᵗʰ cent. BC
Pottery
H8.4 D MAX10.9 cm
Manama, Bahrain National
Museum, main store
Unpublished. Comp.: *Bahrain
National Museum* 1989, nº95

Sometimes described
as "teapots" by archaeologists
as they often have a filter,
these small vessels with
a bridged spout and their
characteristic painted
decoration find their equivalent
in the graves and settlements of
Oman in the Iron Age. They
developed in the first half of the
1ˢᵗ millennium BC along the
foothills of the Hajjar range.
This is the case at Rumeilah,
for example, in the al-Ain
oasis, Emirate of Abu Dhabi
(Boucharlat & Lombard 1985, pl.
50: 1-3). This specimen was very
probably imported from that
region. More generally, this
form is well known throughout
the Iranian Iron Age II period
(Magee 1997, p. 94-96).

**¹⁷⁵ Truncated Cone
Shaped Soft Stone Vessel**
Al-Hajjar necropolis,
Bahraini excavations 1970,
Site I, Grave 7
Late Dilmun, 10ᵗʰ /7ᵗʰ cent. BC
Steatite
H7.5 D MAX10.9 cm (vessel)
H5.5 D3.8 cm (lid)
Manama, Bahrain National
Museum, acc. nº191-2-88a-b
B *Bahrain National Museum*
1989, nº 119/120; 1993, p. 43

The Bahrain Iron Age graves
have revealed numerous stone
vessels carved out of a material
that is softer and of a lighter
colour than the chlorite used
in the Bronze Age (steatite
and derivatives). They are
generally associated
with Omani type painted
ceramics and probably
originate from the same area.
The exceptional quality
of the specimens found
in Bahrain is generally
apparent. This streamlined
vessel with a lid has a very pure
shape and a carefully made
incised geometrical decoration.
It is one of the most beautiful
pieces of this type discovered
in the Gulf region.

176-179 Various Soft Stone Vessels
Al-Maqsha necropolis,
Bahraini excavations 1991-92,
Grave 66/B
Al-Hajjar necropolis,
Bahraini excavations 1970,
Site 1, Grave 7
Late Dilmun, 10th /7th cent. BC
Steatite
H5.3, 10.4, 9.3 and 9 D MAX9.7,
7.2, 6.9 and 5.9 cm
Manama, Bahrain National
Museum, main store and
5168-2-91-7, 212-2-88, 185-2-88
Unpublished and *Bahrain
National Museum* 1989, n° 111

180 Soft Stone Vessel
Al-Maqsha necropolis,
Bahraini excavations 1988,
Grave 12
Late Dilmun, c. 800-700 BC
Steatite
H7.5 D MAX8.7 cm
Manama, Bahrain National
Museum, acc. n°197-2-88
Unpublished

181 Cult Stand

Qal'at al-Bahrain,
"Palace of Uperi" area,
French excavations 1991
(QA91.646).
Late Dilmun, 10th /7th cent. BC
Pottery
H31 D MAX16.6 cm
Manama, Bahrain National
Museum, main store
Unpublished

182 Dagger

Shakhura necropolis,
Bahraini excavations 1992-1993,
Mound 3, Grave 10
Late Dilmun, 10th/7th cent. BC
Bronze
L 47.6 W MAX blade 2.4;
W handle 5.4 cm
Manama, Bahrain National
Museum, main store
Unpublished

Daggers with hollowed-out
handles inlaid with wood or
bone are also a speciality of
the blacksmiths of the Oman
Peninsula, a region where
bronze and copper-based alloys
were used until a very late
period. These traditional
weapons, inspired in turn
by models from the Iranian
Iron Age II period, were
probably produced over a
period of several centuries
(Lombard 1984). This isolated
example, found in an unusual
type of tomb at Shakhura
is, unfortunately, of no help
to us in establishing a precise
chronology.

183-187 Pyramidal Stamp-seals

Al-Maqsha necropolis,
Bahraini excavations 1988,
Grave 3; 1992-93,
Graves 1/B, 66A/4, 66B
Late Dilmun, 10th /7th cent. BC
Semi-fine stones
H0.8 to 1.3 L1.9 to 2.7
TH1.8 to 2.55 cm
Manama, Bahrain National
Museum, acc. nº 2932-2-90,
2944-7-90 and main store
Unpublished

The presence of these pyramidal
stamp-seals Bahrain, of a type
hitherto limited to the sites at
the al-Ain oasis in the Emirate of
Abu Dhabi (Rumeilah, Qarn Bint
Sau'd, cf Lombard 1998, fig. 1 p.
156), confirms the close trading
links between these two
regions in the first half of the
1st millennium BC.

188-200 Votive (?) Figurines
Qal'at al-Bahrain,
"Palace of Uperi" area,
French excavations 1989-93
(QA89.482, 650, 1275; 91.551;
92.44, 45, 380, 402, 403;
93.8, 13, 20, 39)
Late Dilmun, 10th /7th cent. BC
Terracotta
H from 4.5 to 10
E from 1.5 to 3.9 cm
Manama, Bahrain National
Museum, acc. nº 1923-2-89,
1930-2-89, 91-1-3, 92-1-2,
92-1-4, 92-1-5, 92-1-6, 97-1-1
and main store
B Lombard 1994, p. 38: fig. 14

**201 Animal Figurine
with Human Head**
Qal'at al-Bahrain,
"Palace of Uperi" area,
French excavations 1989
(QA89.1597)
Late Dilmun, 10th /7th cent. BC
Terracotta
H8.1 TH3 cm
Manama, Bahrain National
Museum, main store
B *Bahrain National Museum*
1993, p. 37; Lombard 1994,
p. 38: fig. 14

203, 204 Burial Offering
Qal'at al-Bahrain,
"Palace of Uperi" area,
French excavations 1990
(QA90.5, 6)
Late Dilmun, 6th/5th cent. BC
Clay
[H]6.5 and 21.8 [D MAX]17 and 21.7 cm
Manama, Bahrain National
Museum, acc. n° 90-2-1
and 1942-2-89
Unpublished

As in Babylon, the burial
offerings associated
with earthenware sarcophagi
were either placed inside or
at the foot of the sarcophagus.
This is the case for this group
of vases typical of Bahraini
manufacture from the end
of the Late Dilmun period, which
were found in this exact
position, against the outside
wall of a small bathtub-
sarcophagus. Any offerings
placed with the body had
completely disappeared.

**205 Burial Jar with Burial
Contents**
Madinat Hamad necropolis
(NBH4), Bahraini excavations
1989-90, Mound 10
Late Dilmun, 6th/5th cent. BC
Clay, bones
[H]37.5 [D MAX]67 cm
Manama, Bahrain National
Museum, main store
Unpublished

This burial of a child,
remarkably preserved in its
jar with an oval opening,
comes from one of the Bahrain
necropoleis that also revealed
a series of "bathtub"
sarcophagi well known
in Babylonia from the end
of the Neo-Assyrian period
until Achaemenid period
(Baker 1995, p. 213-215).
Identical sarcophagi have been
found at Qal'at al-Bahrain
where their stratigraphic
position clearly attributes
them to the Achaemenid phase
of the island's history,
at the end of the Late Dilmun
period (Højlund & Andersen
1997, p. 145-151; Lombard 1994,
fig. 16 and p. 40).
With the exception of one which
was richly stocked, this type
of grave was frequently subject
to severe pillaging.

**202 Figurine of Horse
and Rider**
Al-Maqsha necropolis,
Bahraini excavations 1978-79,
Grave 3/4
Late Dilmun, 10th/7th cent. BC
Terracotta
[H]15.5 [L]12 cm
Manama, Bahrain National
Museum, acc. n° 856-2-82
[B] *Bahrain National Museum*, p. 35

Plainly belonging
to the same tradition as
the fragmentary examples
from Qal'at al-Bahrain,
this complete piece which
shows a horse rider curiously
armed with an axe (tool,
weapon, or ceremonial?)
is the only figurine of this type
found in a burial complex.

²⁰⁶⁻²⁰⁸ Cone-shaped Stamps and Sealing Bulla
Al-Maqsha necropolis,
Bahraini excavations 1992-93,
Grave 4/A
Qal'at al-Bahrain, "Palace of
Uperi" area, French excavations
1988 (QA88.12)
Late Dilmun, 6ᵗʰ /5ᵗʰ cent. BC
Semi-fine stones, clay
^{H}2 and 2.5; $^{W\,MAX}$1.7 cm (stamps)
^{H}4.8 $^{W\,MAX}$ 2.5 cm (bulla)
Manama, Bahrain National
Museum, acc. n° 2936-11-90,
main store and 88-1-3
Unpublished

These small stamps with
their polygonal section
are the most common form
of seal found in the area of
Babylonian influence
in the Near East, around
the 1ˢᵗ millennium BC –
many have been found
at Bahrain, often in the bathtub
sarcophagi. It is much rarer
to find remains of their
impressions. This sealing bulla
from the settlement site
at Qal'at al-Bahrain has
four impressions from two
different seals (representing the
two sides of a commercial
transaction?) as well as the
mark of twisted cord on the
reverse.

²⁰⁹⁻²¹⁰ "Snake Bowls"
Qal'at al-Bahrain,
"Palace of Uperi" area,
French excavations 1992
(QA92.494 and 502)
Late Dilmun, 6ᵗʰ⁻5ᵗʰ cent. BC
Pottery, bones
^{H}7.5 and 7.7
$^{D\,MAX}$13.5 and 14.5 cm
Manama, Bahrain National
Museum, main store
^{B} Lombard 1994, p. 40: fig. 17

Snake sacrifices were rare,
if not unknown in the ancient
Near East. The snake was a very
popular creature, however,
on the Arabian Peninsula,

where it was generally
associated with the idea
of fertility. The deposits
at Qal'at al-Bahrain do not
resemble any found
elsewhere so far.
They could be the result
of prophylactic practices,
destined to bring divine
protection, fertility and long
life to the inhabitants.
These votive deposits could
also have been a ritual act,
within the walls of a public
and holy place. Snake cults
are known to have existed
in the Iron Age in the
neighbouring Omani culture.

²¹¹ Necklace
Saar necropolis,
Bahraini excavations 1988,
Tumulus 154
Late Dilmun, 6ᵗʰ⁻5ᵗʰ cent. BC
Fine stones (carnelian,
banded agate), glass paste,
gold
^{L}34 cm
Manama, Bahrain National
Museum, acc. n° 1858-2-89
Unpublished

As well as burials
in earthenware jars
and sarcophagi, some
contemporaneous pit-graves
have also been discovered
on the island (at al-Maqsha,
Saar and Qal'at al-Bahrain
in particular). They generally
contained richer and more
varied material, in many cases
including jewellery similar to
that found in the Achaemenid
graves – this is the case with
this necklace made of beads
of different types of ornamental
stones and several gold
elements.

²¹² Silversmith's Hoard

Qal'at al-Bahrain,
"Palace of Uperi" area,
Danish excavations 1961–62
Late Dilmun, 6ᵗʰ–5ᵗʰ cent. BC
Pottery, silver scraps
^{H}21.4 $^{D\,MAX}$21.1 cm (vase)
^{H}2.85 $^{D\,MAX}$2. 2 cm (bezel-ring)
Manama, Bahrain National
Museum, acc. n° 2075, 8575
^{B} Bibby 1964, p. 86:1 and 88:2;
Krauss, Lombard & Potts 1983;
Højlund & Andersen 1997,
p. 175-181; Krauss 1997

This vase and its unusual
contents, deliberately hidden
under the last occupation floor
of the luxurious Late Dilmun
residence at Qal'at al-Bahrain,
has been considered as
evidence of a troubled period
in the history of the island.
Along with other similar
discoveries in various places
in the ancient Near East,
it constitutes an example of the
various proto-coinages in use
in this region of the world
before the appearance
of the first currencies.
The hypothesis was thus formed
that these types of fragments
of silver (cast pieces, broken
or intentionally separated parts
of rings, bracelets and other
objects) were in circulation
and were commonly exchanged
during commercial
transactions. This "treasure"
also contained a ring with
a silver mount, which had
a very clumsily reproduced
hieroglyphic inscription.
This object is generally
considered to be a local copy
of an Egyptian model from
the Late period, dating from
c. 650 BC. From the particular
type of vase that contained this
fragment of silver, the copy
must be considered much
more recent than the original.

²¹³⁻²²² Burial Offering

Qal'at al-Bahrain,
"Palace of Uperi" area,
French excavations 1991,
Intrusive grave
Late Dilmun, 6ᵗʰ–5ᵗʰ cent. BC
Vase: Pottery ᴴ from 18.4 to 6.7
ᴰ ᴹᴬˣ from 18.2 to 7 cm
Incense burner: limestone
ᴴ9.7 ᴸ9.7 ᵂ6.7 cm
Small vase: chlorite ᴴ1.7
ᴰ ᴹᴬˣ5.5 cm
Necklace: frit, fines stones,
pearls ᴸ45.5 cm
Stamp-seal: glass paste, bronze
ᴴ4.4 ᴰ ᴹᴬˣ2.1 cm
Manama, Bahrain National
Museum, acc. n° 89-1-1, 89-1-2,
2074-2-90, 2075-2-90,
2076-2-90, 2078-2-90,
2079-2-90, 2081-2-90
and main store
Unpublished

This set of offerings formed
the main burial offering
deposited in an intrusive pit-
grave at the settlement site at
Qal'at al-Bahrain, and is rather
enigmatic in the sense that it
contained three bodies (an old
man, a very young woman,
and a man of approximately
35 years of age) apparently
buried at the same time.
The three glazed vases as well
as the soft stone dish which
contained the necklace were
all together in a bitumen-
coated basket placed at one
end of the pit. A globular vase,
the jar with a neck (over which
a small bowl had been placed)
as well as the limestone incense
burner had been placed
touching the bodies. The stamp
in vitreous paste (whose
pendant ring bronze mounting
is perfectly preserved)
was apparently hung around
the neck of the younger man.
The iconography of this seal,
of typically Achaemenid
tradition (a crowned figure
with a lot of hair mastering
two rampant lions) as well
as the typology of the ceramics
enable us to place this grave
at the very end of the Late
Dilmun Period.

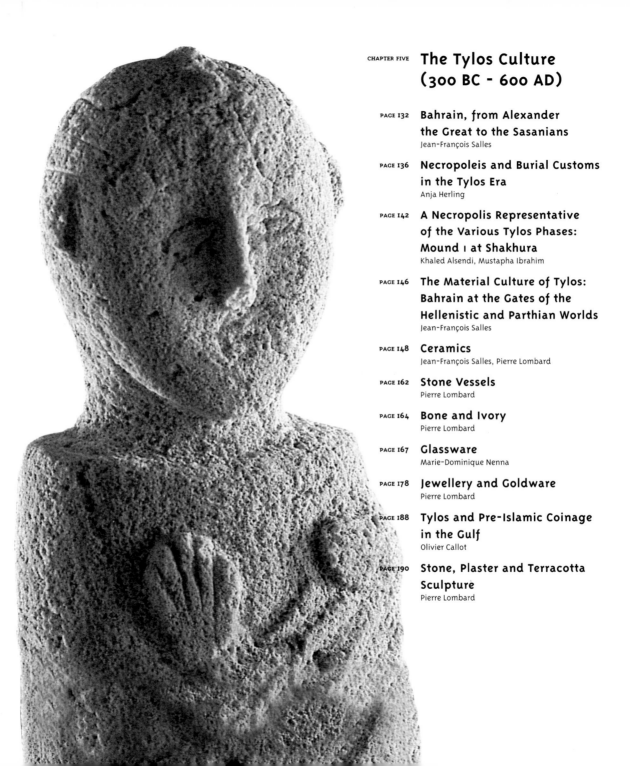

Bahrain, from Alexander the Great to the Sasanians

Jean-François Salles

²²³ Funeral Statuette
Saar necropolis,
Bahraini excavations 1995-96,
Mound 7, Square E3
Middle Tylos, 2ⁿᵈ/3ʳᵈ cent. AD
Limestone
ᴴ 27,3 ᴵ 10,4 ᴱ 7 cm
Manama, Bahrain National
Museum, acc. n° 378
Unpublished

Smaller in size
than the figurative stelae (cf
p. 212-215), but with a similar
iconography, this type
of statuette made
out of fine grained limestone
from Jidda island was
either found outside graves,
or, more rarely, inside.

It was in the wake of Alexander the Great
that the archipelago of Bahrain entered
into Greek literature and the Hellenistic annals
of history. It was said that , on his return from his
Indian expedition, when he was overtaken by a
maritime expedition along the Iranian coast led
by his friend Nearchus, according to Arrian,
Alexander was planning to conquer Arabia - the
truth of this hypothesis lies buried with the hero
himself. But, in any case, Alexander had taken
care to have the Arab side of the Gulf explored
(the "Erythraean Sea") around 325-324 BC,
confident that via trade between India and
the Eastern Mediterranean, the region could
become "as rich as Phoenicia". Archias, Hieron
and Androsthenes were successively responsible
for this task. It is certain that one
of the three expeditions explored the Bahrain
archipelago and probably stayed there for
a while, at least that is what Androsthenes' report
leads us to believe (the text is lost, but was
quoted by several Hellenistic authors).
The island then took the Greek name of Tylos,
probably a transcription of its Semitic name
TLMN (Tilmun).
The island kept its Greek name until
the 2nd century AD, when Ptolemy mentioned
the island in his *Geography* - but the
geographer's sources were almost certainly
derived from Androsthenes, very slightly revised
in the 1st century BC by the author-king Juba
of Mauritania. An inscription of Palmyra dated
from 131 AD is a more reliable source, honouring

"Iaraios, satrap of the Thilouanoi under Meredat,
king of Spasinou Charax", all the commentators
recognised the Thilouanoi as being
the inhabitants of Bahrain. Other later Greek
or Latin evidence are simply glosses of the more
ancient texts, and the name Tylos probably
disappeared from memories shortly after
the 2nd century.

There are few Eastern sources of information
on Bahrain before Islam. We can cite
the controversial expedition by Ardashir I
in 240 to "al-Bahrayn" in the widest sense,
probably including the archipelago,
as well as that of Shapur II in the same region
in 325-326 (a recent reading proposes
the acceptance of the name Samahig
in the narrative of this campaign by the Arab
historian Tabari: Samahig = Masmahig
= Muharraq; the name is also known
in the Babylonian Talmud, no precise date):
the two references simply highlight the logical
integration of the archipelago in the Sasanian
Empire - although no text claims that Bahrain
belonged to the Kings of Kings. A few Syriac
texts make reference to "the isles" of al-Bahrayn
and Jamama (= Eastern Arabia). The names
of the dioceses known from the 5th century
onwards are more precise, found in the synodal
texts of the Oriental Syriac church.
In 410, Batai, bishop of Masmahig, in the "diocese
of the islands" was excommunicated;
in 576 Serge, bishop of Masmahig, was present

at a Nestorian synod; in the middle
of the 7th century, a short time after Islam
was introduced to the islands (between 634
and 640), the bishop of Masmahig, Abraham,
was scolded by the patriarch Iso'yabh III.
Another bishopric may have existed
on the largest island, if the Syriac toponym *TLN*
is taken to refer to the ancient Thilouan/a.
Arab authors, from the 6th century onwards,
designated Bahrain by the name Awal,
but certainly also knew the name Samahig.

Classical sources provide two types
of information on Bahrain, both derived from
reports dating from the time of Alexander the
Great, copied and "corrected" until Ptolemy's
time with no new information – with the notable
exception of a description of Parthia
by the geographer Isidor of Charax, written
at the end of the 1st century BC, of which all
that remains is a very beautiful description
of pearl fishing near a Gulf island whose name
is not mentioned. Strabo and Pliny also mention
the pearls of Tylos.
One type of information describes
the archipelago's vegetation. As early as
the beginning of the 3rd century, the botanist
Theophrastes gathered data collected
by Androsthenes, and Pliny took them up
in his book XII. Date palms, vines, fruit trees
and fig trees are mentioned, all of which
are commonly found on the island today
(apart from vines). Cotton trees are also

mentioned, and other indications show
that the climate of Bahrain was adapted
to the cultivation of cotton for a time.
But the most gripping description is that
of the mangrove, which has almost completely
disappeared today, which the Greek's attentive
examination has enabled us to reconstruct
in precise detail. The writers locate the island
in the Gulf, giving varying amounts of detail
– Strabo and Pliny indicate that there were
two islands.

Strabo provides another piece of information
which has proved problematic: "Tyros [Tylos]
and Arados, where there are sanctuaries
that resemble those of the Phoenicians.
The inhabitants of these two islands confirm
that the islands and the cities of the same
name in Phoenicia are their own colonies"
(*Géo.*, 16, 3, 4; trans. Y. Calvet); the tradition
of a Phoenician origin in the Gulf in
the 3rd millennium BC is also found in many
other classical sources. There is fierce debate
over this reference, which is more significant for
 the history of the Phoenicians than that of the
Gulf itself.

The history of Tylos from the end
of the 4th century BC remains unclear.
One central question is the subject of debate
– did the Greeks/Seleucids, rulers of Mesopotamia
and Hellenistic Iran "occupy" the archipelago
as they were installed on the island of

Failaka/Ikaros at Kuwait? Did they use Bahrain as a port of call or port of distress for the military fleet they maintained in the Gulf? Some data would seem to confirm this. Some inhabitants of the island read Greek, as three documents have been found in the language - a graffito on a jar (proper name ending in -*raios*), an alphabet in relief on a ceramic piece dating from the 2nd century BC, and a grave marker. Totally representative of the archipelago's trading activity and its composite population, the inscription from the end of the 2nd century BC honours a ship's captain called Abdishtar, Phoenician, or Babylonian, son of Abdaios, a Phoenician name. Bahrain probably also had a mint which produced silver Alexander-type tetradrachmas, the typical coinage of the Eastern world, with a Greek inscription. These were perhaps made for Greek mercenaries in Bahrain, or Bahrainis in the Seleucid armies (we know of Arab camel drivers at the battle of Magnesia). Even if these arguments are not conclusive - no more than a few fragments of Attic ceramics with black varnish found in the excavations, they suggest that the archipelago participated in one way or another in the Seleuco-Greek world. At the end of the 3rd century BC, battles were occurring in Babylonia over the ascension to the throne of the king Antiochus III. One of the supporters of the young king was Puthyiades, strategus from the province of the Erythrean Sea (the mouth of the Euphrates, see Mesene *below*) and of "its dependencies" (in Greek, *topoi*, which is vague: the administrative expression designates the places far from the centre of the province, often maritime). These included Failaka/Kuwait, but also probably alliances with Arab "chiefdoms" in Bahrain and in Eastern Arabia (Gerrha). On his return from an expedition in India around 206-205, the same Antiochus III went to Gerrha to "subdue" its people, then stopped briefly at Tylos. A text by Polybus, a source independent of Alexander's acolytes, leads us to suppose that Tylos was sufficiently well-known to readers for it to be unnecessary to situate or describe the island.

The Seleucid empire collapsed towards the middle of the 2nd century BC. The kingdom that established itself in its place was centred on the mouth of the Euphrates and known as Mesene by Greek and Latin writers, or *Maishan* in Aramaic (Syriac sources). Its first sovereign, Hyspaosines, towards 140 BC, was qualified by a Greek author as "king of the Erythrean Sea and its dependencies [*topoi*]". Mesene therefore quickly extended its domination over the Gulf and Bahrain, as the existence of a governor of Spasinou Charax (capital of Mesene at Thilouan/a [*supra*] confirms. The archaeological documents (ceramics, coinage, etc.) which show the closeness of the links between Bahrain and Mesene are numerous, as well as the texts which demonstrate the importance of Mesene's relations with India and Bahrain as a port of call. The island is probably mentioned in the Acts of St. Thomas which describe his apostol mission in India. If Ardashir I's intervention around 240 can be established, the consequence, according to Tabari was the elimination of a *marzban* - Parthian governor of Bahrain - Sanatruk, last "king" of the archipelago.

We have seen that there are no Sasanian sources on the history of the island. Apart from the references to military expeditions in this region, we have to accept that, if the archipelago was really the seat of one or two dioceses dependent on the city Rev Ardashir/ Bushir in Persia, it would be surprising if the island was politically independent from the Sasanian power.

We know of no king of Bahrain from Alexander's time to that of the integration of the island into the Arab-Muslim world. It would certainly be an over-simplification to consider the island as just a "colony" of the Seleucids then the Mesenians and the Parthians, then the Sasanians. The most likely hypothesis is that of an "autonomous" domain closely associated with the successive dynasties who exerted their authority over the merchants and sailors who constantly sailed across the Gulf between the mouth of the Euphrates and India.

Necropoleis and Burial Customs in the Tylos Era

Anja Herling

The graves provide essential evidence for the Tylos period in Bahrain. Rather than textual data, which reflects an outside vision, this particular record provides concrete information on the material and cultural life of the island's inhabitants. Due to the scarcity of remains of settlements from this period, the burial evidence is practically our only source of information.

The most common burial practice in Tylos was individual burial. Cemeteries were placed away from settlements and were above ground. They were built on rocky, uncultivable land. Several of these necropoleis have been excavated by local and foreign teams, under the judicious rescue programme set up by the Bahraini authorities. This has enabled us to determine not just the general principles but also many precise details concerning burial customs.

The Necropoleis

The Tylos cemeteries remained in use for several centuries, and generally included a considerable number of graves, either juxtaposed or superimposed. With time and the increasing number of burials, each of the graves became covered with sand or earth, so the cemeteries became vast groups of extended and irregular mounds of medium height.

Often, at the heart of the necropolis, there was one elaborate grave, over which a particularly imposing mass of earth had accumulated. This made it visible from a distance, and probably indicated that the area had been taken into the possession of a particular group. Among these 'necropolis founders', we have found individuals of both sexes, and their great age is often surprising. The later burials then formed concentric circles around this centre, with much lower sandy mounds. The next tombs were then grouped in different sectors of the cemetery and were superimposed on other, more ancient graves.

The number of necropoleis is impressive, and suggests a large population that may not have been only those people living in Qal'at al-Bahrain. Their progressive extension into the fertile regions (or on the outskirts of them) in the north and west of Bahrain, as well as their concentration close to modern localities such as Saar and Shakhura (whose construction on artificial *tells* show that they date from early antiquity) confirm their close relation to settlements.

At times, several necropoleis close to one another were in use at the same time. The length of use and juxtaposition confirm that each represented an element of a larger community. The number of burials at a given time exceeds the number of people in a family group and their descendants. Isolated families were also found in several necropoleis. This means that only systematic comparison of as many cemeteries as

Saar necropolis,
Typical burial "mound"
from the Tylos period.

possible would enable us to determine the
criteria that guided the choice of burial place.
We hope that analyses being conducted
concerning family ties will provide some
answers.

Grave Construction

The most usual shape is a stone cist cut to size.
Smaller cists made of blocks of stone and mortar
– lime, sand, ash and water, mixed at the time
of construction – are also common.
At the beginning of the Tylos period the inner
walls were frequently lined with limestone slabs
and the base and tops of the walls were plastered
with mortar. Towards the middle of the period,
however only the walls were coated, and the
interior limestone facing slabs no longer used.
The burial chamber was generally covered with
two or three irregular stone slabs, placed flat over
the opening and sealed with mortar.
Occasionally, wooden boards adjusted to fit the
walls were used as covers.

These general principles vary from one cemetery
to another, however, reflecting the tastes of the
period or the builders' skills. With the interior
coating, the depth of the burial chambers went
from 0.50 m to around 1.40 m. Flatter, bath-
shaped tombs then came back into fashion.
In Early Tylos, graves were commonly orientated
east-west, following the path of the sun, as we
can deduce from slight variations (probably due
to the changing seasons). From Middle Tylos

Saar necropolis.
The same "mound"
after excavation
(German archaeological
mission, 1993).

Shakhura necropolis
North-south section of Mound I
(Directorate of Archaeology
and Heritage, 1996).

Saar necropolis. Grave cover-slab
(German archaeological mission, 1993).

onwards, it was purely practical considerations that determined the orientation of the burial chambers, and the orientation varied considerably.

Marks in the floor and wall plaster show that usually, only a few hours separated the completion of the grave and the burial of its occupant. This may also indicate a short amount of time between the death and the burial of the deceased. The building work was not always well done, as we can see from the problems with the covering of certain graves and the fact that old building materials were often used. The flat stone covering and facing slabs, in particular, were apparently rare and precious, which would explain the progressive abandonment of the lining of the interior of the graves. Surprisingly, however, there seems to have been a constant effort employed to improve the quality of the mortar and reinforce the airtight qualities of the graves. Small channels were also dug in the floor, at the feet of the deceased, for liquids to run off (libations? sacrifices?).

A few particularly imposing burial chambers, whose construction in blocks of carved stone was certainly lengthy and costly, imply that social status and personal wealth also influenced the type of grave. Costly funeral furniture - weapons, pieces of armour, rings with an official seal, etc. - indicate the privileged status of the deceased. However, burial of bodies in already 'occupied' graves - sometimes from previous periods (Tylos phases or others) - obviously indicates a lower status, illustrated also by the shallower trenches with walls simply reinforced with a layer of mortar. On burial, babies and young children, like foetuses, were often placed in earthenware vessels, indicating a similar lack of status. The fact that burial of these age groups was rare implies also that other methods were used, and that little importance was placed on this category of deceased.

Treatment and Position of the Remains

Before burial, the body was dressed and adorned, as we can see from the cloths, needles, pin heads, belt buckles, pieces of armour and jewellery found in the graves. Arm rings, ankle rings and earrings, finger and toe rings in silver and bronze as well as pearl necklaces and bracelets of all shapes in all types of materials were popular. Headbands and other gold ornaments were particularly refined. Children were often

Saar necropolis.
Skeleton *in situ*
with burial offering
(German archaeological
mission, 1993).

When burials reused older graves, the remains of the previous burial were piled up or placed to one side, occasionally removed and deposited elsewhere. In some cases, they were hardly decomposed, and in others they dated from centuries before. The structure of the graves shows that their re-use was not always planned. Sometimes there are family associations (mother/child, husband/wife), but just as often they were chosen at random. We cannot say here whether wealth or status had a specific role to play.

Funeral Furniture

Food deposits were apparently an obligatory part of the burial rite, as we can see from pots containing organic remains. Was this the remains of a funeral banquet, provisions for the voyage into the next world, or offerings to a divinity? The fact that this was a regular part of the burial rites implies an obvious link with a certain notion of life after death. The vessels themselves may have had a precise function, but the form simply reflects the fashions of the time. Arabian and Eastern style vessels were replaced little by little by glazed ceramics. Basins and all types of bowls in common clay as well as pitchers, remained popular. Offerings of eggs and small animals, especially small game birds, can also be placed in the funeral food category. Small coins, and single beads placed in the deceased's mouth give an additional indication of local beliefs - obols to facilitate access

adorned with apotropaic amulets. The dead were buried lying on their backs, their arms stretched out along the body, with the hands at hip level, occasionally the hands were placed on the stomach or the chest. The elbows pulled in towards the body often indicate that cloth bands were used, although due to the fragility of the material, these have rarely been preserved. The same is true for wooden biers and coffins, the frequent use of which can be deduced from the marks left on the plastered floors of the graves, and the traces of rope along the walls. In early Tylos, the bodies were placed so as to watch the setting sun. Subsequently, this orientation no longer played a role.

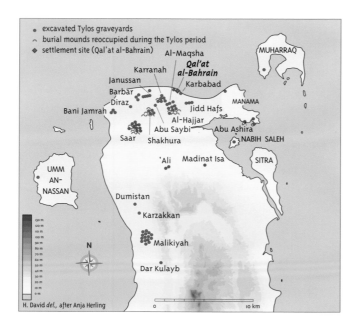

Distribution of the necropoleis from the Tylos period in Bahrain.

Map legend:
- excavated Tylos graveyards
- burial mounds reoccupied during the Tylos period
- settlement site (Qal'at al-Bahrain)

H. David *del.,* after Anja Herling

0   10 km

life or expressed their professional skills. Or perhaps they were considered indispensable for the afterlife. According to current research, weapons only seem to have been placed with male occupants, whereas cosmetics and adornments seem unrelated to the sex of the deceased. The number and quality of these "offerings" seem to imply the social status or wealth of the deceased, but they could also be symbolic of the pain that the living felt or wished to display publicly.

Personal preferences also influenced the type of burial, particularly in Middle Tylos. In the earliest phase, the funeral furniture was limited to ceramics and the usual presence of an obol. Graves of children for all periods contained predominantly ceramics and trinkets, which probably reflects their limited participation in the social life of the community. There were no fixed rules on the placing of these objects. Sometimes they were placed at the feet of the deceased, but also elsewhere. Towards the end of the ceremony, there was a ritual depositing of a receptacle filled with burnt substances (incense? ritual fire?), upturned, next to the grave cover. Sand was then spread over the closed tomb. In memory of the deceased and perhaps also to symbolically protect the grave, a stele was erected. The erection of this on the western edge of the funeral mound, at least in Early Tylos, seems to correspond to

to the afterlife are seen in several cultures, especially in the Greek culture. We can only speculate, however, as to the meaning of the other deposits. These include earthenware or plaster figurines (propitiatory gifts?), and a huge range of everyday objects made out of extremely varied materials. These include incense burners, personal items such as razors, combs, spatulas, perfume or cosmetics containers and also knives, arrow heads, pins, awls, metal ladles, or needles, spindles and spindle whorls, inlaid boxes made of bone, and often net or weaving weights. These objects were not deposited systematically, and often appear to be the deceased's most precious possessions. They probably had a special material or sentimental value. They may have accompanied the deceased during their earthly

the orientation of the remains.
We have no knowledge of the other rites
before, during or after the ceremony.

Conclusion

The care taken over burials is evident during
the Tylos period. It would seem that death
was not considered as the end of life,
but as a rite of passage which required ritual
support. The dead were bade farewell
as one would a living person, taking
into account different aspects
of their personality and their social relations.
Coins, figurines, eggs, coffins,
and the stone plates used to furnish
the tombs are all well-known details
in the Greek world, and represent
the contacts with this world. We know little,
however, about burials in the period
that directly preceded the Tylos period.
Therefore we are unable to judge
the significance of any changes
that occurred with the political transformations,
or to say to what extent the new customs
spread under their influence, or how quickly
they were adopted by the local populations.
In any case, the developments in burial
practices during the Tylos period show
that the island of Bahrain was not
isolated, but much more strongly
integrated in the international systems of
sovereignty that existed at the time than
was once believed.

Shakhura necropolis.
Mound I, funeral stele *in situ*.

A Necropolis Representative of the Various Tylos Phases: Mound I at Shakhura

Khaled Alsendi, Mustapha Ibrahim

The Site

This elevated site, situated about I km to the south of the Budaiya Road, is an integral part of the Tylos necropolis at Shakhura, one of the largest on the island of Bahrain, whose occupation lasted from the 3rd century BC to the 4th century AD. This mound was progressively isolated from the rest of the necropolis following the expansion of the village, particularly in the eastern part.

Overview

Mound I is of a longitudinal shape, orientated north-south. Its dimensions reach 80 x 50 m, with a height that varies from 4 to 12.7 m. It has an irregular profile with several distinct raised parts. Today, this space is occupied by a group of modern dwellings. Before its destruction, Mound I at Shakhura was the object of a systematic salvage dig, conducted from October 1996 to March 1997 by a Bahraini team from the Directorate of Archaeology and Heritage.

The Excavations

The excavations resulted in the discovery of 90 graves that composed a typical cemetery of the Tylos period. Analyses of the plan and the stratigraphy of the site have revealed the existence of an original group of graves in the centre of the mound, the others being placed progressively in concentric arcs around this original core. We cannot therefore define whether these graves were orientated in a specific way, as we can for the funeral chambers of the tumuli of the Bronze Age. The excavations also revealed the remains of three graves from the Dilmun period, placed directly on the rocky substratum. In the same way as other cemeteries from the Tylos period, Mound I at Shakhura was developed on the site of an earlier burial area.

Stages in Grave Construction

From bottom to top, we can determine three stages of occupation of the cemetery, that correspond to three "levels" of graves. -The first group comprised of the eleven most ancient graves, mainly adult graves. They were constructed with great care, and plastered inside and out. Moulding, designed to hold up the covering slab, lined the inside of the chamber. There were sometimes cavities or furrows in the floor, the use of which is not clear. The very first graves of the group are surrounded by the remains of stone perimeter walls, placed against the sandy mound covering themas though to isolate them from the rest of the necropolis or to accentuate their significance or to protect them. The dimensions of the covering slab, of which there was generally only one, and the style of construction of the chamber itself aimed to seal it completely to protect the burial deposit.

Despite this, some of these graves were violated, as we can see by the holes in the walls.
In three cases, coffins were found in which the deceased had been placed.
Made out of dark brown wood, they are rectangular, with a pitched cover, and carefully assembled using a nail-less system of mortice and tenon joints.
This is a unique discovery for the period, even more so since, apart from the base, which has rotted, these coffins are remarkably well preserved. This group of graves provided the greatest wealth of offerings, both rich and spectacular.
-The second group consists of the 57 graves from the intermediate level. They are concentrated in the north-west of the mound and were built in stages. The material used is small pieces of stone, covered with a coating of lime mixed with ash. The floor is also usually coated, except in cases where it was simply compacted. Here, the chambers are covered with three or four juxtaposed slabs, with the cracks filled with small stones bound together with mortar. Some of these coverings have completely disappeared.
These are mostly graves of adults, but a few skeletons of children under twelve have been identified. The absence of offerings of any value (even in the untouched graves) indicates a population that was apparently less wealthy than that of the first group.

N

0   10 m

Dilmoun ancien (vestiges)

Phase I (fin IIᵉ-Iᵉʳ s. av. J.-C. ?)

Phase II (fin Iᵉʳ s. av.-début IIᵉ s. ap. J.-C. ?)

Phase III (IIᵉ-IVᵉ s. ap. J.-C. ?)

Tombes en jarres

Stèle

(Les tombes numérotées ont livré du matériel funéraire mentionné dans le catalogue de l'exposition)

H. David *del.,* d'après Ali Omran

Grave 2 of the necropolis.
A rich example of Phase I burial.

-Finally, the third group consists of 22 graves,
built in a random fashion in stages.
They are simple pit-graves dug into the upper
levels of the necropolis, with walls reinforced
with small stones coated with a layer of mortar.
These are mostly children's' graves,
they are no longer than 50 to 60 cm.
They were visibly built in haste, as fingermarks
can be seen on the inside coating.
Besides these traditional graves, this level
also revealed eight greenish yellow jars,
probably old storage recepticals, which

Wooden coffin
from Phase I.

contained the remains of babies of less than a year old. The jar's opening had been adapted for the body to be placed inside, then closed up with stones or a dish. The small skeletons were adorned with necklaces, bronze rings, or shells. All of the graves of whatever period are individual ones. The deceased was generally laid out on his/her back with the arms out straight along the body.

Burial jar
(Phase III).

Burial Offerings

Several types of objects were deposited with the deceased. The quantity and quality of these varied with the group of graves under consideration. Vases and dishes in glazed ceramics, bronze instruments, objects made of ivory, bone, or alabaster, necklaces of semi-precious stones and various shells have all been found. We also often find an upturned vase which contained incense and ashes on a corner of the grave. These burial deposits were, unfortunately, often pillaged in ancient times, although a few escaped this fate. Grave 2, for example, revealed an exceptional set of objects. It contained the skeleton of an adult woman, who was wearing a necklace of gold beads in the form of grape clusters alternated with smaller beads of amethyst. Another necklace, consisting of long tapered beads in carnelian and onyx was found next to her right thigh. The deceased was also wearing a pair of simple gold ear rings, but most

significantly, on her left hand, she was wearing a gold ring set with a particularly fine Hellenistic or Roman cameo showing a face in profile, which can probably be dated to around the 2nd or 1st century BC. Graves 14 and 47 of the same ancient group contained core-formed glass vessels, which date from the same chronological period, and confirm the dating of the first graves of Mound I at Shakhura to the end of the Early Tylos phase. This type of material also illustrates particularly well the western influences that profoundly marked the island of Bahrain during this period.

The Material Culture of Tylos: Bahrain at the Gates to the Hellenistic and Parthian Worlds

Jean-François Salles

On an island constantly frequented by sailors and merchants from diverse regions, the material culture of the Tylos period could only be a composite of different facets. We will avoid the use of the word "influences" here, by seeking alternative explanations, despite the fact that the archaeological evidence has not yet been found to support these propositions.

At the Bahrain sites, objects have been found that were undoubtedly imported - Hellenistic black-glazed ceramics, egg-shell pottery from Susa in Iran, painted ceramics from Baluchistan, Mesopotamian glass, etc. (not including coins and inscriptions also found). Do these indicate simple trading exchanges, or were these objects destined for the use of specific foreign merchant communities living on the island? Digs have also uncovered finds that were probably manufactured locally which present resolutely non-indigenous characteristics. Those of the Hellenistic Mediterranean world and southern Babylonia can be seen in numerous ceramics, the Parthian kingdom of Hatra in sculpture, etc. Should we consider these imitations of foreign work by Bahraini craftsmen, or the result of technology transfer that would indicate the installation of foreign craftsmen in Bahrain, or Bahraini craftsmen following apprenticeships abroad? Given the cosmopolitan character of the archipelago's population, it is obvious that the lack of excavations of real settlements prevents us from determining the true extent of external contributions during the Tylos period, besides local traditions that seem to have continued for centuries (burial customs, common ware techniques, etc.).

The Tylos material culture did exist, however, in the form of common ware, in terracotta figurines, in the gold and silversmith's art, as well as in the graves with their distinctive character, and probably in traditional dwellings too fragile to have left archaeological traces - unless they are buried under the villages in the north of the island. This culture is very close - apart from the burial customs - to that we can observe during the same period in Eastern Arabia (the references to Failaka/Kuwait remain tenuous) - stone stelae, terracotta figurines, "Arabian" ceramics - it is not always easy to differentiate the original character of each of these groups. Beyond this Bahraini core, we can see well-identified external contributions following a somewhat vague chronology, of which a list follows. We will not enter into the inexhaustible specialist discussions that this list has elicited:
- The Greeks themselves, those of Failaka or further West (ceramics, coinage, inscriptions)
- Babylonia (Seleucia on the Tigris) and Seleucid Susa, end of the 4th century -

middle of the 2nd century BC
(mainly ceramics, some figurines)
- Southern Babylonia, i.e. Seleucid
and Parthian Characene (ceramics, glass,
some coinage), 3rd century BC - 2nd century AD,
the absence of recognised archaeological
remains at Spasinou Charax makes
this identification probable but not proven
- Parthian Mesopotamia (ceramics, glass,
gold and silversmith's art, some sculptures),
1st century BC - 3rd century AD
- Sasanian Iran (ceramics), 3rd - 7th century AD

The crucial point remains the chronology
of the archaeological material from the Tylos
period. By this we mean the division into phases
of the nine to ten centuries of this period of
Bahrain's history. The uncertainty stems from the
fact that the majority of the objects found come
from graves, for which it is impossible
to determine an exact date to within a century.
The stratigraphy of Qal'at al-Bahrain/Tylos was
established forty or so years ago, and the recent
publication of results of excavations does not
provide any definite answers - no other
settlement site has been excavated. Several
proposals concerning the chronology have been
suggested over the last few decades,
including those of the author of this article,
but these remain tentative. With the lack of
objective evidence from the archaeology of
Bahrain itself, these hypotheses are based on
comparative analyses of regional groupings of

material - a method which is always unreliable.
The latest proposal (Herling & Salles 1993), as
uncertain as the others, has the advantage of
defining a "*Bahrain Horizon*" (1st century BC -
1st century AD) which highlights the great
originality of the material culture
of the archipelago within Gulf archaeology
during a given period... But there is a long
archaeological route to navigate before
we will finally be able to fix the dates
of the main phases of Tylos/Bahrain in more
detail than the evidence permits.

Ceramics

Jean-François Salles, Pierre Lombard

We would like here to go beyond the traditional separation of the ceramics from the Tylos period into three categories according to the techniques used (commonware, slipped, glazed), and comment on the great artistic and craft traditions that inspired their manufacture. For the most part, these ceramics were produced locally, with a small proportion coming from imports. The diversity of shapes, and the fact that some types are only found on the island of Bahrain, provide clues to this. It is true that no workshop has yet been discovered, but this is hardly surprising considering that the archaeological data from the Tylos period comes almost exclusively from necropoleis, with a very small proportion coming from the few contemporary levels at the Qal'at al-Bahrain site, the only settlement discovered so far.

First of all, we can highlight the fact that there was a commonware tradition. This represents Bahraini production *par excellence*, and is the most commonly found type in the tombs of Early Tylos, replaced progressively by other types over time, but still found, even in small numbers up to the end of the Tylos period. In this tradition, the shapes are generally simple (open vases, goblets with oblique sides, jugs, etc.) The "Arabian" ceramic tradition is found particularly in early Tylos (300-100 BC). It is characterised, among other things, by a red, sometimes black, slip, usually on the inside

of open vases, and usually accompanied by a highly original decoration done with a burnisher consisting of patterns of bands and stripes (Cat. 226-228). The same slip is found on some closed shapes (Cat. 224-225). This tradition, which originated from the eastern part of the Arabian Peninsula seems particularly well represented at Bahrain, where there was probably a significant production. These polished red slip ceramics are often found side by side with other types, such as conical egg-shell bowls which were also found in the Arabian Peninsula.

Finally, the ceramic tradition most often found at Bahrain is that of glazed ceramics. It appeared progressively in Early Tylos, but mostly developed during the Middle (100 BC-200/250 AD) and Late (250-600 AD) Tylos periods. From Early Tylos onwards, many shapes were inspired by Hellenistic traditions - goblets with a returned border, sometimes with a dip in the middle on the inside, plates for fish, pitchers with a high neck (of Lagynos type), etc. But other vessels characteristic of Mesopotamian traditions are also present: flared goblets, hemispherical bowls, amphora, etc. This double connection, probably taken up by the potters of Bahrain, continued until the beginning of the 1st millennium AD. The truly Hellenistic traditions slowly disappeared, as in Mesopotamia, as well as the close parallels with manufactured goods from Seleucia on the Tigris, emphasizing the decline of the Seleucid influence in the

224, 225 Red Slip Vessels in the "Arabian" Tradition
Madinat Hamad necropolis (BSW), Bahraini excavations 1985-86, Mound 73, Grave 39
Saar necropolis, Bahraini excavations 1991-92, Mound 4, Grave 17
Middle Tylos, c. 1st cent. BC
Pottery
H13.8 and 11.5
D MAX 11.3 and 11.9 cm
Manama, Bahrain National Museum, acc. n° 2563-2-92 and main store
Unpublished

region. A highly characteristic type of ceramic (dark green glaze, giving way to a golden-brown colour) flourished at Bahrain as it did at Failaka (Kuwait) or ed-Dur (United Arab Emirates) at the beginning of the Middle Tylos period. Unless this production originated in the Gulf region, we need to look for its origins to the urban centre most active in the Gulf waters in the 1st century BC, the large merchant city of Spasinou Charax.

At around the same time, more precise parallels were established with the ceramics from Susa, a tendency that increased during the Late Tylos period, even if Bahrain's production continued

to be characterised by its native shapes. It does in fact seem that the artisan potters of Bahrain adapted to the predominant fashions in the Mesopotamian world while at the same time preserving the creativity and inventiveness shown in the course of the previous millennia.

The last point we would emphasize is the rarity of painted ceramics. The rare examples (Cat. 229-230) probably date from the 1st century AD, and may have been inspired by objects from Central Arabia or Iran.

230 Basket-shaped Vase
Shakhura necropolis,
Bahraini excavations 1991-92,
Mound 2, Grave 57
Middle Tylos,
c. 1st cent. BC/1st cent. AD
Pottery
H 11.4 D MAX. 7.5 cm
Manama, Bahrain National
Museum, main store
Unpublished

**226, 228 Red Slip Vessels in
the "Arabian" Tradition**
Shakhura necropolis,
Bahraini excavations 1992,
Mound 2, Grave 14
Karranah necropolis,
French excavations 1986
Al-Hajjar necropolis,
Bahraini excavations 1992-93,
Mound 1, Grave 8
Transition Early/Middle Tylos,
c. 2nd/1st cent. BC
Pottery
H11 D MAX14.2 cmH5.6 D MAX12 cm
H8.7 D MAX24 cm
Manama, Bahrain National
Museum, acc. n° 3756-2-91-6,
2396-2-90 and main store
Unpublished

229 Painted Bowl
Saar necropolis,
Bahraini excavations 1996,
Mound 11, Grave 43
Middle Tylos,
c. 1st/2nd cent. AD (?)
Pottery
H6 D MAX12.8 cm
Manama, Bahrain National
Museum, main store
Unpublished

231-235 Various Jars
Saar necropolis,
Bahraini excavations 1996-97,
Mound 5, Graves 24
and 62; 1995-96,
Mound 7, Grave 34; 1990,
Mound 1, unspecified grave
Madinat Hamad necropolis (E2),
Bahraini excavations 1994-95,
Mound 1, Grave 4

Middle Tylos,
1st cent. BC/1st cent. AD
Glazed pottery
H de 9.2 a 21 D MAX. de 8.5 a 16 cm
Manama, Bahrain National
Museum, acc. n° 4271-2-91
and main store
Unpublished

²³⁶ Footed Bowl
Shakhura necropolis,
Bahraini excavations 1987,
Mound 1, Square D3
Middle Tylos,
1st cent. BC/1st cent. AD
Glazed pottery
^{H}8.5 $^{D\ MAX}$14.5 cm
Manama, Bahrain National
Museum, acc. n° 2539-2-90-6
Unpublished

²³⁷ Footed Bowl
Shakhura necropolis,
Bahraini excavations 1991-92,
Mound 5, Grave 2
Middle Tylos,
1st cent. BC/1st cent. AD
Glazed pottery
^{H}10.7 $^{D\ MAX}$18.5 cm
Manama, Bahrain National
Museum, main store
Unpublished

²³⁸ Tripod Vessel
Saar necropolis,
Bahraini excavations 1991-92,
Mound 4, Grave 30
Middle Tylos, 1st/2nd cent. AD
Glazed pottery
^{H}15 $^{D\ MAX}$20.8 cm
Manama, Bahrain National
Museum, acc. n° 3248-2-91
Unpublished

²³⁹ Globe-shaped Vessel
Shakhura necropolis,
Bahraini excavations 1992-93,
Mound 1, Grave 94
Middle Tylos, 1st/2nd cent. AD
Glazed pottery
^{H}15.8 $^{D\ MAX}$16.5 cm
Manama, Bahrain National
Museum, main store
Unpublished

240-242 *Amphoriskoi*
and Pear-shaped Bottle
Saar necropolis,
Bahraini excavations 1991-92,
Mound 4, Grave 14;
Mound 2, Grave 22
Abu Saybi necropolis,
Bahraini excavations 1983,
Grave 84
Middle Tylos,
1st cent. BC/2nd cent. AD
Glazed pottery
H15.3 D MAX9.3 cm H16
D MAX11.3 cm H8.2 D MAX5.6 cm
Manama, Bahrain National
Museum, acc. n° 3852-2-91
and 921-2-88 and main store
Unpublished

243 "Pilgrim's Flask"
Saar necropolis, Bahraini
excavations 1988, Mound 5,
at the South of Grave 41
Middle Tylos, 2nd cent. AD
Glazed pottery
H17.6 D MAX13.9 cm
Manama, Bahrain National
Museum, main store
Unpublished

244 "Pilgrim's Flask"
Qal'at al-Bahrain,
Danish excavations (A519.SE),
Northern city-wall
Transition Early/Middle Tylos,
2nd/1st cent. BC
Glazed pottery
H17 D MAX17.5 E 7 cm
Manama, Bahrain National
Museum, acc. n° 871-2-88
B *Bahrain National Museum* 1989,
n° 171; Højlund & Andersen 1997,
fig. 817, p. 216

245 *Lagynos*
Saar necropolis,
Bahraini excavations 1991,
Mound 7, Grave 1
Middle Tylos, 1st cent AD
Glazed pottery
H30.8 D MAX22.3 cm
Manama, Bahrain National
Museum, acc. nº 5173-2-91-3
Unpublished

**246, 247 Jugs
with Ovoid Body**
Shakhura necropolis,
Bahraini excavations 1992-93,
Mound 7, Grave 80;
season and grave unspecified
Middle Tylos, 1st cent. AD
Glazed pottery
H29.5 and 26.5
D MAX20 and 17.4 cm
Manama, Bahrain National
Museum, main store
Unpublished

²⁴⁸ "Fish-plate"
Saar necropolis,
Bahraini excavations 1991,
Mound 5, Grave 23
Middle Tylos, c. 1ˢᵗ cent. AD
Glazed pottery
ᴴ5.6 ᴰ ᴹᴬˣ35 cm
Manama, Bahrain National
Museum, acc. nº 5175-2-91-3
Unpublished

²⁴⁹⁻²⁵² Various Jars
Dar Kulayb necropolis,
Bahraini excavations 1993-94,
Mound 24, Grave 2
Saar necropolis,
Bahraini excavations 1995,
Mound B3, Grave 43
Dar Kulayb necropolis,
Bahraini excavations 1993-94,
Mound 24
Madinat Hamad necropolis
(NBH4), Bahraini excavations
1989-90, Mound 10, Grave 41A
Middle and Late (?) Tylos,
between the 1ˢᵗ and the 4ᵗʰ (?)
cent. AD
Glazed pottery
ᴴ from 32.5 to 38.8
ᴰ ᴹᴬˣ· de 20.7 a 23 cm
Manama, Bahrain National
Museum, acc. nº 2010-2-90
and main store
Unpublished

253 Jar with Fluted Body
Saar necropolis,
Bahraini excavations,
season and grave unspecified
Transition Middle/Late Tylos,
c. $2^{nd}/3^{rd}$ cent. AD (?)
Glazed pottery
H31 D MAX17 cm
Manama, Bahrain National
Museum, main store
Unpublished

254, 255 Oil Vessels
Saar necropolis,
Bahraini excavations 1991–92,
Mound 4, Grave 14;
Mound 4, Grave 33
Middle Tylos, c. 1st cent. AD
Glazed pottery
H 9 and 10.9 D MAX. 3.6 and 4.1 cm
Manama, Bahrain National
Museum, acc. n° 91-2-78
and 3799-2-91-3
Unpublished

256 Kylix
Shakhura necropolis,
Bahraini excavations 1996–97,
Mound 1, Grave 81
Middle Tylos, 1st/2nd cent. AD
Glazed pottery
H 11.4 D MAX. 12.9 cm
Manama, Bahrain National
Museum, main store
Unpublished

257 Alabastron
Saar necropolis,
Bahraini excavations 1991–92,
Mound 4, Grave 14
Middle Tylos, 2nd cent. AD
Glazed pottery
H 18.5 D MAX. 7.2 cm
Manama, Bahrain National
Museum, acc. n° 3766-2-91-3
Unpublished

258 Oil Lamp
Al-Maqsha necropolis,
Bahraini excavations, season
and grave unspecified
Middle Tylos,
1st/2nd cent. AD (?)
Glazed pottery
H12.3 l MAX9 cm
Manama, Bahrain National
Museum, acc. n° 91-2-88.
Unpublished

259 Incense Burner
Shakhura necropolis,
Bahraini excavations 1991,
Mound 1, Grave 9
Middle Tylos, 1st/2nd cent. AD
Pottery
H18.8 D MAX10.7 cm
Manama, Bahrain National
Museum, main store
Unpublished

Stone Vessels

Pierre Lombard

Chlorite/steatite, the traditional material used to produce objects in the Bronze or Iron Ages, did not completely disappear during the Tylos period, but apparently gave way to a form of calcite of a creamy whitish colour, wrongly designated as "alabaster", which became the preferred material for the people of Bahrain. Between the 1st century BC and the 1st century AD especially, a whole series of miniature vases were imported from Yemen in particular, (beehive-shaped vessels, alabastra and various goblets) similar to those found in the famous necropolis at Timna or discovered at Hajar bin Humeid in the ancient kingdom of Qataban. These were sometimes copied at Bahrain in a white material that is very different to the veined, translucent stone so typical of southern Arabian work.

262 Footed Bowl
Shakhura necropolis,
Bahraini excavations 1991-92,
Mound 2, Grave 40
Tylos Period, Ist cent. AD
Calcite ("alabaster")
^{H}6 $^{D\ MAX}$14.3 cm
Manama, Bahrain National
Museum, acc. n° 5179-2-91-6
^{B} *Bahrain National Museum*
1993, p. 69

Bone and Ivory

Pierre Lombard

It is not always easy to distinguish between these two materials, both of which were used to make everyday objects, which were often placed with the deceased during the Tylos period. These were usually domestic utensils, mainly found in the tombs of women: fragments of jewellery boxes, kohl tubes, combs, and other personal effects; awls, spindles, whorls, occasionally figurines. Ivory, probably from elephants, is generally harder than bone, and seemed to be reserved for the larger pieces of marquetry, as well as for lathe-turned or hollowed objects, such as cosmetic tubes or conical whorls. This material probably came from the Indian subcontinent, which, during the Tylos period, evidently re-established the contacts with Bahrain that were maintained during the Bronze Age. The numerous spindles discovered were probably used to spin wool, but it is also tempting to associate them with the processing of cotton, whose cultivation is mentioned several times by the naturalists of classical antiquity such as Theophrastes who, in the 3rd century BC, mentions the "wool trees" of Tylos (*History of Plants*, IV, 7, 7-8). Archaeobotanic studies conducted at Qal'at al-Bahrain have proven that cotton bushes were present at Bahrain from the Achaemenid period, as affirmed in the 1st century AD by Pliny the Elder (*Natural History* 12, XXI, 38-39).

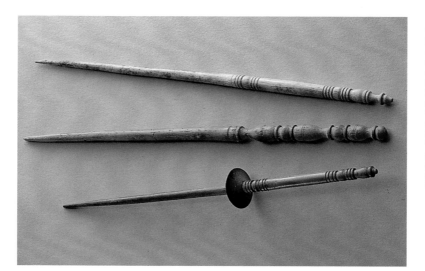

263-265 Spindles
Shakhura necropolis,
Bahraini excavations 1991-92,
Mound 2, Grave 58; 1996-97,
Mound 1, Grave 2
Saar necropolis,
Bahraini excavations 1996,
Mound II, Grave 9
Tylos Period,
1st cent. BC/1st cent. AD
Ivory
L23.2, 23.8 and 21 cm
Manama, Bahrain National
Museum, main store
and acc. n° 397-3-4
Unpublished

266 Set of 25 Spindle Whorls
Shakhura necropolis.
Bahraini excavations 1996-97,
Mound 1, Grave 1
Tylos Period, 1st cent. BC
Ivory
H0.2 to 0.9 D MAX1 to 1.8 cm
Manama, Bahrain National
Museum, acc. n° 397-3-12
Unpublished

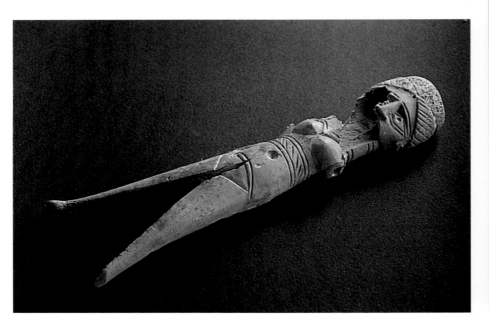

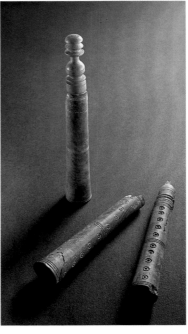

²⁶⁷ Figurine/toy (?)
Shakhura necropolis,
Bahraini excavations 1996-97,
Mound 1, Grave 47
Tylos Period, 1ˢᵗ cent. BC
Bone
ᴴ17.5 ᵂ2.3 ᵀᴴ6 cm
Manama, Bahrain National
Museum, acc. n° 180-2-97
Unpublished

This figurine, which must have
had (articulated?) arms made
out of a perishable material,
probably wood, is at present
the only example found
on Bahrain. It came from a
grave that had not been
pillaged. The grave contained
the skeleton of young
adolescent female, and also
contained pieces of gold and
glassware (cf Cat. 323).

²⁶⁸⁻²⁷⁰ Cosmetic Cases
Shakhura necropolis,
Bahraini excavations 1996-97,
Mound 1, Graves 14, 35 and 2
Tylos Period,
1ˢᵗ cent. BC/1ˢᵗ cent. AD
Ivory
ᴴ13.6, 12. 3 and 10
ᴰ ᴹᴬˣ2, 1.5 and 1.9 cm
Manama, Bahrain National
Museum, acc. n° 397-3-97,
164-3-97 and 15-3-96
Unpublished

Glassware

Marie-Dominique Nenna

The impressive set of glassware discovered during excavations of the necropoleis of the Tylos phase consists mostly of small perfume containers which were part of the offerings to the deceased. Their vast chronological spread, from the 2nd century BC to approximately the 6th century AD bears witness to the long period of prosperity that Bahrain apparently enjoyed during the Hellenistic, Parthian and Sasanian periods. The island's continuing role as a trading crossroads during these centuries is also evoked by the diverse origins of this material - the Eastern Mediterranean, Syria/Palestine, Mesopotamia, Egypt, perhaps even Italy. Finally the collection illustrates the main techniques of Hellenistic-Roman glassware manufacture. This is highlighted by the excellent state of preservation of the pieces, most of which were found intact in the tombs. The most ancient in this collection are the core-formed vessels, represented by a superb *amphoriskos* (Cat. 271), dating from between the middle of the 2nd and the end of the 1st century BC. The free-blown glass flasks (series of *aryballos* and small jugs, Cat. 273-275), simple *unguentaria* in transparent glass (Cat. 292-294), probably originated from the Eastern Mediterranean, and date from the second half of the 1st and the 2nd century AD. The specimens in mould-blown glass of various shapes also date from this period

(*amphoriskoi* Cat. 277-279; dates Cat. 285, 286 etc.), some of the shapes are complex (hexagonal bottle Cat. 280). We can also observe the presence, also from the 1st century AD, of a flat bead in mosaic glass (Cat. 291), certainly produced in Egypt and a small vase in marbled glass, perhaps from Italy. We have found many vases in blown glass dating from the 3rd century to the end of the Sasanian period - they become more and more highly decorated with sometimes thick threads applied in spirals, zigzags or dots, sometimes with mottling. These later flasks must have all been produced in the Eastern Mediterranean. Perfume was among the traditional trade goods in the Tylos era. It is not surprising, therefore, to find only imported glassware in the necropoleis finds. Digs carried out on contemporary settlement sites may one day provide a different picture, and perhaps even some locally made pieces.

271 *Amphoriskos*
Shakhura necropolis,
Bahraini excavations 1996-97,
Mound 1, Grave 14
Transition Early/Middle Tylos,
c. end of 2nd/1st cent. BC
Core-formed glass
H14 D5.6 cm
Manama, Bahrain National
Museum, acc. n° 187-3-97
Unpublished

Two examples of this well-
known type of core-formed
vessel have been found
in Bahrain, in two tombs
at this necropolis, attributed
to the Early or the beginning
of the Middle Tylos Period. Of
Syro-Palestinian manufacture,
these are copies of the Aegean
Hellenistic wine amphorae, and
this specimen from Shakhura
shows many parallels with these
vessels (cf D. Grose 1989,
p. 122-125 and n° 168-176).

272 Flask
Saar necropolis,
Bahraini excavations 1991-92,
Mound 4, Grave 14
Middle Tylos, c. 2nd cent. AD
Core-formed glass
H7.3 D MAX3.9 cm
Manama, Bahrain National
Museum, acc. n° 1973-2-91-1
Unpublished

This small vessel with handles,
a cylindrical neck and an ovoid
body, although produced using
the same technique
as the previous example,
illustrates a shape that is
typologically very different,
and does not have an exact
equivalent among
the traditional core-formed
types. The date of the context
in which it was discovered,
although certain, seems
rather late for this type
of manufacture, perhaps
originating from the Eastern
Mediterranean.

273, 274 Aryballoi
Madinat Hamad necropolis (E2),
Bahraini excavations 1994-95,
Mound 1, Grave 4
Saar necropolis,
Bahraini excavations 1996,
Mound 7, Grave 42
Middle Tylos, c. 1st cent AD
Free-blown glass
H6.7 and 7.2 D MAX5.1 and 5.6 cm
Manama, Bahrain National
Museum, main store
Unpublished

These imports from the Eastern
Mediterranean circulated
throughout the Arabian Gulf,
where they are also found
on the coastal site of Ed-Dur,
in the United Arab Emirates
(cf D. Whitehouse 1998,
n° 78, 75).

275 *Aryballos*
Abu Ashira necropolis,
Bahraini excavations,
season and grave unspecified
Middle Tylos, c. 1st cent AD
Free-blown glass
H8.4 D MAX7.8 cm
Manama, Bahrain National
Museum, main store
B *Bahrain National Museum*
1989, n° 216

276 "Sidonian Flask"
Shakhura necropolis,
Bahraini excavations 1992-93,
Mound I, Grave 17
Middle Tylos, 1st cent AD
Mould-blown glass
H7.2 D MAX4.9 cm
Manama, Bahrain National
Museum, main store
Unpublished. Comp.: *Bahrain
National Museum* 1989, n° 198-
200

The traditional name of this
type of small flask with one
or two handles and a moulded
foliate scroll decoration
on the body comes
from its production area. It is
a shape often found in Bahrain.

277-279 Amphoriskoi
Madinat Hamad necropolis (E2),
Bahraini excavations 1994-95,
Mound I, Grave 2
Al-Hajjar necropolis,
Bahraini excavations 1971,
Site 2, Grave IA
Al-Maqaba necropolis,
Bahraini excavations 1989,
Grave 7
Middle Tylos,
second half of the 1st cent AD
Mould-blown glass
H7.2, 7.8 and 6.6
D MAX2.8, 3.5 and 3.6 cm
Manama, Bahrain National
Museum, main store,
and acc. n° 199, 970-2-88,
2915-14-90
B *Bahrain National Museum*
1989, n° 203, and unpublished.
Comp.: E.M. Stern 1995,
p. 157-159, n° 64-68; p. 150-154,
n° 53-58. D. Whitehouse 1998,
n° 109-111

**280 Unguentarium
with Marbled Decoration**
Madinat Hamad necropolis (E2),
Bahraini excavations 1994-95,
Mound I, Grave 5
Middle Tylos, 1st cent AD
Free-blown glass
H6.8 D MAX3.5 cm
Manama, Bahrain National
Museum, main store
Unpublished. Comp.: *Bahrain
National Museum* 1989, n° 208;
D. Grose 1989, p. 261-262
and n° 608-616

**281 Hexagonal Flask
with Moulded Decoration**
Shakhura necropolis,
Bahraini excavations 1996-97,
Mound I, Grave 4
Middle Tylos, 1st cent AD
Mould-blown glass
H8 D MAX3.7 cm
Manama, Bahrain National
Museum, main store
Unpublished

This small bottle with a flat rim
and a long cylindrical neck
is a typically Syro-Palestinian
production (cf E.M. Stern 1995,
p. 129-135, n° 36-40); its body
in particular shows a complex
moulded decoration organised
in six panels with alternate
patterns of grenadines, bunches
of grapes, cedar apples,
and perhaps a woman's face.

282 Deep Purple Millefiore Pillar-Moulded Bowl, with Opaque White Marbling
Hamla North.
Tylos Period
H4.6 D13.3 cm
British Museum
BM No. 1999-10-30,1
Deposit n° 2693
From the Higham Collection, Tumulus 36.
Courtesy of the Trustees of the British Museum.
B *The Bahrain Tumuli*: An Illustrated Catalogue of Two Important Collections. Elizabeth C L During-Caspers. Leiden 1980.

The bowl has 25 ribs which run from below the rim towards the centre of the base.

283 Amphora
Hamla North.
Tylos period.
H12 D4.1 cm
British Museum
BM No. 1999-10-39,2
Deposit n° 2693
From the Higham Collection, Tumulus 36.
Courtesy of the Trustees of the British Museum.
B *The Bahrain Tumuli*: An Illustrated Catalogue of Two Important Collections. Elizabeth C L During-Caspers. Leiden 1980.

Small millefiore amphora of blue glass ornamented with whitish trails. Originally with two handles, one of which is now broken.

285, 286 Flasks in the Shape of Dates
Saar necropolis,
Bahraini excavations 1996,
Mound II, Grave 20
Shakhura necropolis,
Bahraini excavations 1997,
Mound I, Grave 26
Middle Tylos, 1st cent. AD
Mould-blown glass
H6.2 and 8 D MAX2.9 and 3.6 cm
Manama, Bahrain National
Museum, main store
Unpublished. Comp.:
E.M. Stern 1995, p. 91–94
and n° 84–107

Although one might imagine them to be local as their shape evokes the Bahraini fruit *par excellence*, these small unguent or perfume flasks come from the Syro-Palestinian region where their production is well documented between the middle of the 1st century and the beginning of the 2nd century AD.

284 Flask
Madinat Hamad necropolis
(DS3), Bahraini excavations
1985–86, Mound 73, Grave 1
Middle Tylos, 1st/2nd cent. AD
Free-blown glass
H11.1 D MAX6.4 cm
Manama, Bahrain National
Museum, main store
Unpublished. Comp.:
A. von Saldern 1974,
p. 221, n° 645–646

287 Footed Dish
Saar necropolis,
Bahraini excavations 1988,
Mound 5, Grave 2
Middle Tylos, 1st/2nd cent. AD
Moulded glass (?)
H12.2 D MAX28 cm
Manama, Bahrain National
Museum, acc. n° 421-2-88
B *Bahrain National Museum*
1993, p. 68

291 Bead with Mosaic Decoration
Saar necropolis,
Bahraini excavations 1987-88,
Mound 5, Grave 72
Middle Tylos, c. 1st cent AD
Mosaic glass
AVERAGE D 1.8 TH MAX 0.7 cm
Manama, Bahrain National
Museum, acc. n° 3880-2-91-3
B *Bahrain National Museum*
1993, p. 74

Two specimens of this type
of flat bead with a transversal
perforation and with a
figurative mosaic decoration
(here a woman's head with
stylised features and with hair
standing on end) of Egyptian
production, were found
in the Tylos necropolis at Saar.
This type of object of Egyptian
origin, including beads, pins,
etc. was very popular in the 1st
century AD (J.D. Cooney 1976, p.
138, n° 1711; S.M. Goldstein 1979,
p. 273-274, n° 817-821; E.M.
Stern & B. Schlick-Nolte 1994,
n° 149-154).

288-290 Bowls and Goblet
Saar necropolis,
Bahraini excavations 1985-86,
Mound 5, Grave 12; 1995-96,
Mound 7, Grave 55
Dar Kulayb necropolis,
Bahraini excavations 1993-94,
Tumulus 24 (reutilisation)

Middle Tylos, between
the 1st and the 3rd cent. AD (?)
Free-blown glass
H6.6, 21.5 and 6
D MAX 11.8, 8 and 12.1 cm
Manama, Bahrain National
Museum, main store
Unpublished

292-294 Flasks and Bottles
Madinat Hamad necropolis
(DS3), Bahraini excavations
1985-86, Mound 73, Grave 27;
(E2) 1994-95, Mound 1,
Graves 1, 4, 5
Abu Saybi necropolis,
Bahraini excavations 1983,
Grave 1
Middle and Late Tylos, between
the 1st and the 4th cent. AD
Free-blown glass
H12, 4.7, 12.3
D MAX 7.8, 5.8, 7.5 cm
Manama, Bahrain National
Museum, main store and
acc. n° 950-2-88, 4827-2-90-2
Unpublished

295-300 Jars and Miniature Flasks
Saar necropolis,
Bahraini excavations 1991,
Mound 12, Grave 22 and 6; 1996,
Mound 1, Grave 7; 1987-88,
Mound 5, Grave 49; 1991,
Mound 12, Grave 6
Late Tylos, 3rd/4th cent. AD
Free-blown glass
H4 to 9 cm D MAX 3.9 to 9.1 cm
Manama, Bahrain National
Museum, main store
and acc. n° 429-2-88
Unpublished

The decoration of threads
applied in spirals or zigzags
on the neck and body of these
very small vases shows that they
originated from either the
Eastern Mediterranean or more
probably from Mesopotamia.

303 Baby's Bottle
Saar necropolis,
Bahraini excavations 1996,
Mound 7, Grave 44
Middle Tylos,
c. 1st/2nd cent. AD
Free-blown glass
H6.6 D MAX5 cm
Manama, Bahrain National
Museum, main store
Unpublished

**301, 302 Flask and Jug
with Applied Decoration**
Al-Hajjar necropolis,
Bahraini excavations 1996,
Mound 1, near Grave 9
Late Tylos,
post-3rd/4th cent. AD
Free-blown glass
H12,1 and 10.3
D MAX. 3.6 and 5.4 cm
Manama, Bahrain National
Museum, main store
Unpublished

Discovered out of context,
these two pieces from a late
necropolis of the Tylos Period
are not easy to date. The glass,
originally of a yellowish colour,
is covered with a strong
iridescent layer of a bronze
and black colour.
The decoration consisting
of a large ribbon pinched
at regular intervals across
the shoulder and body
appeared until the Late
Sasanian Period, around
the 6th century AD.

304-306 Miniature Jars
Al-Maqsha necropolis,
Bahraini excavations 1978,
Grave 12
Late Tylos, c. 5th/7th cent. AD
Free-blown glass
H5.7, 3.8 and 2.5
D MAX4.2, 2.8 and 4.5 cm
Manama, Bahrain National
Museum, acc. n° 911-2-88,
962-2-88.
Unpublished and *Bahrain
National Museum* 1989, n° 197.
Comp.: *Bahrain National
Museum* 1989, n° 194, 196

These two small jars which
belong to a late Syrian
production, also found
in Mesopotamia and at Susa
(cf C.J. Lamm 1931, p. 331
and pl. LXXVI:2) confirm
the very long period during
which the Tylos Period
necropoleis were used. The few
graves attributed to this phase,
however, remain rare in
Bahrain.

Jewellery and Goldware

Pierre Lombard

Though they were frequently pillaged, the Tylos era tombs on Bahrain appear to have survived better than the Bronze Age tumuli. This is partly explained by the difficulty in identifying particularly imposing (so probably rich) tombs under the anonymous sandy mounds characteristic of the period, and by the fact that they were situated close to residential areas. Varied adornments have been found in the tombs of many adults and children. In some cases exceptional sets of jewellery or goldware have been found (Tomb 2 of Shakhura Mound 1, discovered at the end of 1996 by a Bahraini team, for example). This jewellery does not, at first sight, seem to have had a specific function in the burial, so we can assume that the deceased were adorned with their favourite everyday or special occasion jewels - it has already been observed that this practice does not seem to be especially linked to the sex of the deceased.

There is no doubt that gold, which began to appear more regularly in Bahrain from the Iron Age onwards (notably during the Achaemenid period, Cat 211), became much more common after the establishment of the Seleucid kingdom. In view of the current research, it would be imprudent, however, to affirm that Bahrain simply reflected the more general state of affairs in the Hellenistic Middle East at that time. From the end of the 4th century BC, gold prices dropped, and availability increased, due to the relaunch of the gold mines at Thrace by Phillip II, and especially to the later dispersion of the Persian "treasures" seized by his son Alexander. Due to its privileged trading position, the island of Tylos could also have had access to the gold mines of western Arabia, perhaps those of the mysterious land of Ophir which, a few centuries earlier, had already attracted the attention of King Solomon. For the source of the numerous precious and semi-precious stones (amethyst (?), certainly garnet, carnelian, chalcedony, agate, onyx) we have to look to the Indian sub-continent, where, in the Cambay region to this day we find workshops specialised in the making of long tapered beads of carnelian (cf Cat. 325).

A few pieces of goldware were probably imported 'as is' (Cat. 307, 320, 322, 323) from regions that we cannot always identify with ease (Parthian Mesopotamia? Ptolemaic Egypt or Bactria?). We can suppose that numerous adornments (necklaces in particular) were probably more usually made locally by craftsmen using imported materials - in several cases, natural Gulf pearls had been added (Cat. 326, 335), creating a type of production typical of the archipelago. Did Pliny the Elder not praise, in the first century AD, "*the island of Tylos, famous for its quantities of pearls*" (Natural History, VI, 148)?

**307 Pair of Earrings
with Pendant**
Shakhura necropolis,
Bahraini excavations 1990,
unspecified grave
Transition Early/Middle Tylos,
c. end of 2ⁿᵈ/1ˢᵗ cent. BC
Gold, fine stones, pearl
ᴸ8 cm
Manama, Bahrain National
Museum, acc. n° 2118-2-90
ᴮ *Bahrain National Museum* 1993,
p. 71

The theme of Eros, here riding
a goat, was particularly
popular in the Hellenistic world
from the 3ʳᵈ century BC
onwards. These exceptionally
finely crafted pieces date
from the end of the 2ⁿᵈ
or the 1ˢᵗ century BC.
The presence here of numerous
coloured precious stones
shows the taste for polychromy
that appeared in Eastern
jewellery from the Parthian
period onwards. The exact
place of manufacture
of this piece has not yet been
determined.

308 Pair of Earrings
Shakhura necropolis,
Bahraini excavations 1996-97,
Mound 1, Grave 2
Transition Early/Middle Tylos,
c. end of 2nd/1st cent. BC
Gold
D MAX 2.2 TH 0.32 cm
Manama, Bahrain National
Museum, acc. n° 1996-3-97
Unpublished

Cf Cat. 320.

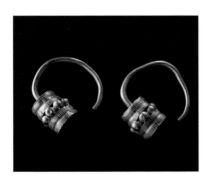

309 Pair of Earrings
Al-Hajjar necropolis,
Bahraini excavations 1992-93,
Mound 2, Grave 31
Middle Tylos,
1st cent. BC/1st cent. AD
Gold
D MAX 2 cm; cylinder: L 1 D 0.8 cm
Manama, Bahrain National
Museum, main store
Unpublished

Several examples of this type
of cylinder-shaped earrings
have been found in the Tylos
graves at Bahrain. They were
also part of a hoard of goldware
and jewellery from near
Dhahran (Potts 1990b. II,
pl. IXa), on the eastern coast
of Saudi Arabia.

310-313 Mouth Bands
Al-Hajjar necropolis,
Bahraini excavations 1992-93,
Mound 2, Graves 11, 34, 31, 30
Middle Tylos,
1st cent. BC/1st cent. AD
Gold
L 5.4 to 7.7 W 1.5 to 2.3 cm
Manama, Bahrain National
Museum, main store
Unpublished

In the best preserved Tylos
graves, this type of oval band
was often found in position,
placed over the deceased's
mouth, originally fixed at both
ends. On one of them,
the schematic trace of the lips
can be seen. This is a common
custom in contemporaneous
graves in the Near East
(cf Toll 1946, p. 115
and pl. XLI, XLVIII).

314-315 Decorated Discs applied to Clothing (?)
Abu Saybi necropolis,
Bahraini excavations,
season and grave unspecified
Middle Tylos,
1st cent. BC/1st cent. AD
Gold
H5.3 and 4.8 W MAX4.1 and 3.9 cm
Manama, Bahrain National Museum
B *Bahrain national Museum* 1993: 71a, b

These two delicately embossed pieces are part of a set of four that reproduce, in pairs, an eagle with its wings spread and a bust of a bearded figure seen in profile. They were found on the chest and shoulders of the deceased, and were perhaps attached to part of their clothing or shroud.

316 Elements of a diadem (?)
Al-Hajjar necropolis,
Bahraini excavations 1971, Site 1,
unspecified grave
Transition Early/Middle Tylos,
c. end of 2nd/1st cent. BC
Gold
Manama, Bahrain National Museum, main store
Unpublished

These various elements, several of which are leaf-shaped and trilobated were fixed, probably with an adhesive, to a headband or a funeral wreath whose base was perhaps made from a plaited branch. Similar adornments have been frequently found in the graves of the Hellenistic and Post-Hellenistic Periods (for example at Dura-Europos, cf Toll 1946, pl. XL, XLII, LVII).

³¹⁷⁻³¹⁹ Bezel-rings
Shakhura necropolis,
Bahraini excavations 1990,
Mound 1, Grave 1
Saar necropolis,
Bahraini excavations 1988,
Mound 104, unspecified grave
Karranah necropolis,
German excavations 1993,
Mound 1, Grave 220
Middle Tylos,
1ˢᵗ cent. BC/1ˢᵗ cent. AD
Gold, fine stones
ᴴ2.4, 2.1 and 1.6
ᴰ ᴹᴬˣ2.1, 2 and 1.5 cm
Manama, Bahrain National
Museum, acc. n° 2120-2-90,
1857-1-89 and main store
ᴮ *Bahrain National Museum*
1993, p. 70 and unpublished

³²⁰ Ring Set with a Cameo
Shakhura necropolis,
Bahraini excavations 1996-97,
Mound 1, Grave 2
Transition Early/Middle Tylos,
c. end of 2ⁿᵈ/1ˢᵗ cent. BC
Gold, fine stone
ᴴ2.55 ᴰ ᴹᴬˣ2.2 cm;
Cameo: 1.2 × 0.9 cm
Manama, Bahrain National
Museum, acc. n° 1996-3-97
Unpublished

The engraving of the cameo
here follows the contours of a
male head with a band around
the forehead. It is fixed
to the mount by a sort
of transparent resin. This fine
piece comes from a woman's
grave discovered intact in 1996
at Shakhura (Grave 2, cf above),
and is stratigraphically
attributed to the early phase
of the necropolis. The necklaces
Cat. 322 and 325, and the ivory
utensils Cat. 265, 266
and 270 were also associated
with this rich grave.

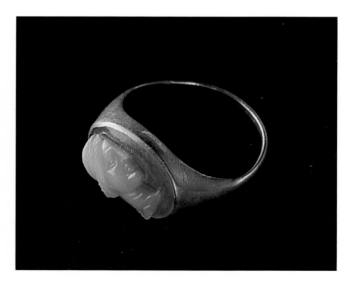

321 Necklace
Saar necropolis,
Bahraini excavations 1995-96,
Mound 7, Grave 44
Middle Tylos, c. 1st cent. AD
Mosaic glass, frit, coral, pearls,
gold
L48 cm
Manama, Bahrain National
Museum, main store
Unpublished

322 Necklace
Shakhura necropolis,
Bahraini excavations 1996-97,
Mound 1, Grave 2
Transition Early/Middle Tylos,
c. end of 2nd/1st cent. BC
Gold, agate, rock crystal,
carnelian, amethyst
L24 L granulation beads 1.4 cm
Manama, Bahrain National
Museum, acc. n° 1996-3-37
Unpublished

Cf Cat. 320.

323 Necklace
Shakhura necropolis,
Bahraini excavations 1996-97,
Mound 1, Grave 47
Transition Early/Middle Tylos,
c. end of 2nd/1st cent. BC
Gold
^{L}23.7 cm
Manama, Bahrain National
Museum, acc. n° 297-3-168
Unpublished

This jewellery was found
in a young girl's grave from
the early phase of the Shakhura
necropolis (cf Cat. 267).

324 Necklace
Shakhura necropolis,
Bahraini excavations 1996-97,
Mound 1, Grave 14
Transition Early/Middle Tylos,
c. end of 2nd/1st cent. BC
Carnelian, agate
^{L}76.5 ^{L} beads 1.8 to 3.3 cm
Manama, Bahrain National
Museum, acc. n° 297-3-57
Unpublished

325 **Necklace**
Shakhura necropolis,
Bahraini excavations 1996-97,
Mound I, Grave 2
Transition Early/Middle Tylos,
c. end of 2nd/1st cent. BC
Carnelian, banded agate
L56.5 Lbeads 1 to 7 cm
Manama, Bahrain National
Museum, acc. n° 297-3-8
Unpublished

Cf Cat. 320. The special nature
of this piece of jewellery lies
in the shape and size
of its long tapered beads
(between 5 and 7 cm),
which are similar to present day
productions from the Indian
subcontinent, the region
from which they were probably
imported. It is not impossible
therefore, that the remarkable
carnelian carving techniques
practised by today's craftsmen
from Gujarat, for example,
are the result of a long tradition
that goes back more than
two thousand years.

326 **Necklace (fragmentary?)**
Shakhura necropolis,
Bahraini excavations 1996-97,
Mound I, Grave 3
Transition Early/Middle Tylos,
c. end of 2nd/1st cent. BC
fine stones (garnet, carnelian),
glass paste, pearls, gold
L10 cm
Manama, Bahrain National
Museum, acc. n° 297-3-358
Unpublished

³²⁷⁻³³² Beads-amulets
Saar necropolis,
Bahraini excavations 1996,
Mound 7, Grave 5
Karranah necropolis,
French excavations 1986-87,
Mound III, Grave C3
Middle Tylos,
1st cent. BC/1st cent. AD
Frit
L1.9 to 2.15 W1.15 to 1.2
TH0.65 to 0.75 cm
Manama, Bahrain National
Museum, main store
Unpublished

These small earthenware
amulets, covered with a typical
blue-green glaze, are generally
considered to be imports
from Egypt. They were very
popular during the Hellenistic
and Roman periods when
they were attributed

prophylactic powers – bunches
of grapes and phalluses were
obvious symbols of fertility
and supposedly guaranteed
this for their wearer. This type
of object is commonly found
in graves in the Near East
between the 1st century BC
and the 2nd century AD,
for example at Dura Europos
(Toll 1946, pl. XLIII, XLIV, XLVI,
IIV), or at Ed-Dur, in the United
Arab Emirates (Haerinck 1991,
p. 50, fig. 28:8).

³³³ Necklace
Al-Hajjar necropolis,
Bahraini excavations,
season and grave unspecified
Middle Tylos,
c. 1st/2nd cent. AD
Glass paste, shell, chlorite
L56 Lbeads 0.9 to 2.3 cm
Manama, Bahrain National
Museum, main store
Unpublished

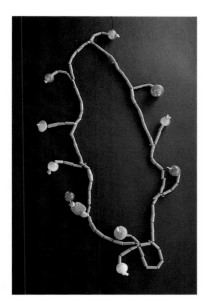

334 **Necklace**
Al-Hajjar necropolis,
Bahraini excavations,
season and grave unspecified
Middle Tylos,
c. 1st/2nd cent. AD
Frit, carnelian, amethyst, agate
L56 cm
Manama, Bahrain National
Museum, main store
Unpublished

335 **Necklace (fragmentary?)**
Shakhura necropolis,
Bahraini excavations 1991-92,
Mound 2, Grave 56
Middle Tylos,
1st cent. BC/1st cent. AD
Carnelian, rock crystal, pearl,
glass paste
L24.5 cm
Manama, Bahrain National
Museum, acc. n° 297-3-160
Unpublished

On this probably fragmentary
necklace there is a fine baroque
pearl that has been carved
into a pendant in the shape
of a bunch of grapes - this
is probably exactly the type
of jewellery set made locally
by the artisan-jewellers of Tylos
(cf also Cat. n° 326).

Tylos and Pre-Islamic Coinage in the Gulf

Olivier Callot

336, 337 Burial Obols
Saar necropolis,
Bahraini excavations 1995,
Mound 4, Graves 2 et 9
Tylos period
Silver
D1 cm
Manama, Bahrain National
Museum, acc. n° 28 and 12
Unpublished

These silver obols
(the smallest Greek monetary
unit) are inspired by
Alexandrine types that
belonged to late pre-Islamic
Arab coins from the 1st century
BC to the 1st century AD.
These small items, generally
found inside the head or close
to the jaws of the deceased
had most likely been placed
inside the mouth. After
the practice of the Greek world,
these constituted the "offering
to Charon", the boatman
to the netherworld, and are
a concrete indication of popular
beliefs in the Tylos Period.

The first pre-Islamic coinage appeared
in the Gulf in the middle of the 3rd century BC.
This coincided with a weakening of the power
of the Seleucids which led the regional powers
– kingdoms or cities – to produce their own
currency for their commercial transactions
or to pay troops. All these currencies were
imitations of the coinage of Alexander the Great,
used in the Seleucid Empire.
We can distinguish some major groups within
these regional currencies, though it is still
difficult to attribute them accurately to a specific
power or territory. Some have been found
on the island of Ikaros (Failaka in Kuwait),
and other examples are also known,
where they are inscribed with the names of Arab
dynasts such as Abi'el, Abyatha or Haritat,
who probably reigned on the coast of what is now
Saudi Arabia. The trading city of Gerrha,
whose exact geographical location is not yet
known, probably also had its own specific
currency. More distant regions like
the Oman peninsula also minted coins
at that time. Numerous examples
of Tylos-Bahrain's own currency were found
in the treasure at Qal'at al Bahrain (Cat. 338).
Production apparently came to a sudden halt at
the end of the 3rd century BC when the Seleucid
power again appeared in the Gulf under the reign
of Antiochus III (223-187). We know that in 205,
on his return from the great expedition destined
to re-establish his authority in the eastern part
of his vast empire, he took Ikaros back by force

after stopping in Gerrha and Tylos. Re-
establishing his authority thus enabled him to
take control over the regional trading routes
again, and to prohibit the local currencies
that challenged his own. This situation did not
last long, however. As soon as his son,
Antiochus IV died in 164, the Seleucid presence
disappeared definitively from the Gulf,
and new, if extremely crudely produced,
currencies appeared. These currencies were still
inspired by those of Alexander the Great,
and used the same weighting system,
and lasted until the first centuries of our era.

Type 1a

Type 2

338 Coin Hoard

Qal'at al-Bahrain,
Danish excavations 1970,
Northern City-wall
Tylos period
Clay, silver
^H17.5 ^{D MAX}15.5 cm (vase)
Manama, Bahrain National
Museum, acc. n° 401
^B Mørkholm 1973; Callot 1990,
1994; Arnold-Biucchi 1991

This jar, discovered in 1970,
contained around 310 silver
tetradrachms of two different
types:
Type 1a (3 examples):
on the front, head of Heracles
facing right wearing the pelt of
the Nemean lion. On the reverse,
Shamash sitting on the right
holding an eagle and a long
sceptre; on the right, written
vertically: ΑΛΕΞΑΝΔΡΟΥ
(ALEXANDROU); on the left
a southern Arabic inscription:
 hꞵꞵ (Shams).
Type 1b (over 212 examples):
identical to the previous coin,
but with the name of Shams
reduced to its first letter
on the reverse side: ꞵ
These are very good imitations,
often over-stamped onto
Seleucid tetradrachms from
the beginning of the reign
of Antiochus III. These coins may
have been stamped at
Tylos-Bahrain around 220-215.
Type 2 (over 76 specimens):
on the front head of Heracles
facing right wearing the pelt of
the Nemean lion; the lion's jaws
form a large horn shape on
his head. On the reverse, Shamash
sitting on the left holding
a drinking horn in the shape
of a horse and a sceptre; to
his left, a small date palm

and various marks. On the right,
a vertical inscription
in Aramaic, part of which
is not clear: "Abi'el son of Tlbs
or Tlsll". This is a clumsier
imitation of an Alexandrine
type stamped in the second
half of the 3rd century by
a dynast named Abi'el.
We do not know where
the workshop was (coast
of Saudi Arabia? Gerrha?).
Like those of Alexander,
all these coins show the head of
Heracles on the front facing
right wearing the pelt
of the Nemean lion and,
on the reverse, a seated figure
holding an eagle and a sceptre.
However, in contrast with the
Greek protoypes which show
a bearded Zeus, the Arabian
specimens show a rather
youthful, beardless figure. This
was probably Shams
or Shamash, who was at the
time the main deity worshiped
in these regions. These Arabian
coins generally follow
the Attican weight system.
We can see here that the authors
did not want to definitively
break away from the kingdom
of Syria, but only to become
a part of its monetary system.

Stone, Plaster and Terracotta Sculpture

Pierre Lombard

Apart from rare architectonic elements, all of the figured, modelled or sculpted evidence from the Tylos period comes from tombs. This record, which has constantly been enriched as the salvage digs of the last few years have progressed, consists essentially of bas-relief figures on stelae, as well as some free-standing pieces (busts or funeral statuettes).

These two categories of objects, all carved in the archipelago's finest calcarenite, are undeniably of local origin. We can extend this (reasonable) premise to encompass most of the figurines modelled in plaster (Cat. 339, 342) or in earthenware (Cat. 340, 344-346), generally considered to be the work of local craftsmen.

As well as the worshipping or weeping figures in the form of small ex-votos, common in the funerary domain, there was seemingly a systematic desire on the part of the populations of the Tylos period to provide an individual representation of the deceased, the best examples of which are seen in the grave stelae in more or less marked relief.

The deeper meaning of this practice, which was far from generalised throughout the island, still escapes us. Inside a given necropolis, not all tombs are associated with a stele, there are many cemeteries where none has been found, whereas the discovery by chance of fifteen or so specimens on a private palm grove close to Qal'at al-Bahrain implies the proximity of a necropolis which perhaps had a special status. These stelae, when found, were generally placed outside the tomb, often under the mound of earth covering the tomb, so their primary function was not to mark the tomb.

There is a first group of monuments with a simple shape that takes its inspiration from the human form. These can be identified as the simple evocations of the spirit of the deceased known commonly in the ancient Near East as stelae-"*nephesh*" ("breath" in Aramaic). A second group consists in more individualised stele-niches which show in greater or lesser relief, figures of both sexes in an attitude prayer, the right hand raised with the palm facing forwards.

Recent excavations have enabled us to identify another group that can be designated as "intermediary", as the stelae are directly inspired by the "nephesh" type, but often show details (often very roughly) of faces and hair. The stele-nephesh is manifestly the most ancient type (one includes a short inscription in Greek dating from the end of the 2nd century BC), but seems to have remained in use in the first few centuries AD (Cat. 347, 354).

The iconography of the stele-niches is, on the contrary, close to the Parthian artistic tradition of the 2nd and 3rd centuries AD, as seen in Mesopotamia (Hatra) or Iran (Elymais) (Cat 356, 361). But these distinct traditions succeeded one another, and probably co-existed for a period. This remarkable craft could also be evidence of Bahrain's multicultural artistic traditions during the Tylos period. The stele-nephesh, indigenous to the island, was progressively 'humanised' through contact with the other regional artistic traditions and the populations that practised them.

339 Mourner Figurine
Al-Maqsha necropolis,
Bahraini excavations 1992–93,
Grave 1
Tylos Period, 2nd /1st cent. BC
Moulded plaster
H24.2 W7.3 TH3 cm
Manama, Bahrain National
Museum, acc. n° 311
Unpublished

340 Female Figurine
Shakhura necropolis,
Bahraini excavations 1991–92,
Mound 1, Grave 10
Tylos Period,
1st cent. BC/1st cent. AD
Terracotta
H7.7 D MAX4.6 cm
Manama, Bahrain National
Museum, acc. n° 91-1-48
Unpublished

341 Horse Figurine
Al-Hajjar necropolis,
Bahraini excavations 1992–93,
Grave 11
Tylos Period,
1st cent. BC/1st cent. AD
Terracotta
H15.3 L17.2 W4.2 cm
Manama, Bahrain National
Museum, acc. n° 86
Unpublished

This piece, the only example
found in Bahrain to date,
was discovered in a grave
which, although apparently
unviolated, did not contain
the rider normally associated
with this type of figurine.
An almost unreadable graffito
(a few cursive Greek letters)
is visible on the upper part
of the animal's neck.

342 Circular Relief
Saar necropolis,
Bahraini excavations 1991,
Mound 6, Grave 3
Tylos Period, 2nd/1st cent. AD
Moulded plaster
D MAX13.6 TH3.4 cm
Manama, Bahrain National
Museum, acc. n° 3878
B *Bahrain National Museum 1993*

Traditionally, during the whole
of the Tylos Period, one
or several female figurines
were placed near the deceased.
They were crudely made
out of plaster in a flat mould,
and decorated with a few bright
colours. They evoke "wailing
women", who probably formed
an important aspect of
the burial ritual. They are
usually represented full length,
dressed in a kind of long *chiton*
pulled in at the waist,
their hands clinging to their
long hair, in a gesture
of profound lament (Cat. 339);
this circular-shaped relief
illustrates a later version
of this highly realistic theme,
limited here to the reproduction
of a dishevelled female bust.
These pieces were undoubtedly
the product of local
and popular craftsmen.

343 Figurine
Al-Hajjar necropolis,
Bahraini excavations 1992-93,
Grave 57
Tylos Period,
1st cent. BC - 1st cent. AD
Terracotta
H15.9 W6.7 cm
Manama, Bahrain National
Museum, main store
Unpublished

344-346 Female Figurines

Saar necropolis,
Bahraini excavations 1991,
Graves 44 and 47
Shakhura necropolis,
Bahraini excavations 1991-92,
Mound 1, Grave 12
Tylos Period,
1st cent. BC - 1st cent. AD
Terracotta
H14.2, 21 and 14. 4 W6 and 5.8
Manama, Bahrain National
Museum, acc. n° 2133-2-90
Unpublished

This series of female terracotta
figurines, some of which show
traces of polychrome painting,
are all represented in the same
posture with the right hand
brought up to the chest.
They are less common than
the moulded plaster figurines,
and came from significantly
later Tylos graves. It is difficult
to say whether they symbolise
the deceased herself, or whether
they were made locally.

347-348 Nephesh Type Stelae

Al-Hajjar necropolis,
Bahraini excavations 1992-93,
Mound 6, Square C4
Karranah necropolis, Mound III
Tylos Period, 2nd /1st cent. BC
Limestone
H51.2 and 62 W21.5 and 23
TH15 cm
Manama, Bahrain National
Museum, main store
Unpublished

349-351 Nephesh Type Stelae
Shakhura necropolis,
Bahraini excavations 1991-92,
Mound 4, Square B6
Abu Saybi necropolis,
Bahraini excavations 1983,
Mound B
Tylos Period, 2nd /1st cent. BC
Limestone
H26, 28 and 20 W12, 11.5 and 13.5
TH6. 6 and 6.5 cm
Manama, Bahrain National
Museum, main store
Unpublished

352 Nephesh Type Stelae
Shakhura necropolis,
Bahraini excavations 1991-92,
Mound 1, Square 1
Tylos Period,
1st cent. BC /1st cent. BC
Limestone
H47 W22 TH12 cm
Manama, Bahrain National
Museum, main store
Unpublished

This very distinctive type
of monument, directly inspired
by earlier ones, probably dates
from the very beginning of the
development of the figurative
tradition in Tylos stelae. This
began with the plainest
nephesh and developed
towards a style influenced
by Parthian art and also western
Graeco-Roman art. We see
the gradual appearance of arm
shapes as well as hair.

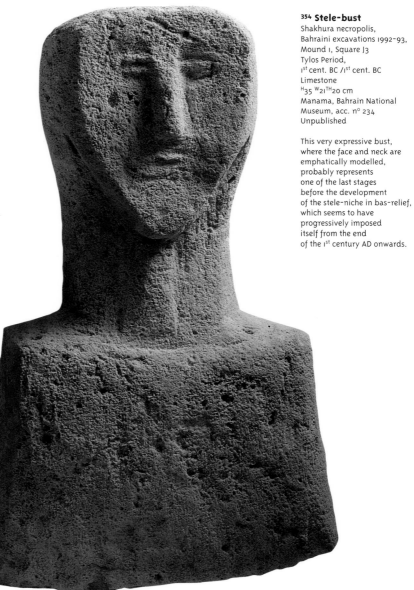

354 Stele-bust
Shakhura necropolis,
Bahraini excavations 1992-93,
Mound 1, Square J3
Tylos Period,
1st cent. BC /1st cent. BC
Limestone
H35 W21 TH20 cm
Manama, Bahrain National
Museum, acc. n° 234
Unpublished

This very expressive bust,
where the face and neck are
emphatically modelled,
probably represents
one of the last stages
before the development
of the stele-niche in bas-relief,
which seems to have
progressively imposed
itself from the end
of the 1st century AD onwards.

353 Nephesh Type Stele
Al-Maqsha necropolis,
Bahraini excavations 1992-93,
Square D12
Tylos Period,
1st cent. BC /1st cent. BC
Limestone
H27.7 W12.6 TH10 cm
Manama, Bahrain National
Museum, main store
Unpublished

This stele, which still conforms
to the general profile
of the Early Tylos prototypes,
has a face on the front
on which, for the first time,
realistic elements appear - eyes,
nose and mouth. The ears are
curiously placed on the sides
of a head which the sculptor,
faithful to the traditional
model, did not really curve
in the round.

355 Figurative Stele
Al-Maqsha necropolis,
Bahraini excavations 1992–93,
Square D12
Tylos Period, 2nd/3rd cent. AD
Limestone
^{H}37 ^{W}17 TH14 cm
Manama, Bahrain National
Museum, main store
Unpublished

From the same iconographical
tradition as the previous
monuments, this stele was
found in an identical context
to that of the stele-niches,
it can practically be described
as a small statue in the round.
In addition to its frontality,
we can observe the treatment
of the curls of the hair that
are so characteristic of the
Parthian art of the first centuries
AD.

357, 358 Figurative Stelae
Qal'at al-Bahrain, Northwestern palmgrove. Chance discovery, 1991
Tylos Period, 2nd /3rd cent. AD
Limestone
^{H}57 and 50 ^{W}30 and 33 TH17 and 19.5 cm
Manama, Bahrain National Museum, acc. n° 97-4-4 and main store
Unpublished

From the middle of the 2nd century AD, men and women are generally represented figuratively, on a pedestal or half-length, dressed in the Parthian style.

356 Figurative Stele
Qal'at al-Bahrain, Northwestern palmgrove. Chance discovery, 1991
Tylos Period, 2nd /3rd cent. AD
Limestone
^{H}34 ^{W}22 TH13 cm
Manama, Bahrain National Museum, acc. n° 97-4-1
^{B} Lombard 1994: 33, fig. 9a

359 Figurative Stele
Shakhura necropolis, Bahraini excavations 1992-93, Mound 1, Square J3
Tylos Period, 2nd /3rd cent. AD
Limestone
^{H}53.5 ^{W}32.5 TH15 cm
Manama, Bahrain National Museum, main store
Unpublished

360 Figurative Stele

Al-Maqsha necropolis,
Bahraini excavations 1992-93,
Square D12
Tylos Period, 2nd /3rd cent. AD
Limestone
H36 W16 TH14 cm
Manama, Bahrain National
Museum, acc. n° 176
Unpublished

This small stele-niche featuring
a young man, is in a style
very much influenced
by eastern Roman sculpture
(bird and bunches of grapes
held in the hand for example),
and was discovered associated
with two stelae (Cat. 355, 361),
of a style more proper
to Parthia. Once again,
this connection is hardly
surprising at Bahrain/Tylos
which, in the first few centuries
AD had evidently regained
its position as a key crossroads
and attracted diverse artistic
traditions.

361 Figurative Stele

Al-Maqsha necropolis,
Bahraini excavations 1992–93,
Square D12
Tylos Period, 2nd /3rd cent. AD
Limestone
H 46 W32 TH22 cm
Manama, Bahrain National
Museum, main store
Unpublished

The full-face rendering
of the character represented,
the treatment of his hair,
beard and moustache, probably
make this burial monument
one of the most representative
of local Tylos productions
inspired by the Parthian
tradition. The piece of cloth
folded and placed on the left
shoulder (cf also Cat. 356, 359)
recalls similar representations
from ancient Elymais,
where this sort of stole is usually
associated with priests.

362, 363 Statue-busts
Al-Hajjar necropolis,
Bahraini excavations 1992–93,
Mound 2, Grave 60
Tylos Period, 2nd /3rd cent. AD
Limestone
^{H}72 and 74.5 ^{W}37.5 TH15 cm
Manama, Bahrain National
Museum, main store
Unpublished

These two statue-busts are
a somewhat strange discovery
for a necropolis from the Tylos
period on Bahrain. They were
found standing side by side
inside a tomb with no skeleton
and practically no burial
offerings. They are unique
on Bahrain, and are difficult
to date accurately.
They could however belong
to the later burial sculpture
tradition (end of the 2nd
and the 3rd century AD),
often found in the north
of Palestine
(cf Skupinska-Løvfet 1983,
pl. LVI:53, LVII:54).

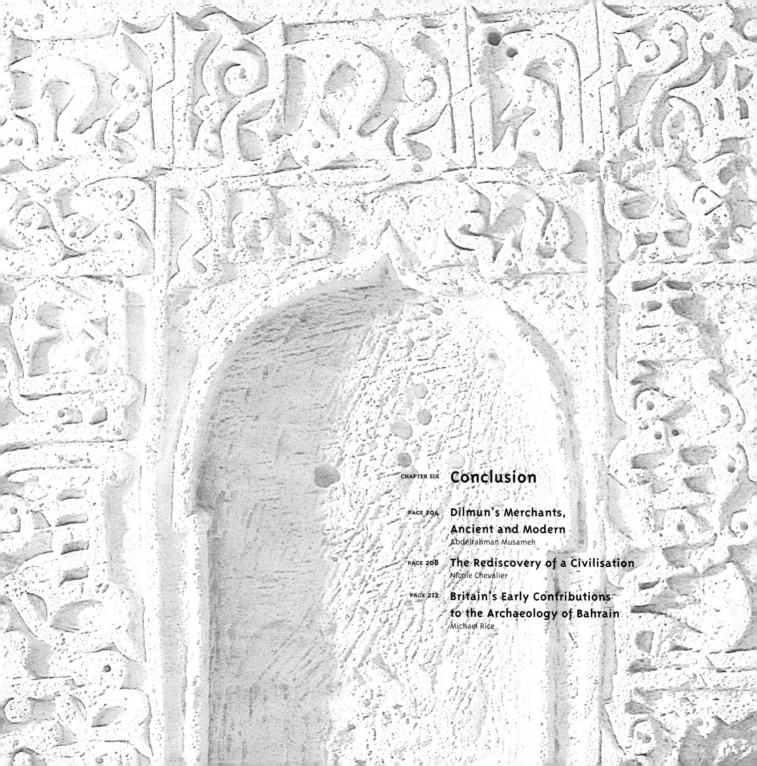

Dilmun's Merchants, Ancient and Modern

Abdelrahman Musameh

As the site of one of the civilisations most recently revealed by Oriental archaeologists, the Bahrain archipelago is rightly arousing a great deal of interest. Bahrain played a vital part in the maritime trade in the Near and Middle East over nearly two millennia, and its culture also played an essential role. As we have seen, two factors facilitated Bahrain's accession to this privileged situation – a strategic position as an island, and abundant sources of freshwater on the land not far from its coast. These freshwater sources enabled a rich agriculture to develop – date palms, fruit, and vegetables. As well as these advantages, the islands of Bahrain had several natural ports in the area of the currents of the Arabian Gulf, and these have always facilitated navigation, particularly from north to south.

The coasts of the islands were – and still are today – also rich in marine fauna. Fish abound, and the oysters of the region provide natural pearls of worldwide renown.

The sea has always been a natural protection for this archipelago, which explains the strong attraction of Bahrain for neighbouring countries as opposed to other areas of the Gulf (except perhaps for the al-Hasa area in the present day Eastern Province of Arabia). So, from the 3rd millennium BC, and for the entirety of their history, these islands have been inhabited by a multitude of peoples, and often even been attacked or conquered by regional powers. It was at the time of the Early Dilmun culture that the land of Bahrain became an active centre of civilisation. For nearly two millennia (from the 3rd millennium to the beginning of the 1st BC), despite occasional periods of relative obscurity, Bahrain played the role of trading intermediary between several Mesopotamian kingdoms (Sumer, Akkad, and Assur), the Indian sub-continent (Meluhha in the Sind region), and the Arabian Peninsula (Magan and Oman). It is during Dilmun's apogee, around 2000/1900 BC, that we can best

364 Mihrab Slab (?)
Suq al-Khamis mosque
Islamic period, 12th cent. AD
Limestone
H72.8 W64.8 TH9.5 cm
Manama, Bahrain National Museum, main store
Unpublished

This limestone slab in the form of a mihrab was found during recent restoration work at the Suq al-Khamis mosque,
the oldest mosque in the Arabian Peninsula. It is part of a series of which two were fixed on the façade of the prayer room (Kervran & Kalus 1990; Kalus 1995). The difference here is that the inscriptions carved on the other stones were compatible with their function as mihrabs, whereas the inscription around the niche of this slab comes from
two surah of the Koran that are usually engraved on gravestones: "We have not assigned to any mortal before thee to live forever; therefore, if thou diest, will they live forever?" (Koran XXI, 34-35.) "Every soul shall taste of death; and We try you with evil and good for testing, then unto Us you shall be returned" (Koran XXI, 34-35).

observe the diversity of the contributions made by its inhabitants to universal civilisation and thought.

First of all, we can see this in the clarification and identification of the particularly varied iconographic repertoire of the circular stamps first known as the "Arabian Gulf" seals, then the "Dilmun" seals. Another point is the creation of several specific types of ceramics, sometimes derived from models from outside the archipelago, but always produced in the local clay with its highly specific composition.

The practice of burying the dead outside towns and villages in tombs underneath tumuli or within huge honeycomb complexes (as at Saar) also remains a characteristic specific to the Dilmun civilisation, and the immense Bahraini necropoleis of the Bronze Age remain a phenomenon that is practically unique on the planet. We have seen that, beneath an identical external appearance, these tombs do indeed reflect differences in internal organisation. This reveals, despite use over a very long period, a basic conception, and probably an unchanging set of religious ceremonial rites that give great insight into the religious beliefs of the period. The creative and pragmatic character of the people of Dilmun invented or adapted all sorts of techniques on this archipelago touched by two seas. In the architectural domain, the fine carvings in the

The town of Manama, seen from the island of Muharraq.

local limestone draw admiration from visitors to the temple at Barbar or the official buildings of early, middle or late Dilmun at Qal'at al-Bahrain. This is also true for agriculture and irrigation – the Bahrain qanats, a local adaptation of the famous underground canals found in Iran or Oman, channel the flow of the largest springs to often-remote palm groves. The ingenuity of the people of Dilmun also played a vital role in domains as diverse as fishing, diving, basketry, jewellery-making and glyptic, and even metallurgy (in particular copper, over which Dilmun long maintained a trading monopoly), astronomy, shipbuilding and navigation. There is one sector in which the people of Dilmun visibly excelled – commerce. They managed to transform their land into an essential trading platform, due in particular to the implementation of domestic and international commercial rules and techniques, particularly in terms of barter.

**365, 366 Vessels
with Glaze-covered
Decoration**
Barbar, Danish excavations,
Well-chamber of the Temple
Bahrain, unspecified origin
(Muharraq?)
Islamic period,
9th and 10th cent. AD
H8.4 and 8.15 D MAX29.3
and 23.3cm
Manama, Bahrain National
Museum, acc. n° 1178-2-88
and 1269-2-88
B Glob 1958: 124, fig. 11; *Bahrain
National Museum* 1993: 84

These two imported vessels
are representative, among
others, of the international
trading position held
by the Bahrain archipelago
from the Abbasid era onwards.
The first with a yellow
and green decoration on slip
and covered with a transparent
lead glaze, comes from Iraq or
Iran. The red and black
decoration on a white
background of the second
includes a traditional
benediction - this piece
apparently originates from
Nishapur (Iran) or Samarkand
(Uzbekistan).

The entry of Bahrain-Tylos at that time,
into the Hellenistic world left by Alexander
the Great was evidently an opportunity to regain
contact with major international trade,
after a brief period of relative decline.
The wealth of funeral furniture found
in the necropoleis, which originated from all
across the Orient, is dazzling proof of this,
and from this point of view, the population
of Tylos was certainly a worthy successor
to that of Dilmun.
This enterprising spirit continued to flourish
throughout the Islamic period. With the
progressive restoration of the Gulf maritime route
from the Abassid era onwards, the Bahrainis took
up their trading activities once more,
even going as far afield as China, whose Ming
porcelain and celadon ware are found
in great abundance in the 14th and 15th century
archaeological levels at Qal'at al-Bahrain,
which was still the island's main international
port (unless urban expansion has removed
traces of other ancient mooring points).
We even know of a 14th century Bahraini trader
called Foliyân who was established in China,
where he lived in order to run his business.
He possessed a merchant fleet of 80 vessels.
He died there, far from his homeland,
abandoning almost "an hundred and thirty
hectolitres of fine pearls" in his residence
at Quanzhou. During the period of the European
Renaissance, Bahrain was regularly mentioned
by travellers who appreciated - and traded in -
the incomparable natural pearls praised by
ancient authors such as Strabo and Pliny.
Present day Bahrain is the Dilmun of yesteryear.
It still enjoys a privileged position in trade
between the Orient and the West. Its people,
while preserving their culture and beliefs,
distinguish themselves by their open and civilised
conduct towards other communities, cultures
and religions.
Like its ancestor, Dilmun, Bahrain is a pioneer.
The archipelago was the first country
of the Arabian Peninsula to enter into the oil era.
The first oil deposit was discovered in 1932
at the foot of Jebel Dukhan.
Curiously, the arrival of this new resource
coincided with the time at which the oyster
industry was practically ruined by the invention

³⁶⁷ **Hoard of Pearls
in a *Murex***
Qal'at al-Bahrain,
"Palace of Uperi" area (surface),
French excavations 1996
(QA96.240)
Islamic period,
15ᵗʰ/16ᵗʰ cent. AD (?)
Shell and pearls
ᴴ3.5 ᴸ6 cm
Manama, Bahrain National
Museum
Unpublished

This *murex* (one of the shellfish
most frequently collected and
consumed in ancient Bahrain)
comes from a disturbed surface
level at Qal'at al-Bahrain.
It contained the impressive total
of 407 very small pearls
(the diameter of the smallest
is no bigger than 0.8 mm!).
This unexpected discovery
can probably be attributed
to one of the last periods of
occupation of the site, and
leads us to imagine a story
behind the find. Perhaps a pearl
fisherman, after patiently
opening the oysters from
his daily harvest stored the most
precious "fruits" in this
small shell, which he hid
somewhere and never came
back to collect…

of cultured pearls by the Japanese, pearls
which defy any aesthetic comparison with natural
pearls, but which are substantially cheaper
to produce. With the beginning of oil production,
Bahrain gained access, followed, slightly later on,
by the rest of the Arabian peninsula, to a new era
of economic, social, cultural and urban
prosperity. Factories, schools, institutes and
universities all multiplied, paving the way for
growth and a prosperous future… when the oil
deposits have run dry.
The post-oil era is therefore under preparation.
It is based on the diversification of sources
of revenue and the dissemination of advanced
technology – heavy metal industries, dry docks
for repairing huge ships, and some light industry
are already in place. The Dilmun/Bahrain
character is still going strong, and adapts to life,
to the obligations and demands of the times.
In the same way as their ancestors imported
copper ore from Oman to work it, but also,
more importantly to re-sell it to Bahrain's bigger
neighbours who had none, today's Bahrainis
import aluminium ore from Australia which
they treat in their factories using natural gas
and sell the finished product to a number
of countries.
During the last third of the 20th century, Bahrain
has made an honourable place for itself
among the Middle East countries. It has become
a world financial and economic centre
of the greatest importance. Due to its strategic
position at the heart of the world's economic

decision-making projects, Bahrain attracts
investors and specialised institutions
who desire to participate in these enterprises.
Bahrain also constitutes a bridge between Orient
and Occident for all kinds of communication.
Its international airport, operational since 1931,
is being expanded to accommodate aircraft
for the major airlines running flights that link
the Far East, Japan, and Australia to Europe,
Africa and America. The same is true of the
country's ports.

The different civilisations that have succeeded
one another in Bahrain have enabled
the country to accumulate a significant
heritage, and to boast of a history at once rich
and universal. It was inevitable
that such a heritage should leave its mark on
the Bahraini people's character.
The Bahrainis are open, welcoming
and courteous, have a sharp business sense,
exhibit a great *joie de vivre* and are always
available for others. This admirable
character was probably that of the
people of Dilmun, too…

The Rediscovery of a Civilisation

Nicole Chevalier

A mere thirty years ago Geoffrey Bibby was at Qal'at al-Bahrain writing the preface to the work that was to reveal the land of Dilmun to the public. One of the discoverers of Gulf archaeology thus ended a long period during which a handful of travellers, the occasional archaeologist and a few epigraphists had been trying to perceive the contours of this ancient civilisation of which Bahrain was the main focus. For centuries ancient writers, Arab geographers, Portuguese conquerors and a few European travellers had described this archipelago close to the coasts of Arabia. However, they sang the praises of its rich banks of pearls rather than of its archaeological remains. Curiously, the archaeological digs carried out in northern Mesopotamia in the mid 19th century were the first to contribute to the revelation of Bahrain's ancient history. The uncovering of the palace of Sargon of Assyria at Khorsabad from 1843 onwards by P.-E. Botta, French consul at Mosul, provided a great number of inscriptions that related that sovereign's military campaigns year by year. Among the growing list of names of cities and vassal, defeated or dependent kings, some of them unknown, figured the mysterious Uperi, king of Dilmun. After the digs at Khorsabad, Nineveh, Nippur and Tello, the references to Dilmun multiplied, arousing the curiosity of scholars of the ancient Near East. Thus, in January 1880, in a short article published in the *Journal asiatique*, the French scholar Jules Oppert concluded, based on writings by ancient authors and the passage from the Khorsabad inscription concerning Dilmun, that the island known as "Tylos" by the Greeks and "Tilvun" by the Assyrians, was in fact the island of Bahrain. According to him, this was even the site for the legendary Phoenician metropolis of Tyre, and it would be well advised to proceed with archaeological digs in Bahrain, as they would certainly be fruitful. After this, until the end of the 1970s, the French contribution to Bahrain archaeology was practically non-existent. The island of Bahrain, being positioned on the route to India was essentially explored only by the British, until the arrival of P.V.Glob's and Bibby's Danish team.

The first to provide information on the remains on the island was Captain E. L. Durand, a young British officer. In 1879, he explored the island in its entirety, studying its flora and fauna, and investigating the political and economic situation of the country. Through this systematic exploration he drew up a very complete inventory of antiquities. His observations, complete with sketches, were transmitted in a report to the Indian government, and then appeared in an abridged form in the *Journal of the Royal Asiatic Society* in 1880.
Among other things, Durand's report described the enigmatic fields of tumuli "that cover the island on all sides", and gave a description of their interior, revealed by somewhat hasty "digs" – he had opened up two large tumuli at 'Ali using explosives. Durand was obviously intrigued by

the number of tombs, and expressed doubt as to whether they were of indigenous origins, preferring to attribute them to the Phoenicians.

His most surprising and decisive discovery was that of a cuneiform inscription on a black basalt stone that he found incorporated in the wall of a mosque. It was presented for inspection by the great epigraphist Henry Creswick Rawlinson. The text, written in old Babylonian, was shown to be a pious proclamation by one Rimum who presented himself as the humble servant of the divinity Inzak, protector of Dilmun. With the help of this inscription, three months after Oppert, Rawlinson expressed his conviction that Bahrain was indeed to be associated with the mysterious land of Dilmun. Many epigraphists remained sceptical that this was indeed the correct identification. It took the work done by the American Peter Bruce Cornwall in the 1940s for any remaining doubts to be dispelled. Like Oppert, Rawlinson was of the opinion that excavations conducted in Bahrain would yield significant results.The years that followed are marked by the passage through the Gulf of two famous travelling couples - Marcel and Jane Dieulafoy, in 1884, and J. Theodor Bent and his wife in 1889. However, the Dieulafoys, too busy with their mission at Susa, or unaware of the archaeological riches of the island and the wishes of Oppert, said nothing about the tumuli. In her *Journal*, Jane mentions that these islands "owe their agricultural richness to artesian wells that pass under the sea, and their trading importance to the banks of pearl oysters already famous in Alexander's time". Bent's clearly stated objective, on the other hand, was to explore this "ocean of tumuli", particularly in the area of 'Ali, where he investigated one of the largest. His work, which he presented to the *Royal Geographical Society*, tended once more to emphasise the Phoenician origin of the population that built the tombs.

Jacques de Morgan, head of the French Delegation in Persia, also wished to extend his investigations to the Bahrain islands. But, held up on his digs at Susa, he was unable to realise this project. Thus, he committed some space in the *Mémoires de la Délégation* to the observations made by André Jouannin, founder of the *Comité de L'Asie française*, who, between 1903 and 1906, carried out several missions in Arabia, Persia and Mesopotamia for the French government. On a brief visit to Bahrain in September 1903, Jouannin gathered information about the tombs mentioned by Bent in his book *Southern Arabia* and visited the tumulus explored by Bent. Impressed by the sheer immensity of the necropoleis, Jouannin decided to undertake research. We glean little from his summary report except that he attempted to show the lack of precise orientation of the tombs, and thought their construction to be attributable to one of the empires of Mesopotamian origin. Morgan based his observations on Jouannin's work, and, in his posthumous work of 1927, *La Préhistoire Orientale*,

Sketches of the 'Ali tumuli, drawn by Captain E. L. Durand in 1879 (from M. Rice, 1983, p.13).

he hastily concluded in his chapter on "The colonisation of Chaldea and Elam": "the ancient necropolis of Bahrain does not teach us anything about the ancient times that we are currently concerned with". In 1905, Colonel F. B. Prideaux, of the Imperial Indian government, was, in turn, charged with solving the mystery of the tumuli. Not only did he rigorously map the great tumuli at 'Ali marking all those already explored, but he energetically investigated nine of the most impressive ones and thirty five smaller tumuli on the outskirts of the village. After studying the means of access to the tombs and recovering material that had often been disturbed – a fact whose meaning he misinterpreted – he confirmed the hypothesis that the tumuli were the work of Phoenicians who lived and died in Bahrain before the era when they emigrated to the coast that was later to be known as Phoenicia. In a remarkable

feat of anticipation, he evoked the possibility that the ruins on the current Qal'at al-Bahrain site might cover Babylonian remains. Finally, the eminent archaeologist Flinders Petrie, following the example of Morgan whom he had confronted over the thorny issue of Egyptian prehistory, became interested in Bahrain, which he planned to explore as early as 1892. Twenty years later, in January 1912, he proposed to T.E. Lawrence, who had temporarily dropped the digs at Karkemish to join him in Egypt, that he undertake digs in Bahrain, under the aegis of the British School. Lawrence gives Petrie's reasons in one of his letters: "He tells me that Bent had performed digs in Bahrain, and that Mesopotamian type bulls' feet had been found in prehistoric layers [...] he maintained that the first dynasties came via the sea of Elam and its region, as far as Egypt, and that Bahrain was on their route." The explorer of

Karkemish declined Petrie's offer – another time and other circumstances were required before Lawrence took the road to Arabia... Finally, it was not until 1925 that Petrie managed to send Ernest J. Mackay who had also worked in Palestine and at Kish, in Mesopotamia – later, he distinguished himself in the Indus valley at the famous site of Mohenjo-daro. Mackay excavated thirty-four tumuli near 'Ali and analysed how they were built. He established a typology for the funeral chambers with a rigour and care noted by today's archaeologists. He advanced the hypothesis that the builders of the tumuli came from close by on the Arabian continent and that they used the island as a sacred burial place. This is why the thesis that Bahrain had, in the past, been a land solely reserved for the dead of neighbouring civilisations became so entrenched. Many years were to pass before this theory could be definitively buried by the anthropologist Bruno Frøhlich, in 1983.

Such was the situation when G. Bibby and P.V.Glob arrived in Bahrain in 1953. After their work had led them to discover the Barbar temple, the city of Qal'at al-Bahrain... and after extending their investigations to Kuwait and Saudi Arabia, Dilmun was no longer a "lost civilisation".

Britain's Early Contributions to the Archaeology of Bahrain

Michael Rice

Interest in the Gulf region from beyond the Moslem world was first stimulated by the competition of the newly-emerging colonial powers, initially the Portuguese who established themselves at the site of Qala'at al-Bahrain and considerably extended its fortifications. After their expulsion, in the early seventeenth century the British became actively involved in the region as a result of their interests in trading with the Persian Empire and later in securing the route to British possessions in India.

A product of the British interest in the route to India was a voyage on Royal Navy ships undertaken by two brothers, William and Thomas Mitchell, in 1856. William was a naval architect and the voyage was undertaken in the course of his work for the Navy. The brothers stayed for some months in Bahrain and William, a very competent draughtsman produced a fine series of watercolour drawings of scenes in Bahrain, taken during their exploration of the islands. The drawings were lost until 1987, when they were acquired at auction for the Government of Bahrain and taken into the national archives.

William Frederick and Thomas Mitchell.

Watercolour drawings by Thomas Mitchell. Courtesy of the Government of Bahrain.

Captain E.L.Durand, during his visit to Bahrain in 1878/9, found a stone inscribed in Old Babylonian script which was one of the key discoveries, revealing the identity of Bahrain as Dilmun. The inscription reads: 'The Palace of Rimun, the Servant of Inzak, of the tribe of Agarum'. Inzak was the tulelary divinity of Dilmun, the son of Enki, the Lord of the Abyss of the Sumerians. From "Extracts from Report on the Islands & Antiquities of Bahrein" by Captain Durand. 1880.

Captain Durand's drawing of the interiors of one of the mounds which he excavated at Aali. From "Extracts from Report on the Islands and Antiquities of Bahrein" by Captain Durand. 1880.

The first published description of the archaeological remains on the islands of Bahrain came from a visit made in the winter of 18789 by Capt. E.L.Durand, 1st. Assistant Resident in the Gulf, an officer in the service of the Viceroy of India. Durand's reports, which survive in two versions, were published in 1879 and contain descriptions and illustrations of the principal antiquities which had survived the centuries. His report, which contains much lively information about life in Bahrain at the time, was commented on by H.C.Rawlinson, then Director General of the Royal Asian Society, who identified Bahrain with the near-mythical land of Dilmun in the writings of the Old Babylonians, the successors of the Sumerians. Durand reserves recognition as the man who first introduced the archaeology of Bahrain to the outside world. His techniques, however, would not be recommended today; describing the excavation of one of the burial mounds at Aali, he records his use of dynamite to remove an inconvenient wall.

An American writer, an early example of the travel journalist, was the next visitor to Bahrain who left a record of the antiquities which he saw there, in 1889. Much of his description, contained in a lecture to the Royal Geographical Society in November 1889, is largely concerned with life in the Bahrain of the day. However, he described the burial mounds in some detail which continued to excite the interest of scholars and lay visitors alike. After Bent's early death, his widow published a book 'South Arabia' which also contains much material relating to their visit to Bahrain.

The new century saw some further interest in Bahrain's archaeology by British and European scholars. Colonel F.B. Prideaux, the Political Resident in the Gulf, residing at Bushire, organised a programme of survey and excavation in October 1906. This was the first scientifically planned expedition to Bahrain, using up-to-date archaeological techniques

Theodore Bent at Aali, 1889. From "The Bahrein Islands, in the Persian Gulf". Proceedings of the Royal Geographical Society. 1890.

Colonel Prideaux' excavations in process. From "The Archaeological Survey of India". 1908-9.

developed by the increasingly skilled and professionally qualified scholars and specialists working on sites in the Middle East. Prideaux produced an accurate plan of the 'Royal Tombs' at Aali, photographed all stages of his excavations and published them with the other findings of his work in the Archaeological Survey of India 19089. Prideaux' report was notable for the attention which it also gave to Eastern Arabia for he rightly considered that, as late as the nineteenth century, much of the eastern Arabian coast had been included in the term 'Bahrain', thus reflecting the situation which had existed in antiquity (when the region was included in the term 'Dilmun').

Petrie however persisted in his interest in Bahrain and in 1925 persuaded E.J. Mackay, who later was to work extensively in the Indus Valley and in Mesopotamia, to visit Bahrain and to produce the first comprehensive and detailed survey of the archaeology of the principal island. His visit was supported by the British Museum and, as a result, the ivory figurine, (Cat. 65) a unique discovery thus far, was handed over to the Museum in return. Mackay's report was published by the British School of Archaeology in Egypt under the title 'Bahrain and Hamamieh' in 1929.

Dilmun - Bahrain: A Comparative Chronology

	Dilmun	Mesopotamia
3000 BC		**Uruk period.** First mention of Dilmun in Sumerian tablets.
2750	Dilmun in Eastern Arabia.	Sumerian City States.
2500	**Bronze Age.**	Myths of Dilmun. Extensive trading contacts.
2250	Centre of Dilmun shifts to Bahrain Islands. City I at Qala'at al Bahrain. City II. Barbar Temple I, II and III.	Sargon the Great of Akkad. Gudea of Lagash.
2000	Saar Town.	Ur III. **Isin-Larsa period.**
1750	Ea-Nasir, the Dilmun Merchant. Decline of copper trade.	**Old Babylonian period.**
1500	Dilmun under Kassite domination.	Kassites in Babylonia.
1250	Tukulti-Ninurta 'King of Dilmun'.	Rise of Assyria.
1000		
750	Uperi, King of Dilmun.	Sargon II. Assurbanipal lists Dilmun as a colony.
500	Last mention of Dilmun in a Neo-Babylonian tablet. **Early Tylos.**	
250	Alexander the Great orders exploration of Arabian Gulf.	Death of Alexander the Great in 323.
0	**Middle Tylos.**	
250 AD	**Late Tylos.**	
500	Conquest of Bahrain before the death of the Prophet Mohammed in 632.	

3000 BC	**2700 BC**	**2500 BC**	**2300 BC**	**2000 BC**	**1500 BC**	**1350 BC**
Invention of writing. First mention of Dilmun. Foundation of the Egyptian State.	Old Kingdom Egypt. Dilmun in Eastern Arabia. Sumerian City States.	Pyramids of Egypt. Urban Civilisation in the Indus Valley. Royal Graves at Ur.	Dilmun in Bahrain. City I.	Dilmun City II. Barbar Temple. Saar. Building of Stonehenge stone circle.	Kassites in Bahrain. New Kingdom Egypt. Minoans in Crete.	Akhenaten. **1330** Tutankamun. **1200** Hittite Empire.

	Iran	**Indus Valley**
3000 BC	**Proto-Elamite period.**	
2750		Harappa and Mohenjo-Daro.
2500		Trade with Dilmun and Mesopotamia.
2250		
2000	Period of Sukkulmahs.	**Late Harappa period.**
1750		Decline of Indus civilisation.
1500	Elamite kings	
1250		
1000	Medes and Persians.	
750	Susa captured by Assurbanipal.	
500	Cyrus the Achaemenid, King of Persia.	
250	Persia conquered by Alexander.	
0		
250 AD		
500		

1000 BC	**550 BC**	**350 BC**	**100 BC**	**50 AD**	**330 AD**	**622 AD**
Phoenicians in the Levant.	Marib Dam built in Yemen. **450** Athens reaches its peak.	**323** Death of Alexander the Great.	**55** Romans invade Britain.	Establishment of Kingdom of Aksum. **125** Building of Hadrian's Wall.	Constantine founds Constantinople.	Beginning of the Moslem era.

Bibliography

A

H. A. Al-Khalifa, 1986,
The shell seals of Bahrain,
in *Bahrain Through the Ages...*
(ed. H.A. Al-Khalifa & M. Rice),
p. 251-261.

H. A. Al-Khalifa and M. Rice
(ed.), 1986, *Bahrain through
the Ages. The Archaeology.*,
KPI, London.

Kh. Alsendi, 1994, *Catalogue
of the Dilmun Seals from Bahrain
National Museum*, Ministry
of Information, Bahrain.

W.Y. Al-Tikriti, 1989, Umm
An-Nar Culture in the Northern
Emirates: third millennium BC
tombs at Ajman, in *Archaeology
in the UAE*, V, p. 89-99.

F. Allotte de la Fuye, 1913,
Documents présargoniques,
fasc. II/2, Paris.

F. Allotte de la Fuye, 1920,
Documents présargoniques,
fasc. suppl., Paris.

B. Alster, 1983, Dilmun,
Bahrain, and the Alleged
Paradise in Sumerian Myth
and Literature, in *Dilmun...*,
D.T. Potts (ed.), BBVO 2, Berlin.

P. Amiet, 1970, Antiquités
du désert de Lut, in *Revue
d'assyriologie* 68, p. 109.

P. Amiet, 1986, *L'âge
des échanges inter-iraniens*,
3500-1700 av. J.-C., RMN, Paris.

Ancient Saar, 1993: *Ancient Saar.
Uncovering Bahrain's Past*, North
Star Publishing, Teddington.

B. André, 1982, Écriture
et civilisation mésopotamienne,
in *Naissance de l'écriture...*
(ed. B. André and C. Ziegler),
p. 194-262.

B. André and C. Ziegler (ed.),
1982, last reprinted 1997,
*Naissance de l'écriture.
Cunéiformes et hiéroglyphes*,
Réunion des Musées nationaux,
Paris.

B. André-Salvini, 1996,
Vocabulaire des arbres,
in *Tous les savoirs du monde.
Encyclopédies et bibliothèques*
(ed. R. Schaer), Paris.

B. André-Salvini
and P. Lombard, 1997,
La découverte épigraphique
de Qal'at al-Bahreïn: un jalon
pour la chronologie de la phase
Dilmoun moyen dans le Golfe
arabe, in *Proceedings
of the Seminar for Arabian
Studies*, 27, p. 165-170.

H. H. Andersen, 1986, The Barbar
Temple: stratigraphy,
architecture and interpretation,
in *Bahrain through the Ages...*
(ed. H.A. Al-Khalifa
and M. Rice), p. 166-177.

C. Arnold-Biucchi, 1990, Arabian
Alexandres, in *Mnemata: Papers
in Memory of Nancy Waggoner*.
The American Numismatic
Society, p. 99-115.

P. Attinger, 1984, Enki
et Ninhursâga, in *Zeitschrift
für Assyriologie*, 74/1.

B

Bahrain National Museum, 1989:
P. Lombard and M. Kervran
(ed.), 1989, *Bahrain National
Museum Archaeological
Collections, I. A Selection
of Pre-Islamic Antiquities
from Excavations 1954-1975.*
Directorate of Heritage
and Museums, Ministry
of Information, Bahrain.

Bahrain National Museum, 1993:
P. Vine, 1993, *Bahrain National
Museum*. Immel Publishing Ltd.,
London.

H. Baker, 1995, "Neo-Babylonian
burials revisited",
in *Archaeology of Death...*
(ed. S. Campbell & A Green),
p. 209-220.

P. Beaumont, G.H. Blake,
J. Malcolm Walstaff, 1988,
*The Middle East. A Geographical
Study*. David Fulton Publ.,
London.

C.A. Benito, 1969,
*Enki et Ninmah and Enki
and the World Order* University
Microfilms, Ann Arbor.

T.G. Bibby, 1965, Arabian Gulf
Archaeology, in *Kuml 1964*,
p. 86-111.

T.G. Bibby, 1969,
Looking for Dilmun,
Alfred A. Knopf, New York.

T.G. Bibby, 1972, *Dilmoun.
La découverte de la plus
ancienne civilisation* (sic),
Calmann-Lévy, Paris
(French edition of the previous
reference).

T.G. Bibby, 1986, The origins
of the Dilmun civilisation,
in *Bahrain through the Ages...*
(ed. H.A. Al-Khalifa
and M. Rice), p. 108-115.

J. Bottéro, S. N. Kramer, 1989
(reprinted 93),
*Lorsque les dieux faisaient
l'homme*, Paris.

R. Boucharlat & P. Lombard,
1985, The oasis of Al-Ain
in the Iron Age. Excavations
at Rumeilah 1981-1983,
survey at Hili 14 in *Archaeology
in the UAE* 4, p. 44-73.

G. Bowersock, 1986,
Tylos and Tyre: Bahrain
in the Graeco-Roman world,
in *Bahrain through the Ages...*
(ed. H.A. Al-Khalifa
and M. Rice), p. 399-406.

G. Burkholder, 1984, *An Arabian
Collection. Artifacts from
the Eastern Province*. GB
Publications, Boulder City.

C

O. Callot, 1990, Les monnaies
dites "arabes" dans le nord
du Golfe arabo-persique
à la fin du iiie siècle
avant notre ère in *Failaka,
fouilles françaises 1986-1988*,
Maison de l'Orient, Lyon,
p. 221-240.

O. Callot, 1994, Un trésor
de monnaies d'argent
et monnaies diverses,
in *Qala'at al-Bahrain 1...*
(ed. F. Højlund
& H.H. Andersen), p. 351-360.

Y. Calvet, 1984, Tylos et Arados,
in *Arabie orientale...*
(ed. R. Boucharlat
and J.-F. Salles), p. 341-346.

S. Campbell and A Green (ed.),
1995, *The Archaeology
of Death in the Ancient Near
East*, Oxbow, Oxford.

M. Casanova, 1991, *La vaisselle
d'albâtre de Mésopotamie,
d'Iran et d'Asie centrale
aux IIIe et IIe millénaires
av. J.-C.*, ERC, Paris.

A. Cavigneaux, 1982,
Mythe de création sumérien:
Enki et Ninhursag, in *Naissance
de l'écriture...* (ed. B. André
and C. Ziegler), p. 236-237.

Cités oubliées de l'Indus, 1988:
Exhibition catalogue
by the Musée national
des Arts asiatiques, Paris

S. Cleuziou, P. Lombard
and J.-F. Salles, 1981,
Fouilles à Umm Jidr (Bahrain),
Recherches sur les grandes
civilisations, A.D.P.F., Paris.

D. Collon, 1986, *Catalogue
of the Western Asiatic Seals
in the British Museum.
Cylinder seals III. Isin/Larsa
and Old Babylonian Periods*,
British Museum, London.

J. Connan, P. Lombard,
R. Killick, F. Højlund, J.-F. Salles
and A. Khalaf, 1998,
The archaeological bitumens
from Bahrain, from the Early
Dilmun Period (c. 2200 BC)
to the 16th cent. AD.
A problem of source and trade
in *Arabian Archaeology
& Epigraphy* 9/2, p. 141-181.

J.D. Cooney, 1976, *Catalogue
of Egyptian Antiquities
in the British Museum 4: Glass*,
London

J. S. Cooper, 1986,
*Sumerian and Akkadian
Royal Inscriptions, I.
Presargonic Inscriptions*,
AOSTS I, New Haven.

H. Crawford, 1991,
Seals from the first season's
excavations at Saar, Bahrain,
in *Cambridge Archaeological
Journal* I, p. 255-262.

H. Crawford, 1998a,
Dilmun and its Gulf neighbours,
Cambridge University Press,
Cambridge.

H. Crawford, 1998b,
Tokens of esteem,
in *Arabia and its neighbours...*
(ed. C.S. Phillips *et al.*),
p. 51-58.

H. Crawford & Kh. Alsendi, 1996,
A Hut pot in the National
Museum, Bahrain,
in *Arabian Archaeology
& Epigraphy*, 7, p. 140-142.

H. Crawford, R. Killick,
J. Moon (ed.), 1997,
*The Dilmun Temple at Saar.
Bahrain and its archaeological
inheritance*, KPI, London.

H. Crawford and R. Matthews,
1997, Seals and Sealings:
Fragments of Art
and Administration,
in *The Dilmun Temple
at Saar...* (ed. H. Crawford,
R. Killick and J. Moon),
p. 47-58.

D

B. Denton, 1994, Pottery,
cylinder seals, and stone vessels
from the cemeteries of Al-Hajjar,
Al-Maqsha and Hamad Town
on Bahrain,
in *Arabian Archaeology
& Epigraphy*, 5, p. 121-151.

B. Denton, 1999, More Pottery,
Seals, and a Face-Pendant
from cemeteries on Bahrain,
in *Arabian Archaeology
& Epigraphy* 10.

B. Denton and K. Alsendi, 1996,
An unusual cylinder seal
from the cemetery of Hamad
Town on Bahrain, in *Arabian
Archaeology & Epigraphy*, 7,
p. 188-194.

P. Donaldson, Prehistoric tombs
of Ras al-Khaimah,
in *Oriens Antiquus* 23, p. 191-312.

J.M. Durand, 1977, in *Revue
d'Assyriologie* 71, p. 169-171.

E.C.L. During-Caspers, 1971,
The bull's head from Barbar
Temple II, Bahrain: a contact
with Early Dynastic Sumeria,
in *East and West*, XXI, p. 217-
223.

E

C. Edens, 1986, Bahrain
and the Arabian Gulf during
the second millennium B.C.:
urban crisis and colonialism,
in *Bahrain through the Ages...*
(ed. H.A. Al-Khalifa
and M. Rice), p. 195-216.

C. Edens, 1992, Dynamics
of trade in the ancient
Mesopotamian "World System",
in *American Anthropology*, 94,
p. 118-119.

J. Eidem, 1997, Cuneiform
inscriptions,
in *Qala'at al-Bahrain I...*
(ed. F. Højlund & H.H.
Andersen), p. 76-80.

R. Englund, 1983, Dilmun
in the Archaic Uruk Corpus,
in *Dilmun...*, D. Potts (ed.),
p.35-37.

F

T. Fish, 1954, "Towards
a study of Lagash "Mission"
or "Messenger" Texts",
*Manchester Cuneiform
Studies*, 4.

H.-P. Francfort, 1989,
*Fouilles de Shortughaï.
Recherches sur l'Asie centrale
protohistorique,*
De Boccard, Paris.

B. Frøhlich, 1986,
The human biological history
of the Early Bronze Age
population in Bahrain,
in *Bahrain through the Ages...*
(ed. H.A. Al-Khalifa
and M. Rice), p. 47-63.

G

C.J. Gadd and S.N.Kramer, 1963,
Ur Excavations Texts 6, London.

P.V. Glob, 1959, Alabaster
vases from the Bahrain temples,
in *Kuml 1958*, p. 138-145.

S.M. Goldstein, 1979,
*Pre-Roman and Early Roman
Glass in the Corning Museum
of Glass*, Corning.

M.W. Green and H.J. Nissen,
1987, *Zeichenliste
der archaischen Texte aus Uruk*,
Berlin.

D. Grose, 1989, *The Toledo
Museum of Glass:
Early Ancient Glass*, Toledo.

H

M.M. Haddu, 1989, Preliminary
Report on the Excavation
of Grave N at Hili (in Arabic),
in *Archaeology in the UAE*, V,
p. 53-71.

E. Haerinck, 1991, Excavations
at Ed-Dur (Umm al-Qaiwain,
UAE). Preliminary report
of the 2nd Belgian season
(1988), in *Arabian Archaeology
& Epigraphy* 2, p. 31-60.

A. Hakemi, 1997, *Shahdad.
Archaeological excavations
of a Bronze Age Centre in Iran*,
ISMEO, Rome.

W. Heimpel, 1987,
Das Untere Meer, in *Zeitschrift
für Assyriologie*, 77/1, p. 22-91.

A. Herling, 1994, Excavations
at Karanah Mound I, Bahrain.
A preliminary report,
in *Iranica Antiqua*, XXIX,
p. 225-239.

A. Herling and J.-F. Salles, 1993,
Hellenistic cemeteries
in Bahrain, in *Materialen
zur Archäologie der
Seleukiden- und Partherzeit
im Südlichen Babylonien
und im Golfgebiet*,
U. Finkbeiner (ed.), Tübingen,
p. 161-182.

L. Heuzey, 1893, Nouveaux
monuments du roi Our-Nina,
in *Revue d'Assyriologie*, III,
p.13-17

F. Højlund, 1995,
"Bitumen-coated basketry
in Bahraini burials"
in *Arabian Archaeology
& Epigraphy*, 6, p. 100-102.

F. Højlund and H.H. Andersen,
1994, *Qala'at al-Bahrain, 1.
The Northern City Wall
and the Islamic Fortress*,
Jutland Archaeological Society
Publications 30:1, Aarhus.

F. Højlund and H.H. Andersen,
1997, *Qala'at al-Bahrain, 2.
The Central Monumental
Buildings*,
Jutland Archaeological Society
Publications 30:2, Aarhus.

I, J

M. Ibrahim, 1982,
*Excavations of the Arab
Expedition at Sar el-Jisr,
Bahrain*, Ministry
of Information, Bahrain.

C. Jarrige, J.-F. Jarrige,
R.H. Meadow and G. Quivron,
1995, *Mehrgarh. Field Reports
1974-1985 from Neolithic Times
to the Indus Civilisation*
Department of Culture
and Tourism, Government
of Sindh, Pakistan, Karachi.

T. Jacobsen, 1981, The Eridu
Genesis, in *Journal of Biblical
literature* 100/4, p. 513 ff.

T. Jacobsen, 1987,
"Enki and Ninsikila/Ninhursag",
The Harps that once...,
New Haven and London.

K

L. Kalus, 1995, "Nouvelles
inscriptions arabes de Bahrain",
in *Archéologie islamique* 5,
p. 133-161.

M. Kervran and L. Kalus, 1990,
"La mosquée Al-Khamis
à Bahrain: son histoire
et ses inscriptions",
in *Archéologie islamique* I,
p. 7-73.

P. Kjaerum, 1994,
"Stamp-seals, seal impressions
and seal blanks",
in *Qala'at al-Bahrain I...*
(ed. F. Højlund & H.H. Andersen),
p. 319-350.

M.A. Konishi, 1996, "Legendary
spring and the stepped
wells of 2000 B.C., Bahrain —
from the excavations,
at 'Ain Umm es-Sujur",
in *Lahore Museum Bulletin*, IX/1,
p. 81-93.

S.N. Kramer, 1945,
"Enki and Ninhursag.
A Sumerian "Paradise" myth"
in *Bulletin of the American
Schools of Oriental Research.
Supplementary Studies* n° 1,
New Haven.

R. Krauss, 1997, "A signet-ring
with hieroglyphs",
in *Qala'at al-Bahrain I...*
(ed. F. Højlund & H.H. Andersen),
p. 176: fig. 779; p. 182.

R. Krauss, P. Lombard
and D.T. Potts, 1983,
"The silver hoard from City IV,
Qala'at al-Bahrain,
in *Dilmun...*, (ed. D. T. Potts),
p 161-166.

L

M. Lambert, 1953, "Textes
commerciaux de Lagash",
in *Revue d'Assyriologie*, 47,
p. 62-63.

M. Lambert, 1976, "Tablette
de Suse avec cachet du Golfe",
in *Revue d'Assyriologie* 70,
p.71-72

C.J. Lamm, 1931,
"Les verres trouvés à Suse",
in *Syria* XII, p. 358-367.

S. Langdon, 1915,
*Sumerian Epic of Paradise,
the Flood and the Fall of Man*,
PBS X:1, 1915.

C. E. Larsen, 1983,
*Life and Land-Use
on the Bahrain islands.
The geoarchaeology
of an Ancient Society*,
Chicago and London.

H. Limet, 1960, *Le travail
du métal au pays de Sumer
au temps de la IIIe dynastie
d'Ur*, Paris, p. 67-68.

J. Littleton, 1995,
"Empty tombs? The taphonomy
of burials on Bahrain",
in *Arabian Archaeology
& Epigraphy*, 6, p. 5-14.

P. Lombard, 1984,
"Quelques éléments
sur la métallurgie de l'âge
du Fer aux Émirats arabes Unis",
in *Arabie orientale...*
(ed. R. Boucharlat & J.-F. Salles),
p. 225-235.

P. Lombard, 1994,
"The French Archaeological
Mission at Qal'at al-Bahrain,
1989-1994: some results
on Late Dilmun
and later periods",
in *Dilmun*, 16, p. 26-42.

P. Lombard, 1998,
"Quand la tradition tue
l'innovation: réflexions
sur la glyptique de l'âge du Fer
à Rumeilah (EAU)",
in *Arabia and its neighbours...*
(ed. C.S. Phillips et al.),
p. 151-164.

P. Lombard and J.-F. Salles,
1984, *La nécropole de Janussan
(Bahrain)*, Maison de l'Orient,
Lyon.

A. Lowe, 1986, "Bronze Age
burial mounds on Bahrain"
in *Iraq*, XLVIII, p. 73-84.

M

P. Magee, 1997, "The Iranian
Iron Age and the chronology
of settlement in southeastern
Arabia", in *Iranica
Antiqua* XXXII, p. 91-108.

V. M. Masson, 1976,
"Altin-depe and the Bull Cult",
in *Antiquity* L, p. 14-19.

S. Méry, C. Phillips, Y. Calvet,
1998, "Dilmun pottery
in Mesopotamia and Magan
from the end of the 3rd
and beginning
of the 2nd millennium B.C.",
in *Arabia and its neighbours...*
(ed. C.S. Phillips et al.),
p. 165-180.

O. Mørkholm, 1973,
"A Hellenistic Coin Hoard
from Bahrain", in *Kuml 1972*,
p. 183-202.

M. R. Mughal, 1983,
*The Dilmun Burial Complex
at Saar: The 1980-82 excavations
in Bahrain*, Directorate
of Archaeology and Museums,
Ministry of Information,
Bahrain.

N, O

M. V. Nikolskij, 1908,
*Dokumenti chozjajstvennoj
ozjajstvenoj otcetnosti
drevnejsej epochi chaldei
iz sobranija N.P. Lichaceva*,
S. Petersburg.

H. J. Nissen, P. Damerow,
R. K. Englund, 1990,
*Frühe Schrift und Techniken
der Wirtschaftsverwaltung
im alten Vorderen Orient*, Berlin.

D. Oates, 1986, "Dilmun
and the late Assyrian empire",
in *Bahrain through the Ages...*
(ed. H.A. Al-Khalifa
and M. Rice), p. 428-434.

E. Olijdam, 1997, "Babylonian
quest for lapis-lazuli
and Dilmun during the City III
period", in *South Asian
Archaeology 1995*, F. R. Allchin
(ed.), New Delhi, p. 155-162.

P

A. Parpola, 1994,
"Harrapan inscriptions.
An analytical catalogue
of the Indus inscriptions
from the Near East"
in *Qala'at al-Bahrain I ...*
(ed. F. Højlund & H.H. Andersen),
p. 304-315.

C. S. Phillips, D. T. Potts
& S. Searight (ed.), 1998,
*Arabia and its Neighbours.
Essays on Prehistorical
and Historical Developments*,
Abiel II, Brepols.

D. T. Potts (ed.), 1983,
*Dilmun. New Studies
in the Archaeology
and Early History of Bahrain*,
Berliner Beiträge
zum Vorderen Orient 2, Berlin.

D. T. Potts, 1990a,
*A Prehistoric Mound
in the Emirate
of Umm al-Qaiwain, UAE.
Excavations at Tell Abraq, 1989.*
Munksgaard, Copenhague.

D. T. Potts, 1990b, *The Arabian
Gulf in Antiquity. I.
From Prehistory to the Fall
of the Achaemenid Empire. II.
From Alexander the Great
to the coming of Islam.*
Clarendon Press, Oxford

D. T. Potts, 1993, "Rethinking
some aspects of trade
in the Arabian Gulf",
in *World Archaeology*,
24:3, p. 423-440.

R, S

J. Reade, 1979.
*Early Etched Beads
and the Indus-Mesopotamia
trade.* British Museum
Occasional Paper n° 2,
London & New York.

M. Rice, 1983, *The Temple
Complex at Barbar*, Ministry
of Information, Bahrain.

M. Rice, 1984,
Dilmun Discovered,
The Longman Group,
London & New York.

M. Rice, 1994, *The Archaeology
of the Arabian Gulf*, Routledge,
London.

J.-F. Salles, 1984 "Bahreïn
hellénistique: données
et problèmes", in *Arabie
orientale...* (ed. R. Boucharlat &
J.-F. Salles), p. 151-164.

J.-F. Salles, 1987,
"The Arab-Persian Gulf
under the Seleucids",
in *Hellenism in the East*,
A. Kuhrt and S. Sherwin-White
(ed.), Duckworth, London,
p. 76-109.

J.-F. Salles, 1996,
"Achaemenid and Hellenistic
Trade in the Indian Ocean",
in *The Indian Ocean
in Antiquity*, J. Reade (ed.),
Kegan Paul International Ltd,
The British Museum, London,
p. 251-267.

V. Scheil, 1939,
*Mélanges épigraphiques
(Mémoires de la Délégation
en Perse*, 28), E. Leroux, Paris.

I. Skupinska-Løvset, 1983,
*Funerary Portraiture
of Roman Palestine.
An Analysis of the Production
in its Culture - Historical
Context*, Paul Åströms förlag,
Göthenburg.

E. Sollberger, 1956,
*Corpus des Inscriptions royales
présargoniques de Lagash*,
Paris.

E. Sollberger and J.-R. Kupper,
1971, *Inscriptions Royales
Sumériennes et Akkadiennes*,
LAPO 3, Paris 1971.

A. A. Soweileh, 1995,
"A typology of Dilmun
burial mounds",
in *The Archaeology of Death...*
(ed. S. Campbell and A. Green),
p. 196-198.

K. M. Srivastava, 1991,
*Madinat Hamad.
Burial Mounds - 1984-85*,
Bahrain National Museum
and Ministry of Information,
Bahrain.

E. M. Stern, 1995,
*The Toledo Museum of Art.
Roman Mold-blown Glass:
The First Through Sixth Century.*
Rome.

E. M. Stern and B. Schlick-Nolte,
1994, *Early Glass from
the Ancient World*,
Ernesto Wolf Collection,
Ostfildern.

T

F. Tallon, 1987, *Métallurgie
susienne I. De la fondation
de Suse au XVIIIe siècle
avant J.-C.*, vol. 1 and 2,
Réunion des Musées nationaux,
Paris.

F. Thureau-Dangin, 1902,
"Notice sur la troisième
collection de tablettes
découverte par M. de Sarzec
à Tello" in *Revue d'assyriologie*,
5, 1902, p. 67-102.

F. Thureau-Dangin, 1903, *Recueil
de Tablettes chaldéennes*, Paris.

F. Thureau-Dangin, 1904,
"Fragments de syllabaires",
in *Revue d'assyriologie* 6,
p. 128-132.

N. P. Toll, 1946, "The Necropolis",
in M.I. Rostovtzeff et al. (ed.),
*The Excavations at Dura
Europos. Preliminary Report
of the 9th season of work
(1935-36)*, Yale University Press,
New Haven.

V, W

C. Velde, 1998, "The Dilmun
Cemetery at Karanah I and the
change of burial customs in late
City II", in *Arabia and its
Neighbours...* (ed. C.S. Phillips
et al.), p. 245-261.

B. Vogt, 1985, "The Umm an-Nar
Tomb A at Hili North:
A preliminary report
on three seasons of excavations,
1982-1984", in *Archaeology
in the UAE*, IV, p. 20-37.

A. Von Saldern et al., 1974,
*Sammlung Erwin Oppenländer:
Gläser der Antike*, Hamburg.

D. Whitehouse, 1998,
*Excavations at Ed-Dur
(Umm al-Qaiwain, United Arab
Emirates), I. The Glass Vessels.*
Leuven.

C. L. Woolley, 1934,
Ur Excavations II, The Royal
Cemetery, London.

Pieces not illustrated in the exhibition catalogue

Unless indicated otherwise, all pieces come from the Bahrain excavations by the Directorate of Archaeology and Heritage and are kept at the Bahrain National Museum

Early Dilmun

(unless indicated otherwise, these pieces date from circa 2000-1800 BC)

368 Jar
Madinat Hamad necropolis, Tumulus 2.40
Clay
H33 D MAX31.5 cm

369 Burial Jar
Madinat Hamad necropolis, season and grave unspecified
Clay
H19.3 D MAX9 cm

370, 371 Goblets
'Ali necropolis, Tumulus 103
Clay
H16.5 D MAX13.2 and 14.6 cm

372 Vessel Stand
Madinat Hamad necropolis, Tumulus 46.2
Clay
H28.4 D MAX26.2 cm
Acc. n° 54-2-88

373 Soft Stone Vessel
Saar necropolis ("Burial complex"), Grave A/A1.2 2.40
Chlorite
H9.7 D MAX8.9 cm (vessel);
H2.5 D MAX6.3 cm (lid)
Acc. n° 348-2-88 and 148-2-88
B Ibrahim 1982 ; fig. 45.1 : 1 ; pl. 53:1

374, 375 Bitumen-coated Baskets
Saar necropolis, Tumulus 1.2
Bitumen
H7.2, 5.5 and 5.8
D MAX 6.7, 6.7 and 4.3 cm
Acc. n° 356-2-88, 453-2-88, 387-2-88

376 Fragmentary Crucible
Qal'at al-Bahrain, Danish excavations (520AAF), Northern city-wall
c. 2200 BC
Clay
D22 cm
Moesgård Prehistoric Museum
B Højlund & Andersen 1994 : 372 ; fig. 1829

377 Axe-Hand Adze
Barbar, Temple Ia, central platform, Danish excavations
c. 2000 BC
Copper
L16.1 W5.8 cm
Acc. n° 1812-2-88
B Bahrain National Museum 1989, n° 40

378 Dagger Blade
'Ali necropolis, Tumulus 96.
Copper
L23.1 W MAX4.4 cm

379 Chisel
Saar settlement, House 51.
British excavations 1991 (K16:51:11)
Bone, alloy, copper
L9.9 W1.04 cm

380 Fish Hook
Saar settlement, House 210.
British excavations 1992 (4130:5)
Copper
L4 W MAX1.5 cm

381 Tool on Ovine Metapodium
Saar settlement.
British excavations (5506:3)
Bone, copper alloy
L15.8 W MAX2.6 cm

382 Votive Ingot
Barbar, Temple Ia, central platform.
Danish excavations (517.FH)
Copper
H2 D MAX12.8 cm
Acc. n° 90-7-2
B Bahrain National Museum 1989, n° 48

383 Mortar and grinder
Madinat Hamad necropolis (DS3, 1985-86), Tumulus 83:7
Limestone
H5 D MAX14.3 cm
Acc. n° 1698-2-88

384 Pounder
Al-Hajjar settlement (1992-93)
Limestone
L32 W15 TH7 cm

385 Discoid Grinder
Al-Hajjar settlement (1992-93)
Limestone
H5 D MAX7.5 cm

386 Spindle-shaped weight
Al-Hajjar settlement (1992-93)
Haematite
L3.6 D MAX0.9 cm We8.32 gr

387-389 3 spindle-shaped weights
Al-Hajjar necropolis (site 2, 1974)
Haematite
L3.2 to 4 D MAX0.8 to 1.3 cm;
We5.61, 8.5 and 16.57 gr
B Bahrain National Museum 1989, n° 56a, b, d

390 Necklace
Al-Maqsha necropolis (1992-93), Grave 3b
Carnelian
L38 cm

391 Stamp-seal
Saar necropolis (1988-89), Tumulus 302
Chlorite or steatite
H1 D2.1 cm

392 Stamp-seal
Barbar, Temple IIb, Well Chamber
Chlorite or steatite
H0.9 D2.2 cm
B Andersen 1986, fig. 43a

393 Stamp-seal
Saar necropolis, season and grave unspecified
Chlorite or steatite
H1.4 D2.7 cm
Acc. n° 2732-2-90

394 Stamp-seal
Saar necropolis (1990), Tumulus 26
Chlorite or steatite
H0.9 D2.6 cm
Acc. n° 2138-2-90

395 Stamp-seal
Al-Hajjar necropolis (1981), Grave 3
Chlorite or steatite
H1.3 D2.5 cm
Acc. n° 4221-2-91-4

396 Stamp-seal
Saar necropolis (1988-89), Tumulus 245a
Chlorite or steatite
H1.1 D2.3 cm
Acc. n° 2850-2-90

397 Stamp-seal
Karranah necropolis. French excavations 1987
Chlorite or steatite
H1.3 D2.6 cm
Acc. n° 2830-2-90

398 Stamp-seal
Karzakkan necropolis (1978), Tumulus 18
Chlorite or steatite
H0.8 D2.2 cm

399 Stamp-seal
Saar necropolis ("Burial Complex"), Grave A/E3.5
Chlorite or steatite
H1.1 D3.3 cm
Acc. n° 2753-2-90

400 Stamp-seal
Madinat Hamad necropolis (BS2/1,1986-87), Tumulus 1
Chlorite or steatite
H1.3 D2.6 cm
Acc. n° 2804-2-90

401 Stamp-seal
Karranah necropolis, French excavations 1987
Chlorite or steatite
H1 D2.9 cm
Acc. n° 3010-9-90

402 Stamp-seal
Qal'at al-Bahrain.
Danish excavations, unspecified location
Chlorite or steatite
H1.1 D2.3 cm
Acc. n° 759-2-90

403 Stamp-seal
Saar necropolis ("Burial Complex"), Grave A/B9.1
Chlorite or steatite
H1.1 D2.8 cm
Acc. n° 2745-2-90

404 Stamp-seal
Saar necropolis ("Burial Complex"), Grave 43
Chlorite or steatite
H1.2 D2.6 cm
Acc. n° 4092-3-90
B Mughal 1983: 96; fig. 23:3; pl. XLVI:3

405 Stamp-seal
'Ali necropolis, season and tumulus unspecified
Chlorite or steatite
H1 D1.9 cm
Acc. n° 3001-10-90

406 Stamp-seal
Saar settlement, House 1
British excavations 1990 (F18:33:15)
Chlorite or steatite
H0.9 D2.4 cm
Acc. n° 2991-3-90
B Crawford 1991: 260 (a)

407 Stamp-seal
Saar settlement, House 205
British excavations 1993 (4025:14)
Chlorite or steatite
H1.34 D2.87 cm

408 Stamp-seal
Saar settlement, House 224
British excavations 1995 (5510:2)
Chlorite or steatite
H0.87 D1 cm
B Crawford et al. 1997: 93, fig. 10

409 Stamp-seal
Saar settlement, House 51
British excavations 1992 (2535:01)
Chlorite or steatite
H0.91 D2.1 cm
Acc. n° 3904-2-91-2

410 Stamp-seal
Al-Hajjar necropolis, season and grave unspecified
Chlorite or steatite
H0.6 D1.4 cm

411 Stamp-seal
Saar settlement, House 55
British excavations 1992
(2144:01)
Chlorite or steatite
^{H}0.8 ^{D}2.2 cm

412 Stamp-seal
Saar necropolis
("Burial Complex"), SW4/3,
Grave I
Chlorite or steatite
^{H}1.1 ^{D}2.1 cm
Acc. n° 3005-2-90

**413 Quadrangular
Stamp-seal**
Saar necropolis
("Burial Complex"),
Grave A/E8.4
Chlorite or steatite
^{H}1.3 ^{L}2.9 ^{W}2.1 cm
Acc. n° 2735-2-90
^{B} Alsendi 1994, n° 50

414 Cylinder-seal
Saar settlement, House II
British excavations 1998 (4741:11)
Chlorite or steatite
^{L}3 $^{D\,MAX}$1.7 cm

415 Seal-blank
Qal'at al-Bahrain,
Northern city-wall.
Danish excavations (520.TK)
Chlorite or steatite
^{H}0.85 ^{D}2.15 cm
Moesgård Prehistoric Museum
^{B} Kjærum 1994: 338, fig. 1751

416 Seal-blank
Qal'at al-Bahrain,
Northern city-wall
Danish excavations (520.AXH)
Chlorite or steatite
^{H}0.85 ^{D}1.75 cm
Moesgård Prehistoric Museum
^{B} Kjærum 1994: 338, fig. 1752

417 Sealing
Saar settlement, Temple
British excavations 1992 (1600:1)
Clay
$^{D\,MAX}$2.3 ^{H}1 cm

418 Sealing
Saar settlement, Block K
British excavations 1990
(E18:15:5)
Clay
$^{D\,MAX}$2.6 TH1.2 cm

419 Stamped Token
Qal'at al-Bahrain
Danish excavations 1964,
Northern city-wall
Clay
^{D}2.15 cm
Acc. n° 4100
^{B} Kjærum 1994: 336-337,
fig. 1749

Middle Dilmun

(unless indicated otherwise,
these pieces date
from the 14th century BC)

420 Vessel
Al-Hajjar necropolis, site I
(1972-73), Unspecified grave
Pottery
^{H}22.4 $^{D\,MAX}$13.2 cm

421 Vessel
Al-Hajjar necropolis, site I
(1972-73), Unspecified grave
Pottery
^{H}8.2 $^{D\,MAX}$7 cm
Acc. n° 1098-2-88

422 Vessel
Al-Hajjar necropolis, site I
(1974), Grave 37
Pottery
^{H}28.5 $^{D\,MAX}$8.6 cm
Acc. n° 102-2-88

423 Vessel
Qal'at al-Bahrain,
"Kassite Palace".
French excavations 1996
(QA96.66)
c. 1450 BC
Pottery
^{H}16 $^{D\,MAX}$18 cm
^{B} Glob 1958: 118, fig. 5; Højlund &
Andersen 1997: 134; fig. 637

424 Vessel
Madinat Hamad necropolis
(BS2, 1984-85), Grave 47D
Pottery
^{H}9 $^{D\,MAX}$6.5 cm
Acc. n° 5496-2-91

425 Vessel
Saar necropolis
("Burial Complex")
Pottery
^{H}10 $^{D\,MAX}$7 cm
Acc. n° 7117-2-91

Late Dilmun

(unless indicated otherwise,
these pieces date
from circa 550-450 BC)

426 Vessel
Al-Maqsha necropolis (1978),
Grave 4
c. 800-700 BC
Pottery
^{H}9 $^{D\,MAX}$11.8 cm

427 Vessel
Madinat Isa necropolis (1968?),
Unspecified grave
c. 800-700 BC
Pottery
^{H}8.4 $^{D\,MAX}$10.5 cm

428 "Snake Bowl"
Qal'at al-Bahrain,
"Palace of Uperi" area
Danish excavations (519.DL)
Pottery, bones
^{H}12 $^{D\,MAX}$8 cm
Moesgård Prehistoric Museum
^{B}Højlund & Andersen 1997: 136;
fig. 644

429 "Snake Bowl"
Qal'at al-Bahrain,
"Palace of Uperi" area
Danish excavations (519.DE)
Pottery, bones
^{H}11.2 $^{D\,MAX}$20 cm
Moesgård Prehistoric Museum
^{B} Højlund & Andersen 1997: 134;
fig. 631, 632

430 "Snake Bowl"
Qal'at al-Bahrain,
"Palace of Uperi" area
Danish excavations (519.DG)
Pottery, mortar, bones
^{H}10 $^{D\,MAX}$18 (approx.) cm
Moesgård Prehistoric Museum
^{B} Glob 1958: 118, fig. 5; Højlund &
Andersen 1997: 134; fig. 637

431 "Snake Bowl"
Qal'at al-Bahrain,
"Palace of Uperi" area
French excavations 1992
(QA92.498)
Pottery, bones
^{H}6.9 $^{D\,MAX}$14.3 cm

**432 Sarcophagus
and Contents**
Madinat Hamad necropolis
(NBH4, 1989-90), Mound 10
Clay, bones
^{H}89 cm^{W}68 cm^{H}59 cm

433 Sarcophagus
Qal'at al-Bahrain
Danish excavations,
Unspecified location
Clay
^{H}58 ^{L}98 ^{W}66 cm
Moesgård Prehistoric Museum

434 Mirror
Qal'at al-Bahrain,
"Palace of Uperi" area,
Danish excavations (519.CU)
Bronze
^{H}14$^{D\,MAX}$12 cm
Moesgård Prehistoric Museum
^{B} Højlund & Andersen 1997: 198;
fig. 846

435 Situla
Qal'at al-Bahrain,
"Palace of Uperi" area,
Danish excavations (519 LH)
Bronze
^{H}24.6 (with handle) $^{D\,MAX}$6.9 cm
Moesgård Prehistoric Museum
^{B} Højlund & Andersen 1997: 198;
fig. 845

Tylos Period

(unless indicated otherwise,
these pieces date from
between the 2nd century BC
and the 4th century AD)

436 Vessel
Shakhura necropolis (1992-93),
Mound I, Square C4
Pottery
^{H}9.5 $^{D\,MAX}$17.2 cm

437 Vessel
Shakhura necropolis,
season and grave unspecified
Pottery
^{H}9 $^{D\,MAX}$16.5 cm

438 Vessel
Saar necropolis (1991-92),
Mound 2, Square C2
Pottery
^{H}10.2 $^{D\,MAX}$15.5 cm

439 Vessel
Madinat Hamad necropolis
(1994-95), Mound I, Square D3
Pottery
^{H}14.5 $^{D\,MAX}$21 cm

440 Vessel
Madinat Hamad necropolis
(E2, 1994-95), Mound I, Grave 3
Pottery
^{H}23.8 $^{D\,MAX}$20.7 cm

441 Vessel
Saar necropolis (1995-96),
Mound 5, Grave 49
Pottery
^{H}8.7 $^{D\,MAX}$7.9 cm

442 Vessel
Saar necropolis (1995),
Mound 4, Grave 9
Pottery
^{H}14.7 $^{D\,MAX}$15 cm

443 Vessel
Saar necropolis (1995),
Mound 4, Grave 30
Pottery
^{H}13.5 $^{D\,MAX}$18.5 cm

444 Vessel
Shakhura necropolis (1993-95),
Mound 7, Grave 8
Pottery
^{H}13.2 $^{D\,MAX}$18.5 cm

445 Vessel
Saar necropolis (1991-92),
Mound 4, Grave 30
Pottery
^{H}6.3 $^{D\,MAX}$24 cm

446 Vessel
Qal'at al-Bahrain,
Northern city-wall.
Danish excavations 1957
(520.MZ)
Pottery
^{H}7.6 $^{D\,MAX}$15.1 cm
Acc. n° 831-2-88
^{B} Bahrain National Museum
1989, n° 169;
Højlund & Andersen 1994:
276, fig. 1545

447 Vessel
Al-Hajjar necropolis (1992-93),
Mound 2, Grave 34
Pottery
^{H}6.3 $^{D\,MAX}$20.5 cm
Acc. n° 5153-2-91-3

448 Vessel
Al-Hajjar necropolis (1992-93),
Mound 6, Grave 15
Pottery
^{H}9.5 $^{D\,MAX}$13.5 cm

449 Vessel
Bahrain, unspecified necropolis
Pottery
^{H}7.2 $^{D\,MAX}$26.2 cm
Acc. n° 881-2-88

450 Vessel
Saar necropolis (1985-86),
Mound 3, Grave 2
Pottery
^{H}10.3 $^{D\,MAX}$14.2 cm
Acc. n° 2248-2-90-3

451 Vessel
Al-Hajjar necropolis (1970),
Site 1, Grave 13
Pottery
^{H}30.2 $^{D\,MAX}$24.2 cm
Acc. n° 1153-2-88

452 Vessel
Shakhura necropolis (1992-93),
Mound 1, Grave 17
Pottery
^{H}7.2 $^{D\,MAX}$4.9 cm

453 Vessel
Karranah necropolis.
French excavations 1986,
Mound 2, Grave 119
Pottery
^{H}7.7 $^{D\,MAX}$16.1 cm
Acc. n° 420-2-88

454 Vessel
Karranah necropolis.
French excavations 1986,
Mound 4, Grave 76
Pottery
^{H}6.3 $^{D\,MAX}$15.3 cm
Acc. n° 479-2-88

455 Burial jar
Al-Hajjar necropolis (1992-93),
Mound 6, Square E2
Pottery
^{H}62 $^{D\,MAX}$44 cm

456 Oil Lamp
Saar necropolis (1995-96),
Grave 8
Pottery
^{H}5 $^{D\,MAX}$13.6 cm

457 "Pilgrim's flask"
Saar necropolis (1996),
Mound 7, Grave 69
Pottery
^{H}9.6 $^{D\,MAX}$8.1 cm

458 "Pilgrim's flask"
Shakhura necropolis (1991-92),
Mound 2, Grave 57
Pottery
^{H}15.8 $^{D\,MAX}$12.7 cm

459 Flask
Madinat Hamad necropolis
(DS3, 1985-86),
Mound 73, Grave 54
Glass
^{H}12.8 $^{D\,MAX}$6.5 cm

460 Flask
Saar necropolis (1987-88),
Mound 1, Grave 39
Glass
^{H}10.5 $^{D\,MAX}$9.9 cm
Acc. n° 387-2-88

461 Flask
Saar necropolis (1996),
Mound 7, Grave 3
Glass
^{H}10.4 $^{D\,MAX}$5.1 cm

462 Flask
Saar necropolis (1991),
Mound 12, Grave 22
Glass
^{H}9.4 $^{D\,MAX}$5.7 cm

463 Flask
Saar necropolis (1996),
Mound 11, Grave 25
Glass
^{H}9.5 $^{D\,MAX}$5.8 cm

464 Flask
Al-Hajjar necropolis,
Site 2 (1971), Grave A/b
Glass
^{H}7.6 $^{D\,MAX}$6.4 cm
Acc. n° 937-2-88

465 Stone vessel
Al-Hajjar necropolis,
Site 2, Grave 28
Calcite ("alabaster")
^{H}7.5 $^{D\,MAX}$11.2 cm
Acc. n° 216-2-88
^{B} *Bahrain National Museum*
1989, n° 109

466 Cosmetics case
Saar necropolis (1996),
Mound 11, Grave 9
Ivory
^{H}7.7 $^{D\,MAX}$1.7 cm

467 Cosmetics case
Saar necropolis (1996),
Mound 11, Grave 9
Ivory
^{H}10 $^{D\,MAX}$1.7 cm

468 Cosmetics case
Saar necropolis (1996),
Mound 11, Grave 9
Ivory
^{H}12.5 $^{D\,MAX}$1.7 cm

469 Spindle
Shakhura necropolis (1991-92),
Mound 2, Grave 31
Ivory
^{L}17.8 cm

470 4 Spindle Whorls
Dar Kulayb necropolis
(1993-94), Mound 24
Ivory
^{H}0.8 $^{D\,MAX}$1.7 to 2.2 cm

**471 Pair of Pendant
Earrings**
Saar necropolis (1988),
Mound 154
Gold, agate, lapis-lazuli, pearl
^{L}5.7 and 4.9 cm

472-474 3 Mouth Bands
Al-Hajjar necropolis,
season and grave unspecified
Gold
^{L}7.2 to 8.7; ^{W}1.9 to 2.3 cm

475 Necklace
Al-Hajjar necropolis,
season and grave unspecified
Frit, carnelian, rock crystal
^{L}51 cm

476 Necklace
Saar necropolis,
season and grave unspecified
Glass paste, frit, pearls
^{L}67 cm
Acc. n° 293-1-31-3

477 Necklace
Shakhura necropolis (1991-92),
Mound 2, Grave 23
Carnelian, agate, frit
^{L}75 cm

478 Necklace
Saar necropolis (1995-96),
Mound 7, Grave 97
Carnelian, shell, frit
^{L}57 cm

479 Figurine
Al-Maqsha necropolis
(1992-93), Unspecified grave
Plaster
^{H}24.2 ^{W}7.3 TH3 cm

480 Figurine
Shakhura necropolis, Mound 1,
Grave 52
Plaster
^{H}25.4 ^{W}4.8 TH8 cm

481 Statuette
Saar, Unspecified palmgrove,
chance discovery
Limestone
^{H}18.4 $^{D\,MAX}$7.3 cm
Acc. n° 97-1-46
^{B}*Bahrain National Museum* 1993,
p. 64

482 Nephesh-type Stele
Bahrain, Unspecified
palmgrove, chance discovery
Limestone
^{H}29.5 ^{W}14 TH12cm
Acc. n° 501-2-88

483 Figurative Stele
Qal'at al-Bahrain,
North-western palmgrove.
chance discovery, 1991
Limestone
^{H}30.2 ^{W}19 TH5 cm
Acc. n° 97-4-3
^{B} Lombard 1994: 33, fig. 9b

484 Figurative Stele
Shakhura necropolis (1992-93),
Mound 1, Square J3
Limestone
^{H}26 ^{W}17 TH12 cm

485 Incense Burner
Shakhura necropolis (1994),
Square D3
Limestone
^{H}26 ^{L}12 ^{W}10 cm

Islamic Period

(unless indicated otherwise,
these pieces date from
the 15th and 16th centuries AD)

**486-488 Chinese Ming
Sherds**
Qal'at al-Bahrain,
Islamo-portuguese Fortress
(1998)
Porcelain
^{H}19. 5 and 5 cm
^{W}14.5, 7 and 5.5 cm

489 Chinese Ming Inkpot
Qal'at al-Bahrain,
"Palace of Uperi" area
French excavations 1989
Porcelain
^{H}4.7 $^{D\,MAX}$4.9 cm

490 Chinese Coins
Qal'at al-Bahrain,
"Palace of Uperi" area
French excavations 1989
(QA89.41),
12th century
(date of production).
Copper
^{D}3.62 TH0.29 cm
^{B} Lombard 1994: 31, fig. 6

491 Koran
Bahrain, 1215 H
Paper, ink, gouache, leather
38, 5 x 29 cm